D1201609

Miracles
of
Mind

Other books by Russell Targ

Mind-Reach: Scientists Look at Psychic Abilities
The Mind Race: Understanding and Using Psychic Abilities

Miracles
of
Mind

Exploring Nonlocal Consciousness
and Spiritual Healing

Russell Targ and Jane Katra, Ph.D.
Foreword by Larry Dossey, M.D.

NEW WORLD LIBRARY
NOVATO, CALIFORNIA

New World Library
14 Pamaron Way
Novato, CA 94949

Cover design by Big Fish
Cover photograph by Photonica
Text layout and design by Aaron Kenedi

Library of Congress Cataloging-in-Publication Data

Targ, Russell.
Miracles of mind : exploring nonlocal consciousness
and spiritual healing / Russell Targ and Jane Katra ;
foreword by Larry Dossey.
p.   cm.
Includes bibliographical references and index.
ISBN 1-57731-070-5 (hardcover : alk. paper)
1. Extrasensory perception. 2. Parapsychology. 3. Mind and body.
4. Mental healing. 5. Spiritual healing. I. Katra, Jane. II. Title.
BF1321.T365   1997   97-31591
133.8--dc21   CIP

First printing, January 1998
ISBN 1-57731-070-5
Printed in U.S.A. on acid-free paper
Distributed to the trade by Publishers Group West

10 9 8 7 6 5 4 3 2 1

Dedication

For Aleta, Elisabeth, Alexander, and Nicholas, whose energy, love, and enthusiasm will help to create a world in which miracles are abundant.

Every man takes the limits
of his own field of vision
for the limits of the world.

— Arthur Schopenhauer

The world of our sense experiences
is comprehensible. The fact that it is
comprehensible is a miracle.

— Albert Einstein

Contents

Foreword

A*lthough we seem to be different individuals inhabiting separate bodies, we are* *intimately connected with each other at some level of the mind.* This image has surfaced consistently throughout human history. It permeates the language of poets, artists, and mystics, and has been repeatedly understood by spiritual adepts of all the great religious traditions.

The view that human consciousness is unified and connected, however, has largely been considered heresy since science began its ascendancy three centuries ago. The predominant belief holds that the mind is a product of the brain, and is therefore confined to the body and to the here and now. This means we are limited by our senses, that we cannot possibly perceive or convey information at great distances or outside the present moment. This point of view has become dogma in our century, and those scientists who have questioned this perspective have often been shouted down as soft-headed, unthinking renegades. In fact, until recently, one of the most insulting, pejorative comments one scientist could make about a colleague is that "he believes in mental action at a distance!"

But, as Aldous Huxley once said, facts do not stop being facts simply because they are ignored. And the evidence has never been greater that consciousness *can* act outside the brain and the present, defying the constraints of space and time.

In *Miracles of Mind*, Russell Targ and Jane Katra provide compelling reasons why the limited view of consciousness must give way to an expanded one in which the mind knows no bounds. Their thesis, which is based both in empirical science and personal experience, is that the mind is *nonlocal* — that is, it cannot be localized or confined to specific points in space, such as brains and bodies, or to specific points in time, such as the present moment. This means that in some sense our consciousness is *infinite* — soul-like and boundless, limitless and immortal.

This book, therefore, goes beyond new scientific facts and technical breakthroughs. It sheds new light on the Great Questions humans have always asked — questions about our essential nature, our origin, our destiny, and the meaning of life. So, dear reader, be forewarned: In this book you will be handling spiritual and philosophical dynamite.

In the modern era, the belief in the infinite nature of consciousness has been considered illusion at worst or a matter of faith at best. But as Targ and Katra show, it is now a matter of *data*. And in our culture, in which science is so highly valued, this four-letter word makes an immense difference.

We thus stand at a landmark period in human history. Because of the accumulating evidence of an expanded view of consciousness, we are poised to make great progress in human affairs — if we can find the courage to honor and engage the data that Targ and Katra present. And we *are* finding the courage. Perhaps this is most obvious in the field of medicine. For example, as of this writing, eleven premier U.S. medical schools within the past two years have developed courses devoted to exploring "spirituality and clinical practice," including the effects of distant, intercessory prayer in healing. Conferences on spirituality, prayer, and healing are being held at some of the most prestigious medical schools in the country. Elite scientists are now investigating the nonlocal healing power of consciousness. The role of love, empathy, and compassion in healing is now considered a fit subject for research. The primary reason underlying these developments is the subject of *Miracles of Mind* — our expanding view of the nonlocal nature of human consciousness.

When Alfred Russel Wallace, the co-discoverer, with Charles Darwin, of the theory of evolution, encountered the distant effects of consciousness in the nineteenth century, he did not believe them at first. Yet he courageously investigated them and eventually concluded, "The facts beat me." If the facts are to speak to us, as they did to Wallace, we must put aside our biases about how we believe the human mind *ought* to behave, and allow ourselves to become vulnerable and open to new truths. If we do so, we may discover something more glorious about our nature than we have recently believed.

André Malraux, the French novelist, remarked that the twenty-first century will be spiritual or it will not be at all. If he is correct, there is great urgency in taking seriously the material in this book, because it holds the promise not just of an expanded view of science but also of a respiritualization of the human vision.

Geoffrey Madan, the English writer, once said, "The dust of exploded beliefs may make a fine sunset." Let us therefore not lament the fading of the old views but celebrate the glorious emergence of new ones — in which we will recognize ancient wisdom as well.

— Larry Dossey, M.D.
Author of *Prayer Is Good Medicine, Healing Words,*
and *Recovering the Soul,* and executive editor of
Alternative Therapies in Health and Medicine

Acknowledgments

The authors wish to acknowledge and thank the following people, without whose contributions and support this book would not have been possible:

Most especially, and with deep gratitude, to Dean Brown for his profound scholarship, willingness to share his wisdom, and unflagging devotion through the years it took to write this book; and to William Braud for his inspirational and pioneering work in direct mental interaction with living systems, and great encouragement to us in the early days of this project.

Willis Harman, George Pezdirtz, Edgar Mitchell, and the Institute for Noetic Sciences, who all played essential parts in creating a home for this work at Stanford Research Institute; Judy Skutch Whitson for bringing us the miracles that were necessary for our collaboration on this book; Nicholas Targ for hours of loving persistence in dealing with the CIA maze to free the once SECRET data, and Allan Ebert for leading us through the arcane avenues of the Freedom of Information laws.

Harold Puthoff for fending off the many internal and external assaults on the SRI program, and making it possible for work to continue; Ingo Swann, who insisted that our psi abilities were not limited, but could span all of time and space; Gary Langford, who shared his extraordinary gifts of psi mobility and precision; Charles Tart for his good humor under duress and his many insights on the psychology of psi; Ed May and James Spottiswoode for stimulating conversations on the physics of psi; Joe McMoneagle for his unparalleled and indefatigable remote viewing for nearly two decades; Michael Murphy for his continuing inspiration, and his generosity in making the Esalen Institute available to us for many meetings and workshops; Larry Dossey, Larry LeShan, Dora Kunz, Stanley Krippner, and Janet Quinn for their years of work and contributions toward our understanding of nonlocal healing; Ken Ring for knowing that near-death experiences were worth studying, and for sharing his ideas of their value with the rest of us. Jerry Jampolsky for helping both of us to change our minds; Phyllis Butler for her astute and insightful editing of this manuscript; our literary agent, Doug Latimer, and our publisher, Marc Allen, for their help in bringing this book to light; and our editor, Jason Gardner, for his skill and patience in dealing with the complexities of the authors and this manuscript.

Wendy Wiegand, and Skip and Linda Durham for their unconditional love, hospitality, and support throughout this project; Molly May Butler for introducing Russell to the teachings of Vedanta and Theosophy more than forty years ago, and for her recent insights from Nagarjuna teaching us that we are "both here and not-here"; Teri Klein for her inspiring thoughts concerning spirituality and Jewish Renewal; Bing Escudero for his scholarship and commitment to expanding awareness; Robert Hackman for his education and support of Jane at the University of Oregon, and for his nurturance of her early healing practice; Mike, Becky, and Gary Williams for their generous caring and all-encompassing contributions to the life and well-being of Jane; Kit Green and John McMahon for their courageous and unfailing support of the SRI program; and Richard Bach and Werner Erhardt for financial support when it really counted.

Thanks also to Jeffrey Mishlove, for his thoughtful review of this manuscript, as well as to Larissa Vilenskaya, Hélène Tricker, Bonnie Lamont, Peggy Leising, Greg Wilson of the Seattle Friends of the International Association of Near-Death Studies; Reverend Stan Hampson of Palo Alto Unity Church, and all the people who came to Jane with trust and acceptance for spiritual healing.

Miracles
of
Mind

Introduction

The Illusion
of Separation

There are only two ways to live your life:
One is as though nothing is a miracle.
The other is as if everything is.
I believe in the latter.

— Albert Einstein

This book is about connecting to the universe and to each other through the use of our psychic abilities. These abilities, known collectively as *psi*, from the Greek word for soul, reveal numerous kinds of connections — mind to mind, mind to body, mind to the world, and what some would call one-mindedness with God. The idea that our "separation is an illusion" is not new — it has been a core premise of wisdom teachings for centuries, even before the time of Buddha, 2,500 years ago. Our ancient ancestors knew that the essence of our nature is consciousness. Extrasensory perception, or ESP, is one way of experiencing the mystery inherent in this consciousness that connects us across space and time. Spiritual healing reveals the powerful effects that our consciousness can have in the presence of peaceful receptivity, trust, and loving intentions.

It is not necessary to hold any particular beliefs about spirituality or anything else in order to be psychic. No special rituals are necessary. And, contrary to what some writers or misguided friends might tell you, using psychic abilities is not something reserved for a select few talented individuals; it does not make a person go crazy, nor does it require having a near-death experience. Our experience and laboratory data clearly

I

demonstrate that psychic abilities are part of our inherent nature. Psychic research from the past fifty years shows conclusively that our universe is both far more grand and more subtle than our science can presently explain.

The authors of this book have devoted most of their professional lives synthesizing the ideas presented here. Russell Targ was a pioneer in the development of the laser, and he is presently a senior staff scientist at the Lockheed Martin Research & Development Laboratory, pursuing the peaceful applications of lasers for remote sensing of the wind. He was also a co-founder of the Stanford Research Institute (SRI International) remote-viewing ESP program.

Dr. Jane Katra has been a practicing spiritual healer for more than twenty years, using her gift of mind-to-mind connection to heal and alleviate pain in others, both nearby and at a distance. She is also a university instructor with a doctorate degree in health education, who has taught nutrition and mind-body health both in private practice as an "immune-system coach," and at the University of Oregon.

"Remote viewing" refers to our psychic ability to experience and describe activities at distant places that are blocked from ordinary perception, and it reveals quite clearly the connection that exists between our minds and the universe. It is this same connection, which we call the "nonlocal mind," that we believe to be the means through which spiritual healing takes place. Because the SRI remote-viewing experiments provided such dramatic proof of the existence of nonlocal mind, we describe them in the first part of this book. Some of these experiments, which have only recently been declassified, took place as part of a series conducted by Targ and others as "ESPionage" for the CIA during the Cold War.

There are many states of nonlocal consciousness available to humankind, just as there are a variety of states of awareness within ordinary space-time. For example, right and left hemispheric tasks — such as the activity of a dancer compared to an accountant, involve quite different mental states, though both are available in "local" sensory consciousness. Dr. Katra experiences kinesthetic, or physical, sensations and direct knowing in connection with her practice of spiritual healing. Her work is also characterized by an experience of serenity that can be described as universal love. Entering into a receptive, nonthinking, nonsensual state of awareness, which could be called a state of meditation or prayer, enables a spiritual healer to become a vehicle carrying healing information to her patients.

Jane Katra's work as a healer was largely responsible for the collaboration that resulted in this book. That partnership actually began in the winter of 1992, when co-author Russell Targ was diagnosed with metastatic cancer. Russell was sickly pale, and he had been losing weight. After two weeks of CAT scans and x-rays that revealed numerous ominous spots on Russell's internal organs, the doctors at his friendly HMO wheeled him out on a gurney cart. They gave him instructions to put his affairs in order, and to begin chemotherapy as soon as possible. Instead, he contacted Jane, whom he had met at Parapsychology Association conferences, and asked her if she would work with him in the dual roles of spiritual healer and immune system coach.

Acting on her intuition, Jane felt compelled to tell Russell that he was not sick, and that he should not empower that concept by saying he was sick, or that he had cancer. "All we actually know is that there were spots on some film," she said. Russell had received the frightening diagnosis just a few days before Christmas, but the chemotherapy team was fortunately unavailable until after the first of the year. In addition to her spiritual healing, Jane worked with Russell exploring the theory of changing the host so the disease could no longer recognize him. During the ensuing weeks, she wrote out a five-page prescription for Russell's healing treatment, based on research literature and her experiences concerning immune system enhancement. She recommended changes affecting the physical body, as well as changes in attitudes, emotional expression, and social and spiritual connections.

In addition, Jane did many healing meditations with Russell, and taught him to focus his thoughts with self-healing imagery and affirmations. She got him to try many new and unfamiliar behaviors: early morning jogging; expressions of gratitude, such as saying grace at mealtime; and even prayer. Healing experiences that involve union with a universal consciousness do not arise out of any particular beliefs, rituals, or actions, except one:

quieting one's mind. These practices were foreign to Russell. Jane also recommended that he get reacquainted with his "community of spirit," which is one of the important aspects of what the health trade calls "social support." Local as well as nonlocal caring connections are important for healing, as well as health.

Russell followed these new behaviors, and he has been well ever since. He never returned to the hospital for medical treatment of cancer and never took any chemotherapy. Ensuing blood tests and x-rays showed no indications of illness. We will never know if he actually had metastatic cancer, or if it was a misdiagnosis, as some people believe. What we do know is that Jane's interaction with Russell saved him from chemotherapy, which could have killed him, even in the absence of cancer. Jane's part in this spiritual healing can be more fully understood by reading Chapters 7 and 8 about "The Making of a Healer" and "The Healing Experience."

Physician Larry Dossey has delineated three distinctively different "eras" of medicine, which distinguish the ways we have viewed the relationship of mind and body: physical, psychosomatic, and transpersonal. With our recognition of the nonlocal mind — our consciousness that is unconfined by either space or time — we have now entered Dossey's third era, which recognizes the importance of mind-to-mind connections for healing. We are just beginning to realize the potential effects of mind both within each person and between people, for information gathering (as in remote viewing), and for information sharing in psychic and spiritual healing. Regarding the effects of our thoughts, physicist David Bohm says, "A change in meaning is a change in being."[1] In other words, thoughts have effects in the physical world.

Because we still do not fully understand the mechanisms underlying spiritual and psychic healing, many people dismiss the possibility of their effectiveness. However, we believe that different states of nonlocal awareness allow us to access levels of information unavailable through our ordinary senses. We will see this demonstrated by the remote viewing and other psychic data reported later in this book. A mystic might call the healing information "universal love."

The practice of quieting one's mental noise and creating coherence with a patient allows a healer's caring intentions and state of consciousness to become an avenue of this spiritual healing. The healing is available from a distance, whenever a patient is receptive to it. A healer's prayerful state makes available a type of "healing template," which appears to activate a patient's own self-healing capabilities. Thus, we believe a spiritual healer interacts with a distant patient by sending or revealing a *healing message*, rather than healing "rays." It is actually an information *transaction*, involving a relationship in which need, helping intentions, and quiet minds are the important elements. Spiritual healing, when done in the presence of a patient, may also involve the transfer of a little-understood "vital life energy" from a healer. Such "energy healing" is postulated to occur during other forms of psychic healing, when the healing practitioner is not distant from the patient.

Psychic and spiritual healing are gaining new credibility in contemporary medical circles as well as governmental agencies. The National Institutes of Health have established an office to investigate alternative medicine, and physicians and hospitals are participating in double-blind clinical trials of spiritual healing. In this book we present the encouraging data from recently published experimental trials with both cardiac and AIDS patients. Such healing research has prompted Larry Dossey, physician, author, and executive editor of the new journal *Alternative Therapies in Health and Medicine*, to comment that:

> After scrutinizing this body of data for almost two decades, I have come to regard it as one of the best kept secrets in medical science. I'm convinced that the distant, nonlocal effects are real and that healing happens.[2]

We begin this book with Russell's autobiographical descriptions of a variety of extrasensory phenomena that point to the existence of mind-to-mind and mind-to-matter connections. We then broaden the evidence by examining the scientific basis provided by some astonishing remote-viewing experiments conducted by Russell at Stanford Research Institute. In these carefully controlled experimental tests spanning two decades, many different subjects sat in a windowless office, closed their eyes, and explored the world outside. These individuals were consistently able to experience and accurately describe distant scenes and events from coast-to-coast and even continent-to-continent, in both present and future time. The SRI experiments demonstrated unequivocal evidence for extrasensory perception and the existence of the nonlocal mind, outside the brain and body. The ability of human awareness to make remarkable connections apparently transcends the conventional limitations of time and space.

One of the most astonishing examples of remote viewing that we include in this book is a particular experiment in a series that was covertly funded by the CIA over a period of many years. In this case, a talented subject named Pat Price was given only the latitude and longitude coordinates of what turned out to be a secret Soviet atom bomb laboratory in Semipalatinsk, Siberia. With no other information of any kind to guide him, Price immediately described and sketched the plant with incredible precision. Not only did his drawings show previously unknown external structures that later were confirmed by satellite photography, but he also described, in remarkable detail, a complicated assembly process being conducted *indoors*, inside a secure building. The existence of this completely secret process was verified by satellite photography several years later, after Price died, when the structure was moved outside.

This particular example of remote viewing occupies only a few pages in the book, but its importance far transcends the amount of space devoted to it. Price's drawings, which were recently declassified and obtained by Russell under the Freedom of Information Act, have never before appeared in book form. (Although initial support for Russell's work came in 1972 from the CIA; by 1995, a multitude of governmental agencies had joined in, including the Defense Intelligence Agency, the Army, Navy, and NASA, all of whom were stunned and impressed by the results.) Price's amazingly accurate drawings and descriptions, as well as the CIA acceptance of remote viewing as a way of penetrating the Iron Curtain, are a powerful testament to the existence of nonlocal mind.

As further evidence of these capabilities, we describe our personal experiences with high-quality psychic functioning, and Jane's involvement in spiritual healing interactions. We deal with psi inside and outside of the laboratory, as well as healing inside and outside of hospitals, during the past two decades. Physical models for psychic functioning are explored, as are the potential impacts of psychic abilities — the mind-to-mind and mind-to-world connections — on our society.

Psychic abilities and remote viewing are probes into what Carl Jung called our collective unconscious, and what the authors call our *community of spirit*. The reason we have a passion for our work with psi is that it allows us, as scientists, to keep one foot firmly in the materialistic twenty-first century, and at least one toe in the "Divine." The data for our ability to share the feelings and experiences of others who are apparently separated from us show clearly that the Biblical idea of spiritual community can have a contemporary scientific meaning. We believe scientists will not come to a full understanding of the nature of consciousness until they recognize that there is no real separation between the observer and the so-called outside world they think they're observing. It's not an exaggeration, in our opinion, to say that the reliable laboratory demonstration by worldwide parapsychological researchers of our human connectedness is an accomplishment on a par with the most notable scientific achievements of the twentieth century.

The field of psi research has its critics, of course. Despite irrefutable evidence for the existence of psi, it has been repressed and ridiculed in Western society because its mechanism is not yet understood. Magicians have gained fame and fortune assailing the ostensible spoon bending of Uri Geller. Many scientists who claim to understand nearly all of the phenomena of the physical universe apparently perceive psi to be a threat to their omniscience. Historically, much opposition to psi has been based on fear rather than intellect. Many leaders of organized religions have viewed psi abilities as a kind of freelance spirituality they could not control.

In this book, we choose not to deal with spoon bending, astrology, or unidentified flying objects. The research we present here has appeared in the world's most prestigious scientific journals: *Nature, The Proceedings of the*

Institute of Electrical and Electronics Engineers (IEEE), The Proceedings of the American Association for the Advancement of Science (AAAS), and the *Psychological Bulletin* of the American Psychological Association (APA). The work we describe has been scrutinized and accepted in the halls of Congress, and by the House Committee on Intelligence Oversight, as described in Chapter 2. Our own view of psi functioning has been strongly influenced by the work of the distinguished physicist David Bohm, whose holographic model of the universe could be summarized by saying that any event that occurs is immediately available anywhere as information. That is, each portion of space contains information about all others.[3]

We hope this book will help to overcome fear of our mind-to-mind connections, and inspire people to appreciate, use, and enjoy their natural abilities. Although we know that psi, like any other human ability, is not perfectly reliable, the experimental data discussed here show convincingly that it is widely distributed in the general population. ESP should no longer be considered elusive. It is available and can be used.

Our psychic and spiritual capacities enable us to explore an important part of our true nature. Accepting and learning to use our nonlocal minds is important because it gives us direct access to the wider world in which we reside. It shows us that our consciousness knows no boundaries. We can each personally contact this expansive dimension of life, which evokes in us a greater sense of what our purpose here might be, and inspires us to reach for our highest potential as conscious beings.

We each create the reality that shapes our perceptions and experiences of everyday life. Daily, we are given the opportunity to decide if there will be psi in our lives. Our mental software, however, may need an upgrade in order to create this remarkable future. Otherwise, we will not be able to run the new programs and be part of what we envision as a Psychic Internet: the mind-to-mind connections available to all who wish to log on. If the truth be known, we are all already hooked up. We just have to decide to pay attention.

One of our objectives is to help you to do this, by giving you the essential tools to expand your own potential. We do not promise that you will become more "psychic," but we can teach you to become more aware of the psychic aspects of your own mental processes. We can show you how to achieve a nonlocal connection with others, unlimited by space and time, acquired through trust, acceptance, and regular practice. Spiritual healing is one of the most important of these connections.

In this book, we include strong evidence for distant healing of both humans and animals, as well as theories and studies of noncontact, ostensible "energy healing" techniques such as Therapeutic Touch. We report studies of people affecting living systems from a distance, of remote mental-influence research in the former Soviet Union, and provocative accounts of remote diagnosis. All are further demonstrations of the range of our versatile human capabilities. Discussions of the roles of love, prayer, and surrender in spiritual healing; mental techniques used in studies of distant influence; and the differences between psychic and spiritual healing are also included.

In addition, we address the idea of precognition and the nature of time, and ask, "What does it mean to look into the future?" We explore the question of whether psychic abilities are sacred, or a secular expansion of our sensory awareness. Finally, we describe how a single-pointed focus of attention can be applied to helping others through healing. The basis of this spiritual healing resides in an attitude of openness and attunement to a greater universal mind, working through a person with helping intentions, in an environment of trust and surrender of personal ego.

We describe the many ways the magic of mind transcends our ordinary understanding of the space and time we live in. We hope to share our wonder, gratitude, and our experiences with you, and we invite you to join with us in the adventure of examining the relationship between what a physicist might describe as our "holographic quantum interconnectedness," and what a healer calls "God and our mutual community of spirit." Our goal is to open a door to all the riches of experience available in the world of mind-to-mind connections, and provide the tools to enable you to walk through that door.

His Holiness the Dalai Lama, the Tibetan spiritual and political leader in exile, has written that our strongest tool for achieving peace among nations is education of our shared awareness. He has called upon scientists to assist in educating people of the world concerning our interconnected nature, and the interdependence of life.[4] We hope that this book will further that endeavor. It is partly through learning to quiet our minds that we become peaceful world citizens, and it is also through silencing our thoughts, memories, imagination, and sensations that we become aware of our mind-to-mind connections.

Sir Arthur Eddington (1882-1944) has been described as the most distinguished astrophysicist of his time. His view of the significance of these connections is one with which both the physicist and the healer can agree:

> If I were to try to put into words the essential truth revealed by the mystic experience, it would be that our minds are not apart from the world: and the feelings that we have of gladness and melancholy and our other deeper feelings are not of ourselves alone, but are glimpses of reality transcending the narrow limits of our particular consciousness. . . .[5]

chapter one

What I See
When I Close My Eyes

How *does a physicist happen to co-write a book about healing and the nonlocal mind?* As a graduate student at Columbia, I (Russell) was greatly influenced by philosopher Alfred J. Ayer, who said if a thing can't be measured or verified, it can't be sensibly discussed.[1] Ayer made a great contribution to logical thinking by giving us the tools to determine which kinds of arguments could be resolved, and which kinds would go on endlessly. Although he might be appalled by our current view that we have mind-to-mind connections, and are one with a community of spirit, the data we present here meet all of his criteria for independent verifiability by a fair witness.[2] The idea of nonlocal mind is a contemporary metaphor from quantum physics. It is a congenial match for the phenomena examined through many decades of laboratory parapsychology, as well as the related examples of spiritual healing occurring in hospitals, churches, and clinics.

Ayer also said that if a claim cannot be verified by one's senses, then it should rightly be considered a "non-sense" proposition. In this book, the authors tell you things about which they have direct, personal sensory experience, or firsthand information. We don't, for example, write about the seventeenth-century levitations of St. Joseph of Copertino, or the nineteenth-century seances of D.D. Hume, as much as we might like to.[3] Many said that D.D. Hume was a conjurer. Our opinion is that if he were a magician, he used sleight of hand only to augment his already extraordinary psychokinetic feats. In the same vein, charismatic healers throughout history have likely used combinations of hypnosis and stagecraft to augment their genuine healing gifts.[4] Stage magicians doing mental magic, on the other hand, have a much easier tasks to perform.

Perhaps I should admit here that I am an amateur magician. In fact, my initial interest in psi came from my college days, when I was a performing amateur magician. Almost every magician has had the experience of standing on the stage, doing mental "magic," and suddenly realizing that he knows more about a person in the audience than his trick should have told him. For example, I was often on stage doing an effect (a trick) called billet reading: I held an envelope up to my forehead and tried to answer a question that someone in the audience had written on a slip of paper and sealed inside. In reality, I managed to get a surreptitious peek at the question earlier in the trick, and would just recite it from memory. But standing there with my eyes closed, "mind-reading" the question from a lady who wanted to know where to find her lost dog, for example, I may also have received a sudden mental picture of a large brick house with a line of trees in the front yard. Trusting the quality of this mental picture, after reciting her question I astonished her even more by describing her house. Every magician I have talked with who does mental magic on the stage has received this kind of ESP gift while performing their tricks. After I had several such experiences both on stage and in front of small groups, I became interested in the work of J.B. Rhine at Duke University, who seemed to be doing real magic without any sleight of hand.

One of the paradoxes of psychical research pertains to the difference between a psychic and a magician. When a stage magician enters an ESP laboratory, he is very likely to try using trickery to supplement whatever psychic ability he has. Conversely, it often happens that a magician on the stage will supplement his tricks with whatever ESP might come his way.

I am a good visualizer. When I close my eyes I usually see reasonably sharp and clear pictures — often clearer than I see with my eyes open. My corrected vision with glasses is only about ten percent of normal. Let me share some of my thoughts about psi perception, from the unique point of view of a legally blind researcher.

A person with poor visual resolution like my own regularly experiences the world in a similar way to a participant in a remote-viewing experiment. The images I see are not out of *focus*, but are simply projected onto a film — my retina — that is of too coarse a grain to resolve the fine details. I believe that a number of misconceptions have been formed about psi functioning from the expectation that psi should work like vision. A normal eye can resolve down to one milliradian, the width of a single hand at the distance of a football field.

When I am looking out over an audience, I can see well enough to be absolutely confident that I am talking to people, rather than stuffed animals. But from the stage I cannot identify anyone by sight unless they have unusually distinctive properties of size, shape, or hair. The people are not out of focus, they are just too far away for me to see them clearly. This is an important distinction, because it pertains to the way most people perceive psi images or experimental targets. My personal visual experience coincides with the fragmentary images perceived initially by remote viewers in the SRI data. This fact is consistent with the ideas presented by authors René Warcollier in *Mind to Mind* and Upton Sinclair in *Mental Radio.*[5]

The initial fleeting and fragmentary images experienced during remote viewing are also similar to the process called "graphic ideation," described by Robert McKim in his book, *Experiences in Visual Thinking.*[6] McKim explains how solutions to mechanical engineering problems are extracted from the unconscious through the process of sketching meaningless doodles, with the expectation that the answers will gradually appear in the drawings. Even though it may not be recognizable in early sketches, something will eventually appear that can be identified as the solution to the problem. McKim's book makes it clear why artists are often the best psychic subjects. It is not that they are necessarily more psychic than the rest of us, but that they have much greater control over their visual imagery processes.

Psychic data in visual form may well be mediated by these same processes. Artists are also experienced in stabilizing and examining their visual images. Those of us involved in psi should probably learn and then teach mental imagery skills as part of our parapsychological research.

The process of remote viewing is often similar to the results we have seen from hospital patients who have had their cerebral hemispheres surgically disconnected from each other. These patients are asked to draw a picture of something that they are reading about with one eye open, while holding their pencil in the hand on the opposite side of the body. The drawings they produce are accurate, but the subject's mind is unable to identify the object after they have drawn it. This task illustrates the disconnection that can exist between the knowing and the doing parts of the brain.

Fragmentation appears to be a natural method for extracting information from the unconscious. One should not necessarily expect an object to have the same projection on the psychic plane as when seen by the eyes. I am not using the term "psychic plane" here in a metaphysical sense. I use it as a reminder that, although every day we learn more about the elements of the psychological processes that facilitate psi, we still know nothing about the physics of the interactions between distant and/or future targets and our awareness of them.

Although the production of fragmentary images is a frequent phenomenon in psi, especially with people who are new to it, there is no reason to believe that it is an absolutely necessary characteristic. More experienced viewers are often able to consolidate these fragments mentally, allowing them to produce a single, surprisingly coherent image. Perfect examples of this are the amazing sketches made during a remote viewing by Joe McMoneagle, shown in Figures 10 and 11 in Chapter 2.

My own clearest psi experiences have been spontaneous. My first clear psi perception came to me in 1956, when I was riding in a car with my employer, who was driving me home from the Long Island laboratory where we both worked. The sun was shining brightly in my eyes. When I closed my eyes to avoid the glare, I suddenly had a vivid mental picture of a page of Hebrew writing. (I don't read Hebrew.) I saw white characters written on a black background, with little red flowers with green leaves near the edge of the page. Associated with this was an oval table with candles on it. I related this image to my employer, who knew of my interest in psi. He said that it sounded to him as though I were describing the library of his friend, Professor Schriber, a Hebrew scholar in Brooklyn. He called Schriber that night and obtained a copy of the manuscript that Schriber had been working on at that time. It was a white-on-black photostat of a Hebrew book, which Schriber had annotated by marking the correct parts with green checks, and putting red balls next to the parts that he thought should be changed. There were no actual red and green flowers, but the correspondence to what I had seen in my mind was remarkable when I finally saw the pages a few days later. That is probably the sharpest image of text that I have ever perceived. I will never know if I could have read it, if it had been in English, but it was so clear that I feel I could have.

An even more complete image came to me in a dream while attending a scientific conference several years later, where I was to present a technical paper. I dreamt that the person who was going to speak just before me was dressed in a tuxedo with a red carnation in his lapel, and that he was going to sing his paper! This dream, unlike many that people have, certainly did not reflect any wish fulfillment or residue of the previous day's experience, and it had the unique clarity and bizarre nature that I have come to associate with precognitive dreams.

On my way to breakfast the next morning, I went to the conference room to see what it looked like, and there, at the lectern, stood a man in a tuxedo wearing a red carnation in his lapel. I went right up to him and asked him if he was going to sing. "Yes," he said, "but not until later." He turned out to be a band leader, and he would be conducting in our conference room later in the day for a banquet!

I can think of only one psi event in which I clearly recognized a particular person. About fifteen years ago, I decided to do a practice precognition experiment. I bought a racing form, and I am mildly embarrassed to say that I proceeded to do my meditation on the eighth race at Bay Meadows the next day. I didn't look at the names of the horses at all before the meditation. I just sat down with my candle, and after a few deep breaths, the head and shoulders of Michael Murphy, the founder of Esalen, appeared to me. Mike's face was so close to me that I could easily recognize him (a situation that doesn't occur very often in my everyday life). He said nothing, but just looked at me. About twenty minutes later, I finished my meditation and looked at the paper, eager to see if I could find any correspondence between Mike Murphy and the eight horses running in the eighth race. It turned out that one of the horses was named "Friend Murph." My son Nicholas went to the track the next day and bet five dollars for me on Friend Murph. He came in first at five to one, winning twenty-five dollars!

These three personal experiences are examples of spontaneous psi. The conditions under which each occurred would all be considered psi conducive: The one with the sun in my eyes was a hypnagogic state. Another was while dreaming, and the last was meditative. I am sorry to say that these experiences, like most of my other precognitive dreams, have not taught me any deep lessons. Usually, even the highest quality precognitive events in my life have been more humorous than meaningful. Nonetheless, they have had a great impact on me by serving as constant reminders that psi is in my life, and that this is the area I should be working in. They have also been important to me because of the firsthand knowledge they have offered regarding the form and substance of psychic perception. I don't have to rely only upon other people's descriptions of their mental experiences, because I have my own personal data to work with.

For the past several years, I have been attempting to bring psi under conscious control, so it could be used with confidence. It is important that experimenters share trust, love, and grace in order to achieve reliability in psi functioning.[7] Accuracy will come from time to time without these conditions, but not with consistent reliability. We all have an idea of what is meant by trust and love. What I mean by grace is a feeling of harmony, and even more importantly, unequivocal gratitude, and the acceptance of the gift of psi among the group doing the experiment. Ken Wilber describes this kind of transparent relationship in his remarkable book, *No Boundary*.[8]

Until we have a significantly better description of the interaction of psi targets with our perception of them, I will continue to view psi experiences as miracles masquerading as data. The gestalt is the patterning force that holds the psychic image together and provides meaning to the viewer. One day I hope we will get beyond the holistic and gestalt types of psi data, in which only forms, feelings, and icons are perceived. Analytical data, such as the names and uses of objects and locations, are not yet generally available in psychic research. We know that analysis, imagination, and intrusive memory are the enemies of psi, but we must learn to make use of them constructively if psi is to be brought to consciousness and volitional use.

With this goal in mind, several of us in California formed an informal group of experienced researchers who are willing to share their own introspections about personal psi in experimental situations. Although these exercises are carefully conducted, they are not all double-blind, and we are exquisitely aware of the potential problems of unintentional cues. In our experimental situations, the only comment an interviewer is permitted to make is either, "Tell me more about what you are seeing," or "What are you experiencing that makes you say 'such and such.'" This is all process-oriented research, free from the analytic requirements of sponsoring corporations to achieve statistically significant "P values," variations from standard probability curves. These informal sessions later led us into highly successful, formal, double-blind experiments.

Under this friendly telepathic protocol, I have described many objects in boxes and mental pictures thought up by one of our group. Trying to psychically create visual pictures associated with a psi target is often like searching for a memory. You try to remember a forgotten name; you struggle and struggle. The more you struggle, the farther away the name recedes. Finally you give up. Soon after, with the release of your effort, the name will spontaneously appear.

In the case of searching for psi images, one looks for incongruous and surprising pictures so that they can be separated from old pictures residing in one's memory. However, the process *feels* the same. In one case you are trying to remember something you have known before, while in psi you are trying to "remember" something for the first time. Physicist Gerald

Feinberg thought that precognition was a case of "remembering" one's own future mind.[9]

Larry Dossey, in his book *Recovering the Soul*, says that we do this by reaching into the vast inner space of our eternal, nonlocal mind.[10] We know from our own parapsychological research that this mind exists, and that it transcends both space and time. Nonlocality has come to the forefront recently in quantum physics, with credible laboratory experiments to demonstrate its existence. For example, in these experiments, when one measures the polarization of a pair of photons born in the same interaction, but traveling in opposite directions, the polarization of one photon appears to be *altered* by the mere act of *observing* the other. Since the two photons are traveling away from each other at the speed of light, this startling correlation appears to be a strong violation of Einstein's special theory of relativity. Einstein correctly recognized this effect, and thirty years before the experiments were performed, he wrote (mistakenly, it turned out) that this violation of special relativity was a demonstration of a weakness in quantum mechanics. David Bohm calls this demonstrated nonlocal interaction "quantum interconnectedness."

A more down-to-earth occurrence of nonlocality is the phenomenal connection between identical twins separated at birth and reared apart from each other. A fascinating book I read many years ago described the reunion of male twins meeting each other for the first time at age thirty, after growing up on opposite coasts of the United States. Each had become a telephone company linesman, married a woman named Linda, and had a dog named Penny. When they were brought together for the first time, both were wearing blue work shirts, white pants, gold-rimmed glasses, and had mustaches. Doubtless, the coincidence was due in part to their common genetics, but their truly incredible commonality certainly supports the idea of a psi connection — a bridge between their nonlocal minds.

This "collective unconscious mind" has been called by many names, and described by philosophers for millennia. Two thousand years ago Patanjali, the Hindu philosopher and Sanskrit writer of the *Yoga Sutras* (aphorisms or teachings), taught that we obtain psi data by accessing what has become known as the *akashic* records, the aspect of nonlocal mind that contains all information past, present, and future.[11] One accesses it, he said, by "becoming it," with a single-pointed focus of attention. His writings provide us with a mental tool kit to accomplish this. Patanjali tells us that in order to see the world in our mind, we must quiet our mental waves (*vriti* in Sanskrit).[12] We have learned to call these waves *mental noise.*

While the Buddhists say that most of our troubles come from making distinctions where in fact there are none, Patanjali taught that, to be in control of our own consciousness, we must learn to make distinctions among our mental states. If we cannot control our own mind, how can we hope to control our interactions with the outside world? He described five states of mental functioning, and made it clear that we should always know which state we are in. He said we must discriminate between right thinking, wrong thinking (errors), sleeping or dreaming, remembering, and imagining.[13] These correspond precisely to our concept for learning to separate the psi signal from memory, analysis, and imagination, the principal sources of mental noise we encounter in remote viewing.

This model of psi functioning suggests that the information we access is always with us, and therefore always available. It is not a new theory, but it seems to fit the data I've observed better than the "information transmission" model, in which one person sends a psychic message to another.

In order to familiarize ourselves with the experience of psi, the authors carried out a series of experimental trials, in preparation for the double-blind study later described in Chapter 5. In one, I had to describe a target that was only shown to me sealed in a cardboard box. I looked at the package, closed my eyes, and clearly saw a star filling the box. The unknown remote-viewing object was in fact a papier-mâché star. I believe that with targets that are archetypes, such as a star, or a doll, we instantly fill in the rest of the picture from memory gestalts. We have come to consider these as "hot" targets, which we almost always describe correctly. Examples of these from recent experience include: an apple corer, eyeglasses, a collapsible silver cup, dolls, stars, shiny things, a Swiss army knife, a magnifying glass, Santa Claus, a Coke bottle, land/water interfaces, and windmills. Our brains are hardwired to see faces and to recognize other geometrical shapes, so these archetypes come partly from visual cortex structure, and partly from memory.

My next target in that series was an object in a shopping bag. I described what looked to me like a "furry stuffed animal, perhaps a teddy bear." I was then asked, "What do you see that makes you say 'teddy bear'?" I took a break to clear my mental slate and ready it for a new image. (A break simply means that I opened my eyes, and took a few deep breaths. Taking a break like this is an essential part of the remote-viewing process.) Then I looked again and saw what seemed to be a bear standing up on two feet, like the "honey bear" of the familiar plastic honey container. I described this, saying also that it reminded me of a "troll." I was asked if there was anything further to see, and I offered that the doll seemed to be wearing a crown on its head and a smock-like dress. My target was, in actuality, an angel troll with a halo sewn to her hair!

The final object in the series was a perfectly smooth spherical silver ball with a bell inside it. I described it as some kind of crystal with sharp edges and facets. It was as though the featureless ball had no hooks or handles to mentally grab on to, even though a ball could be considered an archetype. I believe that seeing a featureless ball had no surprise value for me, so I created something more interesting.

It now seems clear that if a target has no distinctive features and cannot be easily described or conceptualized, it is much more difficult to bring into awareness. A target that is an archetype seems to resonate with special brain cells or memories. For example, in electrical engineering one speaks of a matched filter, into which you can put a very noisy signal, but only a prescribed signal can come out. If any of that signal is present in the input noise, you will get a pure distillation of it in the output. I believe the star was a perfect example of that kind.

Telepathy experiments — from one mind to another — are more problematic than remote viewing, because there is an inherent uncertainty as to what the target really is. In one such trial, I was asked to describe the "object" that the interviewer (Jane) had clearly in her mind. I closed my eyes and immediately came up with a picture of a "blue house with white trim." I went on to describe the house as having "two stories, with a peaked roof, and a gable on one side." Jane replied, "That's my house in Eugene, Oregon [which I had never seen], and that's not a gable you're seeing — it's a solar heating panel." The intended target she was trying to project was her little dog, which lives in the house. I never saw the dog at all. It is apparently difficult to separate out a single image from the jumble that is in another person's mind.

Color is often an important and correct perception for me in this type of trial. Recently in an experiment with Jane, I had clear mental pictures of a "red wooden doll," "two blue bottles," and a "green mass with bright orange above." The first two targets were hidden objects, and were absolutely correct. The latter was a mental marigold, but I saw only the colors, not the flower itself. (This is, perhaps, because from across a room I could recognize such a plant visually from its colors, although I would not be able to see the leaves.)

I then decided to turn the tables on Jane. I told her that I thought I could hold and stabilize a mental image for her to receive on her mental screen. Jane, who had never been the subject in a remote-viewing or telepathy experiment, described it first as a totem pole, saying "It's tall and has only one face on it." Then she went on to describe various curving, green sinuous shapes or robes that didn't jell for me into a matchable description. As an interviewer, I always try to continue a session long enough so that some future judge will be able to differentiate among several possible target descriptions. Usually, of course, I would not know what the target was.

I almost always interview with my eyes closed, so that I can share in the viewer's images. I asked Jane to drift above the target and look at the overall setting. I had told her that it was an outdoor target. She said that she now saw a large chessboard, with a queen, wearing a crown, standing on it. She then went back to her curving images, mentioning wavy hair and flowing robes. I opened my eyes, and saw her right hand raised high above her head. I asked her why she was doing that. She said that she didn't know, but it had something to do with the curves. The target in my mind was the Statue of Liberty!

From our experiments, I am convinced that the reason targets with fewer and bolder elements in the visual field are much easier to describe has nothing to do with ESP. The advantage of high contrast is common to all of our ordinary visual, perceptual processing capabilities and habits. One of the keys to separating the psychic signal from mental noise is that the image of the psi target usually has greater surprise value than the noise from memory or imagination. In addition, one is able to move and shift one's point of view for true psi images, especially large outdoor targets.

For example, I recently correctly described an island target as "covered with fir trees, except for an area that is clear-cut down to the orange-brown earth by the sea." I then described a house by the shore, and some of its contents. I had started out with a mental picture of a very large building in a city, until I saw the sea at the edge of my mental field of view. At that point I was whisked out to sea, where I found myself looking down on several islands, of which I described the largest. The clear-cut area was *totally unknown* to my interviewer, but was confirmed by an unexpected phone call the following day.

In addition to our experiments in the Soviet Union, which were videotaped, I have carried out many remote-viewing demonstrations live on television, where the television host was the viewer. Our success rate is much higher on TV than it is in the lab. Successful trials have been done on the *Phil Donahue Show, 60 Minutes — Australia*, and several evening news programs. Researcher Charles Honorton found a similar pattern of TV success when he was director of the Psychophysical Research Laboratory at Princeton, New Jersey. Although the remote viewer feels plenty of "performance anxiety" under such conditions, the excitement and the need for success seems to get the psychic juices flowing. This is further evidence that psi is not an analytic ability, because nobody is able to do mathematical calculations better on TV than in a quiet, private place. I believe that the stimulation of being on TV parallels Yoda's advice from *Star Wars*, when Luke Skywalker was trying to psychically levitate his starship from the mud: "There is no trying — there is only doing."

In April, 1973, we were just beginning to explore the effect of increased distance on remote-viewing accuracy. In one of our experimental series, Hal

Puthoff was on a combined business and pleasure trip to San Jose, Costa Rica. A total of twelve remote-viewing descriptions were collected during Hal's trip, six from each of two viewers, one of whom was Pat Price. Police officer Price, whose incredible work is described in Chapter 2, was one of our most gifted viewers. He conclusively proved the ability of the human mind to make remarkable and far-reaching connections by showing us how well remote viewing could be performed. I was Price's interviewer as he described an assortment of churches, market squares, and volcanic mountains such as one would expect to find in a mountainous Central American country like Costa Rica. After the experiment was concluded, we found that Hal had indeed visited the market, the volcano, etc., on the days that Price had experienced them in the lab.

On one of these days I was waiting in our little electrically shielded room for Price to come and carry out the scheduled 9:00 a.m. experiment. It was almost time to begin and I had already put the introduction on the audiotape: "This is a remote-viewing experiment with Pat Price and Russ Targ. Today is April 12, 1973, and we are in the shielded room in the Radio Physics Building at SRI." But Price never showed up. We considered these first long-distance trials to be part of an important experiment, so in the spirit of "The show must go on," I decided to do the remote-viewing trial myself.

Although I had had many psychic experiences in my life, I had never taken part in any formal experiment before. As I restarted the tape recorder and closed my eyes, I saw what looked like an airport with an "ocean at the end of the concrete runway." I went on to describe an airport building with an overhang on the left, and grass and sand on the right side of the runway, which I drew.

All of this turned out to be correct, except that I "saw" a Quonset-hut type of building with an overhang, where in actuality it was a flat-roofed building. However, when I first saw the photo of the place Puthoff had visited on a one-day, unplanned trip to Colombia, shown in **Figure Ia**, my poor physical vision made the semi-circular patch of grass look to me like a Quonset hut. This raised the interesting question of whether I had been psychically looking at the place Hal was visiting, or at the feedback picture that I was shown several weeks later!

FIGURE 1a. AIRPORT ON AN ISLAND off the coast of Colombia, used as a remote-viewing target.

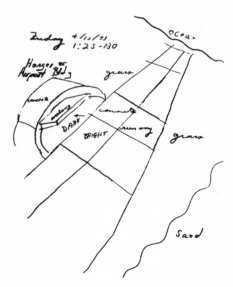

FIGURE 1b. SKETCH PRODUCED BY SUBJECT TARG with San Andreas, Colombia, airport used as remote-viewing target.

In the experiment, we received no feedback after each viewing, but had to wait for Hal's return to find out where he had been when each of the viewings was done. This is a difficult mode of operation, because a viewer likes to clean his mental slate, and usually needs to reach closure of one experiment before starting the next. However, this trial clearly showed that even an inexperienced physicist could function psychically if he is strongly motivated, and if the necessity level is high enough. Since that time hundreds of remote-viewing trials have been carried out successfully by dozens of other inexperienced people from all over the world — evidence that the nonlocal mind exists in all of us.

In her 1995 report, prepared at the request of the CIA for an evaluation of the remote-viewing work conducted over the past two decades, statistics professor and textbook author Dr. Jessica Utts concluded the following:

> Using the standards applied to any other area of science, it is concluded that psychic functioning has been well established. The statistical results of the studies examined are far beyond what is expected by chance. Argument that these results could be due to methodological flaws in the experiments are soundly refuted. Effects of similar magnitude to those found in government-sponsored research at SRI and SAIC have been replicated at a number of laboratories across the world. *Such consistency cannot readily be explained by claims of flaws or fraud.* [Emphasis added.][14]

Vision is not the only sensory modality available to psi. We recently had an almost purely telepathic demonstration in our informal psi research group. We were discussing the extent to which psi was a memory-like phenomenon, and our host, Dr. Dean Brown, said it interested him that people can instantly tell if they have ever heard a word or name before. How can we search the entire contents of our memory so fast? "For example," he said, "Who knows what 'churk' means?" Five of us held up our hands. He protested, "How could you know what it means? I just made up the word!"

The surprising explanation was that five of us (not including Dr. Brown) had just eaten dinner at a Cuban restaurant. The waitress had told us that the specialty of the house was catfish with "churk" sauce, which some of us had ordered. The only plausible place that our host could have accessed that word was from the minds of the five of us who had just experienced it for the first time, half an hour before. (In a follow-up investigation, I discovered that there is no such thing as "churk" sauce. The restaurant manager explained that our waitress was from El Salvador and doesn't speak English very well. The sauce was really "jerk" sauce, and appeared that way on the menu.) This event is therefore an example of almost pure telepathy, in that the only possible other source for "churk" would be *retrocognitive clairaudience!* (This is the experience of psychically hearing something that had occurred in the past.)

In sharing these personal experiences, I do not think for a moment that they substitute for laboratory research. However, I do think that researchers have a unique perspective to bring to the interpretation of their own experiential psi data. As psi researchers over the past two decades, our accomplishment has been the discovery that psi is no longer elusive. It can be called upon when needed. Our task now is to discover where this phenomenon comes from.

Over my thirty years of work in psi research, my goal has become twofold: first, to develop the capability to integrate psychic abilities into my life. Through this, I hope to gain the knowledge to allow me greater contact with that life-sustaining extended consciousness, the source of psychic healing and all other psi — our community of spirit. My colleague in parapsychological research, Dr. Bill Roll, calls this concept of our interlinked selves the "longbody."[15] He tells us that this concept originated with the Iroquois Indians, who used it to refer to the great web of living connections among tribe members both living and dead.

Secondly, as a scientist, I am convinced that we significantly misunderstand our universal interconnectedness, and the place in the universe of space-time where we appear to be residing. Parapsychological researchers were the first to devote their scientific energies to exploring the nature of this, our nonlocal universe. I hope to continue to help us find our place, and to make these connections.

chapter two

Our Astonishing
Nonlocal Mind:

*On a Clear Day
We Can See Forever*

A miracle *is usually thought of as an event that appears to contradict known* scientific laws. Another interpretation of a miracle is a significant occurrence that seems to be inexplicable by the laws of nature, and is therefore attributed to supernatural causes. A miracle is always a surprise. This book is about the miracles of our mind, which have been demonstrated throughout recorded history, and more recently, through a hundred years of psychical research. However, even though psychic abilities have been documented in laboratories, their real importance to us comes from their natural occurrence in our daily lives.

We are writing about events that come from an awareness expanded beyond the ordinary — unlimited by distance or time. Our ability to forecast future happenings, and to psychically influence healing at a distance, may be seen as miracles because they seem to contradict presently understood laws of science. We believe, however, they are caused not by the supernatural, but by the capabilities of what physicists have come to call our "nonlocal mind." This fascinating and not yet fully understood phenomenon that connects us to each other and to the world at large allows us to describe, experience, and influence activities occurring anywhere in space and time.

In our everyday consciousness, this ability to open the psychic door to our universal connectedness is generally unavailable to us because of the noisy distractions of our ongoing thoughts. Nevertheless, some people, through talent and practice, have sharpened their ability to access information that seems unobtainable through ordinary sensory perception. Whenever any one person does this and demonstrates an ability beyond the ordinary, it is an inspiration to the rest of us, as an indication of our immense and still largely unexplored human potential.

This chapter centers around this astonishing and, by now, well-documented human capacity known as clairvoyance or remote (distant) viewing. A discussion of remote viewing is an appropriate introduction to the subsequent topic of healing, in that distant healing and distant viewing are but two different manifestations of our nonlocal minds. The connection between remote viewing and psychic healing is further suggested by Djuna Davitashvili, a renowned Russian psychic healer, whose remarkable clairvoyant ability is described below.

FROM THE COLD WAR TO COLD BORSCHT

In 1976, Hal Puthoff and I (Russell) wrote a paper for the *Proceedings of the IEEE* (Institute of Electrical and Electronic Engineering) describing the government-sponsored extrasensory perception research we were carrying out at SRI.[1] This paper described the clairvoyant spying process for which we had coined the name "remote viewing." Because of the remarkable data we presented, the paper was immediately translated and published in the Soviet Union. When the Russians found that it was possible to take psychic peeks into distant locations hidden from ordinary perception, it was a discovery of shockingly great significance in a country obsessed with secrecy. As a result, I was eventually invited to demonstrate our work for the Soviet Academy of Sciences. After my presentation, a well known Soviet physicist asked me, "Doesn't your work mean that it's not possible to hide anything anymore?" I had to tell him: "Yes, that's just what it means."

Another question surprised me. A distinguished Soviet scientist asked,

"In your country, is it necessary to believe in God to do the work you are doing?"

I usually try to be very forthcoming with questioners, but this one really brought me to a standstill. I finally told him that I, like Einstein, Spinoza, and many others, believe that there is a transcendent organizing principle, or intelligence, in the universe. Today I would add that our psychic research strongly supports the idea of a universal mind-to-mind connection, or community of spirit, which some people associate with God. Of course, I did not choose to tell my Soviet colleague that it was the Central Intelligence Agency's desire to peer into the depth of his country that had begun leading me to these newfound spiritual insights. There is a great American tradition for finding God after being a spy for the CIA!

The following year, my colleagues and I were taking part in the first Soviet-American collaboration to investigate psychic remote sensing. Soviet psychology professor Rubin Agazumson, from Yerevan in Soviet Armenia, convinced his superiors at the Academy of Sciences in Moscow to invite us to demonstrate the remote-viewing abilities. Before we arrived, Agazumson had already replicated our remote-viewing findings, working with his graduate students. Remarkably, he had managed to integrate his passionate Eastern Orthodox religious faith with his excitement over his psi research. His main interest was in exploring the generality of man's community of spirit, rather than the more specific function of remote behavior modification, which, unfortunately, was the application that most interested his government and associates.

After our visit to the Academy, we went to a Moscow apartment and got ready to send a psychic probe halfway around the world to the streets of San Francisco. With the obligatory glass of vodka in hand, I was about to participate in an experiment in a land where psychic experiences have been taken for granted for centuries.

Date: October 17, 1984
Location: Moscow, USSR
Time: 6:00 p.m.

Viewer: Djuna Davitashvili
Client: USSR Academy of Sciences

Ronald Reagan was president of the United States, Andropov (former head of the KGB) was premier of the Soviet Union, and we were in the icon-decorated living room of the famous Soviet healer, Djuna Davitashvili. Djuna's home is a symphony of red: red velvet wall covering, red brocade chairs, and red silk lamp shades. (In Russian the word for red, *crasni*, is the same as the word for beautiful!) Djuna enjoys great celebrity and privilege from her successful work as a psychic healer, an important part of which involved keeping Premier Breznev alive through many of his grave illnesses. Djuna is a beautiful, generous, and charismatic woman, with the large, dark eyes and long, black hair of her Gypsy forebears from Soviet Georgia. She is proud of her Gypsy roots, though now she often wears a white lab coat over her embroidered dresses. These days Djuna is a researcher as well as a subject of research in healing at the Soviet Academy of Sciences. Her spacious apartment is on Arbat Street, in an artistic Moscow district not far from the Academy of Sciences. The overheated living room was crowded with more than forty people, and filled with electronic birdcalls from her doorbell that kept chirping to announce new guests. What appeared to be a party was actually a scientific experiment to demonstrate remote viewing for the Academy of Sciences. A videotaped record would be made of the event.

The Russians had offered us their famous telepathic subject, Karl Nikolaev, for the demonstration, but I preferred to work with someone who had never experimented with ESP before. Our research had taught us how to carry out this type of experiment successfully, and we would rather not have to convince someone that they should follow our approach rather than the method they had been using for years. Although Djuna was a psychic healer, she had never done anything like remote viewing. In fact, that actually became somewhat of a problem.

The American guests included my daughter, Elisabeth, who was a Russian translator and medical student at the time (she is now a psychiatrist),

Jocelyn Stoller, who organized the trip for us, translator Anya Kucherev, and Carol Daniels, an American filmmaker. Apart from Djuna, the key people in the Soviet party were our host, Andrei Berezin, a biophysicist from the Academy of Sciences, and his film crew. (Agazumson was not present.) **Figure 2** shows Berezin seated between Djuna on the right, Elisabeth Targ on the left, and Russell at the far left.

FIGURE 2. MOSCOW-TO-SAN FRANCISCO REMOTE-VIEWING EXPERIMENT: In Djuna's Moscow apartment are, from left to right, Russell Targ, Elisabeth Targ, Andrei Berezin from the Soviet Academy of Sciences, and Djuna Davitashvili.

Also present was Joseph Goldin, an enigmatic and courageous Soviet impresario who had been sent to a psychiatric prison two years previously, for creating a real-time video satellite "space bridge." This space bridge had included young people playing music in Red Square who were able to see and talk to similar happy folk at a park in San Francisco through the medium of video screens. The Soviet police argument was: "Anyone who would do such a thing in the USSR in 1982 must be crazy." It was akin to a failure of reality testing. Fortunately, Joseph had many friends and was released from prison after a few months. It was he who had found Djuna for us after we had turned down the offer of Nicholaev.

We thought it ironic that we were about to attempt to do psychically precisely what Joseph had been sent to prison for attempting with TV satellite technology. Our experiment would be a "consciousness bridge," in which a remote viewer in Moscow — Djuna — would try to describe and experience what our colleague was simultaneously experiencing at an unknown location in San Francisco. Although remote viewing is, of course, not always 100 percent reliable, we were confident we could carry out a successful demonstration.

We hadn't told Djuna exactly what we had in mind, and it was only after the video lights began focusing on her favorite chair that she finally realized we expected *her* to do the viewing. Until then she had thought that we were the psychics, not her, and she didn't want to jeopardize her comfortable position with the Academy by getting involved with a crazy-sounding American experiment.

Elisabeth gradually worked her charm on Djuna, telling her that we knew she had never done anything like this before, and that we would take full responsibility for the experiment if it failed. If she would just follow Elisabeth's step-by-step instructions, everything would be all right. (We reassure all our viewers in this same way.) We told Djuna that our distant American colleague, whose photo she would be shown, had previously selected six interesting locations within San Francisco. In two hours, he would be walking around one of those locations. We would like Djuna to describe that place to us and tell us what it felt like to her. We also told her that the specific target location had not yet been selected; in fact, our research partner was still asleep. When he awakened, he would throw a die on the floor of his room and use that number to determine which one of six places would be his destination. Those of us in Moscow had no prior knowledge of his six possible target locations, although we carried with us six numbered, sealed envelopes containing photographs of each site.

Djuna finally realized that we were asking her to cast her attention ten thousand miles to the west, and two hours into the future, and then tell the awaiting video cameras what she saw. "Who needs this?" she complained. But in the end we prevailed, and Djuna settled into her chair to await further instructions.

After a long period of silence, Elisabeth was able to coax a few hesitant sentences from Djuna. Again and again, Elisabeth asked her to describe her mental pictures of the secret place our San Francisco colleague would be visiting. "I see a small plaza with something round in the center.... Walkways extend out of the plaza but are connected to it.... Small buildings with pointed roofs...the buildings look similar and are connected together."

Elisabeth then asked her to drift up in the air and look down upon the site, a strategy that is often successful, probably because of its surprise value. Djuna said, "From above, I see a green circle with a light circle around it.... I see a white couch or divan.... I see the profile of an animal's eye, with pointy ears."[2]

Two hours after Djuna gave her description, we called our colleague's answering machine in California to get the number of his target destination: the machine said, "number six." When we opened envelope number six, we saw that the target was, in fact, the merry-go-round on the little plaza at Pier 39 on the San Francisco waterfront. We found many dramatic correspondences between the target picture and what Djuna had seen: the merry-go-round, the wooden buildings with the pointed roofs, and even the wooden animals on the merry-go-round. Later, in the formal evaluation of Djuna's thirty-three comments about the target, we found that her associations were so significantly matched to this target that the odds of this occurring by chance were better than 200 to 1. We were all very excited. We felt that we had indeed created a consciousness bridge. A picture of the merry-go-round and Djuna's sketch of it are shown in **Figure 3**. Her remarkable drawing of the animal's eye and ears is shown in **Figure 4**, next to a photo of one of the merry-go-round horses.

Djuna had described the target in Russian as a "cupola." A cupola, of course, is a decorative, dome-topped, cylindrical structure made of pillars and latticework that sits on top of many Victorian and Renaissance buildings. It looks a lot like a carousel, and might easily be mistaken for one under difficult viewing conditions. Djuna's comment reminded me of another time a remote viewer had spoken of a cupola. Remarkably, in that instance the actual target had also been a merry-go-round.

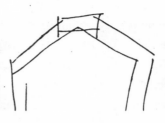

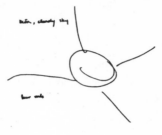

Figure 3. THE TARGET FOR THE MOSCOW-TO-SAN FRANCISCO remote-viewing experiment, October 10, 1984, is the merry-go-round on Pier 39, at Fisherman's Wharf. Djuna's sketch of the "circular area" is on the right, and her pointed-roof building is above it. Djuna said, "I see a small plaza with something round in the center. Walkways extend out of the plaza, but are connected to it.... Small buildings with pointed roofs... like a historical monument outside the city.... The buildings look similar and are connected together.... From above, I see a green circle with a light circle around it. I see a white couch or divan." (There is a white couch on the merry-go-round.)

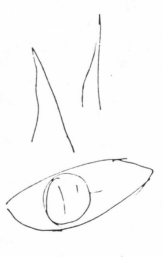

FIGURE 4. EXCERPT FROM DJUNA'S TRANSCRIPT for the Moscow-to-San Francisco remote-viewing experiment: "I see the profile of an animal's eye, with pointy ears." The illustration shows Djuna's drawings of these items.

In 1995, many years after our experiments with Djuna, I was the remote-viewing subject myself at a workshop at Virginia Beach organized by retired U.S. Army General Burt Stubblebine and Lyn Buchanan. I described the target I saw as a merry-go-round. My target turned out to be a cupola! Cupolas and merry-go-rounds seem to be interchangeable in the visual-to-verbal dictionary of psychic functioning. It is as if we are witnessing the emergence of a psychic dictionary that is evolving from translations of the real world into psychic images.

Two days after the Moscow-to-San Francisco merry-go-round experiment, we carried out a second trial with Djuna. This time she got right into the spirit of it, and seemed to be fascinated by the target she was describing. She went on and on, describing, "A building associated with a famous man.... There is a famous book associated with this place.... There is a statue of this man outside the building.... There is a painting of him inside the building. It is not the kind of place where people live. They just come and go.... I think they are having a party. I see lots of candles."

The target was St. Mary's Church in San Francisco! Once again, the sixty different concepts Djuna mentioned in her narrative also matched her target to a mathematically significant degree. Djuna loved the idea that she had so many correct things to say, without realizing at the time that her target was a church. We celebrated our success and mutual pleasure with a sumptuous Russian feast of vodka, cognac, herring, caviar, cabbage salad, and lots of dense black bread with cold borscht.

What particularly impressed me back in 1984 was the friendship and party-like ambiance that we experienced with the Soviet Academy of Sciences, where only a few years before, psychic abilities had fueled part of the Cold War between the Soviet Union and the U.S. For example, one Congressman discussing our remote-viewing work in 1979 said:

All I can say is that if the results were faked, our security system doesn't work. What these people "saw" was confirmed by aerial photography. There is no way it could have been faked.... Some of the intelligence people I have talked to know that remote viewing works, although they still block further work on it, since they claim that it is not yet as good as satellite photography. But it seems to me that it would be a hell of a cheap radar system. And if the Russians have it and we don't, we are in serious trouble.

— Congressman Charles Rose

Rose was Chairman of the House Subcommittee on Intelligence Evaluation and Oversight, and was interviewed in *Omni* magazine on the subject of the SRI long-distance remote-viewing experiments.

Two years later the House of Representatives was still worried about Soviet psi research and the implications of applied remote viewing, as evidenced by the following report from a Congressional investigation of the subject:

SURVEY OF SCIENCE AND TECHNOLOGY ISSUES
PRESENT AND FUTURE
COMMITTEE ON SCIENCE AND TECHNOLOGY
U.S. HOUSE OF REPRESENTATIVES
NINETY-SEVENTH CONGRESS
JUNE, 1981

Recent experiments in remote viewing and other studies in parapsychology suggest that there is an "interconnectedness" of the human mind and other minds and with matter.... Experiments on mind-to-mind interconnectedness have yielded some encouraging results.... The implications of these results is that the human mind may be able to obtain information independent of geography and time.... Given the potentially powerful and far-reaching implications of knowledge in this field, and given that the Soviet Union is widely acknowledged to be supporting such research at a far higher and more official level, Congress may wish to undertake a serious assessment of research in this country.

HOW IT ALL BEGAN

The first U.S. government support for our ESP research had its origins in April of 1972, on a windswept pier at St. Simon's Island off the North

Carolina coast. I (Russell) had just finished talking to a hundred futurists at a NASA conference on Speculative Technology about experiments my partner David Hurt and I had done with an electronic ESP-teaching machine.[3] After my talk, I walked down to the water's edge with Astronaut Edgar Mitchell, rocket pioneer Werner von Braun, NASA Director James Fletcher, science fiction writer Arthur C. Clarke, and NASA's New-Projects Administrator, George Pezdirtz, who had organized the conference. I was looking for a way to leave my job in laser research at GTE Sylvania, where I had worked for the past decade, in order to start an ESP program at SRI.

I had been kept later than I had expected at the lecture hall, answering questions about ESP research, while everyone else had gone off to put on sweaters to counter the chilly evening ocean breeze. As I stood in my short-sleeved shirt on the pier, I tried to remember my Kundalini meditation in order to summon up enough warmth to keep from freezing. I struggled not to shiver while I explained the concepts of contemporary psi research to the men I knew could determine my entire future as a psychic researcher.

In my experience trying to interest people in supporting ESP research, I have often found that the top people in an organization know that psi is real, and they are willing to admit it. Edgar Mitchell had carried out some ESP card-guessing experiments from space, and had a spiritually transforming experience viewing the earth while standing on the moon.[4] Werner von Braun told us of his beloved psychic grandmother, who always knew in advance when someone was in trouble and needed help. Fletcher was concerned that the Russians were ahead of us in psychic research, a fear based in part on the recently published book *Psychic Discoveries Behind the Iron Curtain*.[5] Only the science fiction writer Clarke expressed skepticism, despite his hugely successful book *Childhood's End*, which was all about psi.[6]

In the end, with Mitchell's great assistance and continuing help from Dr. Pezdirtz at NASA, physicist Hal Puthoff and I were offered a contract to start a research program. The inauguration of our program was not without controversy. When we first undertook our remote-viewing investigations at SRI, several prominent scientists, and Martin Gardner from *Scientific American* magazine, wrote angry letters to the president of SRI in an effort to get Hal Puthoff and myself fired — a kind of professional death. When an influential scientist, a vice-president of Hewlett-Packard, eventually had an opportunity to review the data presented in an *IEEE* paper written by Hal and myself, he wrote, "This is the kind of thing that I wouldn't believe, even if it were true!"

Although NASA, an early first sponsor, most of our subsequent support came from the CIA and other agencies of the federal government. We still cannot identify some of them, because to do so would violate our secrecy agreements. Of course, none of the work described in this book is presently classified, but some of it was secret until the middle of 1995. It is all representative of the kind of remote viewing that we saw day after day.

Journalists in this country and abroad have speculated on our work for the CIA ever since our earliest successes in psychic research at SRI. Syndicated *Washington Post* columnist Jack Anderson was one of the most avid followers of our psychic adventures. Although I cannot comment about the truth or falsity of individual items in these columns, a reader with even a modest amount of ESP will find it interesting to sort through Anderson's speculation about our work. One of the odd things about Jack Anderson's provocative columns is that no one paid the slightest attention to them at the time. Apparently, they were simply felt to be too unbelievable to be true!

THE RACE FOR "INNER SPACE"
by Jack Anderson

U.S. Intelligence agencies won't talk about it, but they are rushing to catch up with the Soviet Union in what one scientist jocularly calls the "race for inner space" — psychic research.

Parapsychology is a field so full of pseudoscientists, flakes and outright charlatans, that it's easy to debunk the whole idea.

But, there are legitimate laboratory projects that may eventually unlock the mysteries of the human mind. One of the most promising is the testing of "remote viewing" — the claimed ability of some psychics to describe scenes thousands of miles away.

The CIA and the Pentagon have an obvious interest in this phenomenon. If they could get psychics to throw their minds behind the

Iron Curtain there'd be no need to risk the lives of human agents.

The CIA sent representatives to a parapsychology conference in Virginia last December. Besides the usual spoon bending — which professional magicians have debunked as a fairly simple trick — there was serious discussion of remote viewing. In fact, the CIA is now seriously pondering the possibility of raising "psychic shields" to keep Soviet remote viewers away from our secrets.

I asked my skeptical associates Dale Van Atta and Joseph Spear to find out how remote viewing has become almost universally accepted in the intelligence community. They gained access to top-secret briefings on the subject. This is what they learned:

The CIA's latest remote viewing project was code-named "Grill Flame," and was carried out in part by two respected academics: Harold Puthoff, formally with the National Security Agency, and Russell Targ, formally with Stanford Research Institute in Menlo Park, California.

Puthoff and Targ conducted at least two tests that produced astonishing results. They gave one psychic the latitude and longitude of a remote location, and told him to project his mind there and describe the scene. He described an airfield, complete with details — including a large gantry and crane at one end of the field.

The CIA was impressed, but critical. There was indeed an airfield at the map coordinates the psychic had been given. The site was the Soviet's ultra-secret nuclear testing area at Semipalatinsk, Kazakhstan. But, there was no gantry or crane there.

Still, it had been a while since any U.S. spy satellites had taken a picture of the Semipalatinsk base. So, the CIA waited for the next set of photos — and sure enough, there was the gantry and crane, just as the psychic had described them. No one in the U.S. intelligence agencies had known the equipment was there, so the information couldn't have been leaked to him.

The second test involved a Soviet Tu-95 "Backfire" bomber, which the CIA knew had crashed somewhere in Africa. They were eager to find it before the Soviets did, so they could take photographs and perhaps purloin secret gear from the wreckage. So one of project Grill Flame's remote viewers was asked to locate the downed bomber. He gave the CIA the location within several miles of the actual wreckage.

In this chapter we show that there are no secrets. It doesn't matter that the government won't release all the information in its possession about long-distance remote viewing. We have enough, and I am not even going to speculate on what the Freedom of Information Act data would reveal regarding the tens of thousands of pages not yet released. After all, going to prison is too high a price to pay for telling a secret that isn't a secret. On the other hand, according to Reuters, former President Carter confirmed Jack Anderson's story about our finding a missing Soviet airplane, in his September 1995 speech to college students in Atlanta. Thank you, Mr. President.

Pat Price, whom we mentioned briefly in the preceding chapter, was a gift to our program at SRI. One day in June of 1973, Pat called Hal Puthoff to say that he had been following our research. He felt that he had been doing the same kind of psychic work for years, successfully using remote visualization to catch crooks when he was the police commissioner in Burbank, California. He told us that he would sit with the dispatcher in the police station, and when he heard a crime reported, he would scan the city psychically and then immediately send a car to the spot where he saw a frightened man hiding!

After we began working with Price we realized that this exceptional man actually lived his life as a completely integrated psychic person. We had worked with many other talented individuals, but we never met anyone else who showed the same continuous psychic awareness of the world around him. We show a photo of Pat Price together with out-of-body researcher Robert Monroe in the laboratory at SRI in **Figure 5**.

Here is just one example of Pat's amazing ability to scan the entire globe with his mind: During the Yom Kippur War of 1973, the Israelis were being badly beaten because the Egyptians had radar-guided anti-aircraft guns that were shooting down their planes. One day, as we were walking to lunch (which for Price was usually French fries, cherry pie, and a Coke), he told us that the direction of the war was about to turn. He knew this because his remote vision had seen new pods being fitted to the wings of Israeli planes, and he guessed correctly that these were electronic jammers to be used against the Egyptian radar. This top-secret development was the decisive event of the war, but it wasn't revealed by the Israeli government until months after the war was over.

FIGURE 5. PHOTO OF PAT PRICE AT SRI, working with an electronic ESP teaching machine developed for NASA. On the couch (left) is Robert Monroe, author of the pioneering book *Journeys Out of the Body*. Russell Targ is on the right. Photo by Hella Hammid.

Price was a likable, easygoing Irishman with much warmth and humor about him. One day a secretary, who had been typing his psychic descriptions of distant targets, asked him if he was also able to follow her psychically into the ladies' room. He chuckled and replied, "If I can look at anything I choose, anywhere on this entire planet, why would I want follow you into the ladies' room?" We all laughed.

In the experimental protocol that we established at SRI, our laboratory director Bart Cox oversaw all our early experiments. His staff had put together a box of sixty file cards, each containing a target location somewhere within a half hour's drive from SRI. After the remote-viewing subject had been properly sequestered, Cox would use an electronic calculator with a random number feature to choose one of the target locations. Then he would go to the target location, usually with Hal Puthoff.

Since I do not drive, I was almost always the one to stay with the remote-viewing subjects in their electrically shielded room and work with them to create a description of the location the travelers were visiting. I viewed myself as a kind of psychic travel agent, whose job it was to get the viewer to describe his mental picture of the place Puthoff and Cox were visiting. After the viewer had described the target and the travelers had returned, we would all go to the site together so that the viewer could learn which parts of his or her mental picture had accurately matched the target. In one of the formal studies, I sat with Price in a "Faraday cage" — a small electrically shielded room covered with copper screen — on the second floor of the SRI Radio Physics building, while Hal and Bart went to Bart's office on the ground floor. They chose a card from a target pool of which I had no knowledge. The target turned out to be a swimming pool complex at Rinconada Park in Palo Alto, about five miles from SRI.

After the allotted thirty minutes had elapsed, I told Price the travelers had probably reached their destination. He polished his gold wire-rimmed glasses with a white linen handkerchief, leaned back in his chair, and closed his eyes. Price then proceeded to describe a circular pool of water about 100 feet in diameter. (The large pool at Rinconada Park is actually 110 feet in diameter.) He also saw a smaller, rectangular pool about 60 by 80 feet on a side. (This second pool happens to be 75 by 100 feet.) He went on to describe a concrete-block house, which was also part of the Rinconada Park swimming pool complex.

Price's drawing of this site is shown in **Figure 6**. Its remarkable accuracy was one of the hallmarks of his work. However, this illustration also shows one of the problems that must sometimes be dealt with in remote viewing. Having described the physical aspects of the target site with great accuracy, Price then told me he thought the target was a water purification plant. He went on to draw some nonexistent water-storage tanks, and to put rotating machinery into his drawing of the pools.

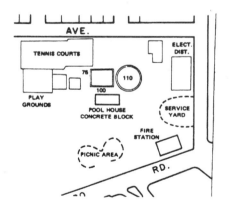

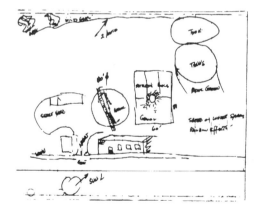

FIGURE 6. REMOTE-VIEWING EXPERIMENT WITH PAT PRICE, in a Faraday cage shielded room, at Stanford Research Institute, Menlo Park, California, 1973. The target is a swimming pool complex at Rinconada Park in Palo Alto. At the left is the Palo Alto city map of the area, and on the right is a drawing of Price's psychic impression from five miles away. His dimensions for the round pool and the rectangular pool are within 10 percent of the correct value. The water tanks shown at the top of the figure were described by Price, but had been removed fifty years earlier.

That was the story as I understood it when Price told it, and up until March 15, 1995. However, on March 16th, I received the *Annual Report of the City of Palo Alto*, celebrating its centennial year. On page 22 of the report I was stunned to read that, "In 1913 a new municipal waterworks was built on the site of the present Rinconada Park." The accompanying photograph showed those two water tanks, exactly where Price had drawn them!

For years we had assumed Price had simply made up an erroneous water purification plant. In reality, he had looked back fifty years in time and told us what had been there at that time, before the swimming pool complex was even built! This amazing phenomenon demonstrated the ability of the non-local mind to travel not only through the three-dimensional world, but also to penetrate the barriers into the fourth dimension — time! It also taught us the lesson that in remote-viewing targeting, one must specify not only the target location to be observed, but the time frame as well.

Pat Price died in 1975 at the age of 57. Two years later Admiral Stanfield Turner, then Director of the CIA, told reporters about his encounter with a man who sounds suspiciously like Price:

WASHINGTON — The CIA financed a program in 1975 to develop a new kind of agent who could truly be called a "spook," Director Stanfield Turner has disclosed.

The CIA chief said that the agency had found a man who could "see" what was going on anywhere in the world through his psychic powers.

Turner said that CIA scientists would show the man a picture of a place and he would then describe any activity going on there at that time.

The tight-lipped CIA chief wouldn't reveal how accurate the spook was, but said that the agency dropped the project in 1975.

"He died," Turner said, "and we haven't heard from him since."

— *Chicago Tribune*
Saturday, August 13, 1977

UNEQUIVOCAL PROOF OF PSI — STRANGER THAN FICTION

Admiral Turner knew what he was talking about regarding the CIA's psychic spooks. In 1974 Hal Puthoff and I briefed CIA officials at the highest levels about our work. The consensus among the operationally oriented people then was that we were "wasting our time" viewing U.S. targets when we could be looking at Soviet sites. The Deputy Director for Intelligence at the CIA at that time was John McMahon, who listened to our story and believed our remote-viewing data. After our briefing, he told us that he had one particular site in the Soviet Union that he would like us to investigate for him.

Now, after sixteen months of correspondence with the Freedom of Information Act folks at the CIA, and the help of two Congressmen, two lawyers (one of whom was my son Nicholas), and a senator, I am finally able to relate the following story, which is one of our most remarkable adventures with Pat Price and the CIA. Their letter to me is on page 62.

In the fall of 1974, one of our "monitors" from the CIA came to SRI with the coordinates for what he described as a "Soviet site of great interest to the analysts." Price and another of our most gifted viewers, Ingo Swann, had already demonstrated that they could describe distant locations that a co-experimenter was visiting. We had just begun a series of new and more difficult experiments to describe distant sites, in which the remote viewers were given only the site's geographical coordinates of latitude and longitude. Our government's security agencies wanted any information we could give them, and they were eager to find out if we could describe a target ten thousand miles away.

Armed with a slip of paper bearing only the coordinates, Price and I climbed to the second floor of SRI's Radio Physics building and locked ourselves into the small electrically shielded room that we used for our experiments. I joked with Price that this trial was just like the Rinconada Park experiment, only further away. As always, I began our little ritual of starting the tape recorder, giving the time and date, and describing who we were and what we were doing. I then read Price the coordinates.

UNCLASSIFIED

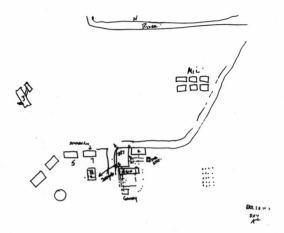

FIGURE 7a. SUBJECT EFFORT at building layout.

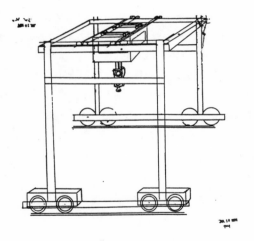

FIGURE 7b. SUBJECT EFFORT at crane construction.

FIGURE 7. PAT PRICE'S SKETCH OF BUILDINGS (Figure 7a) and a crane (Figure 7b), from his remote viewing of a Soviet weapons factory 10,000 miles away, in 1974 investigation of applied *psi* at SRI. What the CIA labeled "subject effort," we consider a miracle.

UNCLASSIFIED

As was Pat's custom, he polished his spectacles, leaned back in his chair, and closed his eyes. He was silent for about a minute, and then he started to laugh. He said, "What I see reminds me of the old joke that starts with a guy in his penthouse looking up at the 3rd Avenue elevated train." Pat then began his description: "I am lying on my back on the roof of a two- or three-story brick building. It's a sunny day. The sun feels good. There's the most amazing thing. There's a giant gantry crane moving back and forth over my head.... As I drift up in the air and look down, it seems to be riding on a track with one rail on each side of the building. I've never seen anything like that." Pat then made a little sketch of the layout of the buildings, and the crane, which he labeled as a gantry. Later on, he again drew the crane as we show it in the recently released illustration, **Figures 7a** and **7b**.

After several days we completed the remote viewing. We were astonished when we were told that the site was the super-secret Soviet atomic-bomb laboratory at Semipalatinsk, where they were also testing particle-beam weapons.

The accuracy of Price's drawing is the sort of thing that I, as a physicist, would never have believed, if I had not seen it for myself. The drawing at the top of **Figure 8** was made by the CIA from satellite photography of the Semipalatinsk facility. At the bottom of that figure we show Price's drawing, together with an enlargement of the crane from the CIA photo. Price went on to draw many other items at the site, including the cluster of compressed gas cylinders shown in the satellite photo, and at the top of his drawing in **Figure 9**.

One of the most interesting things Price saw was not in the CIA drawing at all, because it was inside the building that he was psychically lying on top of, and unknown to anyone in our government at the time. In this experiment he described a large interior room where people were assembling a giant, sixty-foot diameter metal sphere. He said that it was being assembled from thick metal "gores," like sections of an orange peel, but they were having trouble welding it all together because the pieces were warping. Price said that they were looking for a lower-temperature welding material. We didn't get any feedback on this for more than three years. Then we discovered how

FIGURE 8a. ARTIST TRACINGS OF A SATELLITE PHOTOGRAPH of the Semipalatinsk target site. Such tracings were made by the CIA to conceal the accuracy of detail of satellite photography at the time.

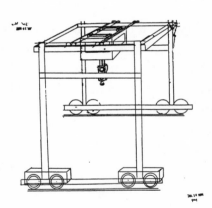

FIGURE 8b. PAT PRICE'S ESP-BASED DRAWING of a gantry crane at the secret Soviet R&D site at Semipalatinsk showing remarkable agreement with Figure 8c.

FIGURE 8c. CIA DRAWING BASED ON SATELLITE photography (Figure 8a). Note, for example, that both cranes have eight wheels.

accurate Price's viewings had been when the sphere-fabricating activity at Semipalatinsk was eventually described in *Aviation Week* magazine.[7]

> SOVIETS PUSH FOR BEAM WEAPON ... The U.S. used high res-
> olution photographic reconnaissance satellites to watch soviet techni-
> cians dig through solid granite formations. In a nearby building, huge
> extremely thick steel gores were manufactured. These steel segments
> were parts of a large sphere estimated to be about 18 meters (57.8 feet)
> in diameter. U.S. officials believe that the spheres are needed to capture
> and store energy from nuclear driven explosives or pulse power genera-
> tors. Initially, some U.S. physicists believed that there was no method
> the Soviets could use to weld together the steel gores of the spheres to
> provide a vessel strong enough to withstand pressures likely to occur in
> a nuclear explosive fission process, especially when the steel to be welded
> was extremely thick.

Although we were happy to receive this confirmation, unfortunately, Pat Price had died two years earlier. So, from the point of view of the experiment, he made his perception of the sixty-foot spheres and "gores" without any feedback at all. Price's drawing of the sphere sections he psychically saw is shown at the bottom of Figure 9. This shows that Price's remarkable perception was *a direct experience of the site.* He was not reading the mind of the sponsor, because no one in the United States knew of the spheres. Nor could Pat have been precognitively looking at his feedback from the future, because he died before the details of the sphere he saw were independently confirmed.

The way we described this miracle in our report to our sponsors back in Washington was as follows:

> The exceptionally accurate description of the multistory crane was
> taken as indicative of probable target acquisition, and therefore the
> subject (Price) was introduced to sponsor personnel who collected
> further data for evaluation. The latter contained both additional phys-
> ical data which were independently verified by other sponsor
> resources, thus providing additional calibration, and also initially
> unverifiable data of current operational interest. Several hours of tape

transcript, and a notebook full of drawings were generated over a two-week period. The results contained noise along with signal, but were nonetheless clearly differentiated from chance results generated by control subjects in comparison experiments carried out by the COTR (Contracting Office Technical Representative).[8]

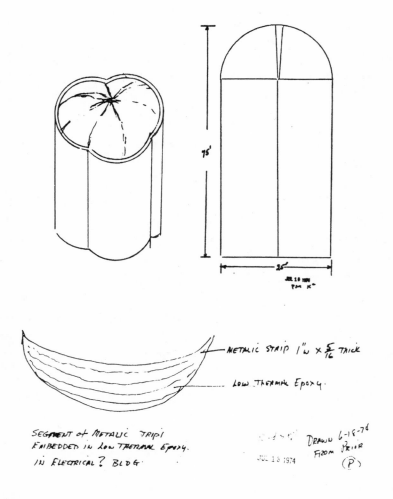

FIGURE 9. DETAILS SEEN BY PRICE include a cluster of gas cylinders shown at the top of this figure and in the satellite photo. The 60-foot steel gores for the sphere construction are shown at the bottom. *Their existence was amazingly not discovered until three years later.* Price had the size correct to within 18 inches.

We would consider Price to be in the ranks of the psychic superstars, and it was a privilege to have been involved in the series of transcendent experiments we carried out with him. I have been longing to talk about them for more than twenty years; until now the secret was so tightly held that I could discuss it with no one outside of our very small group of SRI researchers and CIA sponsors. I feel extremely fortunate to be able to describe these extraordinary events in my lifetime, and to pay homage to Pat Price's abilities — abilities I now believe we all possess, yet some are able to demonstrate so much more obviously, and even brilliantly, than others.

Since the news broke that government scientists at SRI were conducting ESP experiments, various media ranging from *The New York Times* to Phil Donahue have let out a trickle of information. Several other national TV shows have called me requesting information that I can't give them, since most of the work we did is still highly classified. I have tried diligently for more than a year to gain access, through the Freedom of Information Act, to the day-to-day government work in which I participated for the CIA and other agencies during the 1970s and 1980s, but so far I have only been successful in obtaining the CIA data described above.

Perhaps the most important secret about the government's ESP program was already revealed to me for public disclosure in a fortune cookie a couple of years ago. Before opening the cookie I had asked the question, "What is the government doing with ESP?" My cookie's answer was, "There is no secret. There never has been." It told the truth. It reflected the shocked realization of the Soviet physicist mentioned earlier in this chapter, who shouted, "Doesn't this mean that you can't hide anything anymore?"

"THAT'S JUST MENTAL TELEPATHY"

By 1974 Hal Puthoff and I had seen some remarkable results from our remote-viewing experiments. We had made arrangements to brief certain high-ranking military and civilian decision makers at the Pentagon building in Washington, D.C. I clearly remember the day we arrived. I was very ill, suffering with a persistent flu. Too weak to walk unaided, I hauled myself hand-over-hand up the banisters at the sides of the broad, sloping ramps inside the Pentagon building, as men delivering messages on huge tricycles sped by, ringing their little silver bells. It all seems a little surrealistic now, and today the trikes have been replaced by little electric carts.

Our meeting room was inside a vault with a heavy steel door that opened and closed with a combination lock like that of a bank safe. The room itself was spacious, with rows of comfortable, red leather armchairs, and the walls were covered with blue velvet drapes. Of course, there were no windows.

Hal and I had been carrying out our first experiments with the artist Ingo Swann, an exceptional remote viewer whose work we described in our earlier book, *Mind-Reach*.[9] In those studies, government scientists had given us geographical coordinates of latitude and longitude in degrees, minutes, and seconds, and asked us to psychically describe what was there. Ingo called this "*Project Scanate.*" In one celebrated trial we could more or less tell from the coordinates that the target was on the east coast of the U.S., but Swann went on to describe the layout of buildings, roads, a flagpole, and even an underground building. A week later, after Swann's drawings had been analyzed, we learned that he had psychically viewed a highly classified government facility with remarkable accuracy — so much so, that it gave rise to a searching investigation of our activities by the owners of the buildings. We received far more attention than we knew how to handle, but it didn't insure our funding.

So in 1974, we went to Washington to talk about Ingo's striking success. We went for the same reason that every professional consultant and scientist goes to Washington: We hoped to obtain a government contract to continue the research. We had already conducted dozens of experiments similar to Ingo's with several viewers, and we had quite an exciting story to tell. Now the Pentagon wanted to hear about it.

As I looked out over the sea of stern faces before me, I wondered whether they would believe us, or think we were just some silly people from California. After we finished our description of miracles wrapped in the scholarly trappings of laboratory data, the room fell silent. In the customary fashion, everyone waited for the ranking general officer to ask the first question. A tall, white-haired man with a chest full of medals pulled himself to his feet and boomed out, "How do you know that this remote-viewing stuff isn't simple mental telepathy, with your psychic just reading the mind of the guy who gave you the coordinates?" He then sat down, and folded his arms over his well-decorated chest. He had asked an astute and thoughtful question that implicitly accepted the validity of our data. Nothing could have pleased us more.

Later that day, the general related to us the event that had made him a believer in psychic phenomena: a frighteningly vivid dream his wife had had about him years before, on the very night his airplane was shot down in Korea. We got the contract to continue our remote-viewing research, and we spent more than a decade trying to answer some of the questions that were raised in that meeting. The following month we had a remarkably similar meeting at the CIA, in the very room where the ill-fated Bay of Pigs invasion was planned.

If you believe, as I do, that ESP exists, then you believe that everyone already knows, or at least can know, anything. Based on what I have seen in the laboratory, I believe that you can ask an experienced psychic any question at all, and if your question is well-posed and actually has an answer, then the psychic can help you to determine what it is. How, then, could you keep a classified ESP research program a secret? Our contractual ground rules were that we could tell people we had government support for our program, but we couldn't discuss whether it was classified, or which agencies were supporting us. If a reporter asked, "Is your program classified?" we would decline to answer, and let him draw his own conclusions.

One humorous example of the folly of trying to keep the existence of our program secret occurred when the well-known consciousness researcher Dr. Charles Tart joined our program during a year-long sabbatical from the University of California at Davis. He gave the names of six members of the Parapsychological Association as character references, so that he could obtain a security clearance from our sponsor. As a result, six American ESP researchers each received a visit from a friendly security inspector inquiring into Charlie's affairs. Of course, each one of the researchers had to tell at least a few friends, who would tell a few more friends — and so on, until half the country seemed to know about our work.

On another occasion, our shadowy SRI program received a visit from an Under Secretary of Defense. His discreet arrival, with his adjutant officer carrying his briefcase, necessitated clearing the entire parking lot to give his helicopter a place to land. So much for keeping a low profile!

WHAT WILL CONGRESS SAY?

Although we now had fairly continuous support from various government agencies, they were always worried about what Congress would say. Never one to hide good scientific data, I urged that we be given a chance to tell Congress what we were doing. But, whom could we tell? It turned out that we got to relate our entire story to the House Committee on Intelligence Oversight. Our sponsors helped us to present and substantiate our best data. The Congressmen asked questions, and in the end, everyone's fears about getting Wisconsin Senator William Proxmire's Golden Fleece Award ridiculing the greatest publicly funded boondoggles went up in smoke. To summarize Congressman Charles Rose's conclusions after seeing all the data: "All I can say is that if the results were faked, our security system doesn't work. What these people 'saw' was confirmed by aerial photography. There is no way it could have been faked...."

VIEWER 372 NOW IN THE TARGET AREA

In June, 1978, we found the greatest natural psychic ever to walk into our laboratory. I carried out several truly astonishing remote-viewing trials with Joe McMoneagle, code-named "Viewer 372." He had served in South Vietnam, Thailand, Germany, Italy, and other countries as a warrant officer. In 1984 he retired from his last posting at the U.S. Intelligence and Security Command (INSCOM), where he had worked as a Special Projects Intelligence Officer. That agency was then commanded by General Bert Stubblebine, who is now retired from the military and travels around the U.S.

giving workshops on how to do remote viewing.

I remember Joe as a highly intelligent and enthusiastic colleague. Ten years ago he was drinking a cappuccino in my living room and telling me about his out-of-body and near-death experiences from a sudden, mysterious illness when he had been stationed in Germany. It was his experience of psychically looking down on his body, which was lying on the pavement, that led him to become interested in remote viewing.

Joe completed very successful trials with us in 1979, when we did experiments with five other participants that Hal and I had recruited from the same Army Intelligence organization where Joe worked. This series showed us that psi abilities come in all sizes and shapes. Four of these inexperienced participants achieved independent statistical significance in their six trials, giving odds of better than 1 in 10,000.[10] This outstanding result recapitulates the kind of data that we reported in our original paper published in the *IEEE Proceedings* in 1976. All of these military people went on to teach many others in the U.S. Armed Services how to successfully do remote viewing. Two of these men have written books about their adventures in what eventually became a surprisingly large cadre of psychic spies.

After we last worked with him in 1978, Joe continued to apply himself to improving his psi abilities. Some recently released data shows him doing remote viewing with an almost photographic accuracy even more precise than the remarkable drawings he did for us, two of which are described below.

NATIONAL LEGION OF MERIT AWARD FOR JOE MCMONEAGLE

In 1984, Joe was granted a National Legion of Merit Award for excellence of performance in his career in military intelligence. It was awarded on the following basis:

> ...McMoneagle served most recently as a Special Projects Intelligence Officer for the 92nd Military Intelligence Group, as one of the original planners and movers of a unique intelligence project that is revolutionizing the intelligence community. He used his talents and expertise in the execution of more than 200 missions, addressing over

150 essential elements of information [EEI]. These EEI contained critical intelligence reported at the highest echelons of our military and government, including such national level agencies as the Joint Chiefs of Staff, DIA [Defense Intelligence Agency], NSA [National Security Agency], CIA, DEA [Drug Enforcement Agency], and the Secret Service, producing crucial and vital intelligence unavailable from any other source....[11]

The series of technology-related experiments with Joe followed the "classical" remote-viewing protocol. Joe and his interviewer were closeted in the laboratory at SRI. Neither knew anything about the actual targets, except that they would pertain in some way to technology. This general aspect knowledge was not thought to be a source of possible information leakage to the remote viewer, because the San Francisco Bay Area is full of possible technological target locations such as airports, radar installations, electrical plants, linear accelerators, military and naval bases, as well as high-technology manufacturing sites and a number of radio telescopes. Joe's task was to sit quietly in the dimly lit laboratory, designed for us by Ingo Swann a decade before, and describe his mental impressions about the location and present time experience of the two SRI experimenters and the representative of the sponsoring agency, who were visiting the distant target sites.

THE WEST GATE OF THE LAWRENCE LIVERMORE NATIONAL LABORATORY

The two remote-viewing trials we describe here were in many ways the culmination of fifteen years of continuous remote-viewing research at SRI. Joe's target in the first of the two trials was the Lawrence Livermore Laboratory, the world-famous hydrogen bomb research laboratory directed by Edward Teller. In the experiment carried out at SRI by psi researcher and physicist Dr. Edwin May, Joe made a drawing of this complex nearly a hundred miles away, showing many of the buildings and other structures that can be seen from the West Gate side. All of the data in the following paragraphs has never been published, and was generously made available to us by Dr. May.[12]

Among the many items the sponsor wanted Joe to describe were the various buildings he saw, with their specific shapes, and the freeway adjacent to the laboratory. As you can see from the scoring chart below, Joe left his sponsor well pleased.

ITEMS AT LAWRENCE LIVERMORE NATIONAL LABORATORY TARGET	JOE'S SCORE
Multipurpose laboratory complex	80%
Six-story administration building	100%
T-shaped, six-story building	100%
Large parking lot just west of tall building	100%
Segmented, one-story buildings north of tall building	20%
Tall building	100%
Building with cylindrical roof	40%

ITEMS DESCRIBED, BUT NOT AT SITE	
Swimming pool	0%
Large mountain	0%
Overall accuracy from all concepts	85%
Overall reliability from all concepts	95%

Joe's drawing of the West Gate target is shown in **Figure 10**. His accurate three-dimensional rendering of the T-shaped, six-story administration building is indicative of the extraordinarily high-quality remote viewing that he and other experienced viewers have produced. His overall drawing of the complex is especially striking when one considers all the other totally different sites in the area that could have been chosen as his target. One such example is the windmill site we describe next.

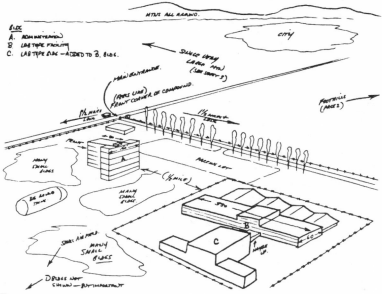

FIGURE 10. LAWRENCE LIVERMORE NATIONAL LABORATORY target site photo, with sketch by viewer a hundred miles away, showing T-shaped, six-story administration building next to a row of trees, with a road separating it from a row of trees.

WINDMILL ELECTRIC POWER FARM

After the traveling team spent their required half hour at the West Gate target, they proceeded on to a windmill farm in the foothills of the Livermore Valley. When Joe focused his attention on this, his third target of the day, without any interim feedback at all, a completely new set of pictures came to him. In the table below, we note the poles, hills, and rotating blades that the sponsor wanted to see in Joe's transcript, compared with what Joe experienced.

ITEMS AT WINDMILL FARM	JOE'S SCORE
Rotating blades	100%
Multiple wind generators	100%
Wind-Powered Electrical Generation	90% for the concept
Poles scattered in hills	100%
Poles connected in a grid	100%
Foothills	100%
Electrical grid	100%
Overall accuracy of all concepts	94%
Overall reliability of all concepts	100%

Joe's drawing of the windmill farm target with its poles, hills, and power grid is shown in **Figure 11**. It is apparent from this sketch and the previous drawing that a remote viewer sitting quietly with his eyes closed can indeed focus his attention more or less anywhere he chooses.

This remarkable accuracy has been achieved with the viewer targeted on anything from a known person to a photograph of an unknown person, a specific site like the Lawrence Livermore Laboratory or the Windmill Farm, or even nothing more than a set of geographical coordinates. Remote viewing appears to be an entirely goal-oriented task. That is, the subject is able to describe the target to be viewed no matter what information is given to demarcate it. The overall reliability is reported as 75 percent. I take this to

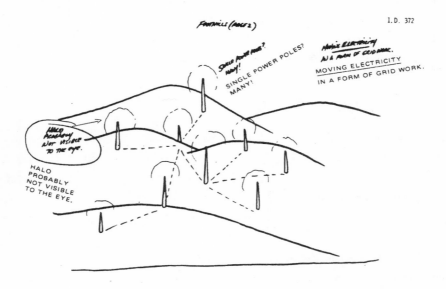

FIGURE 11. LIVERMORE VALLEY FOOTHILLS WINDMILL FARM target site photo, with sketch by viewer Joe McMoneagle one hundred miles away, showing poles, hills, "electricity in the form of a grid," and "halo probably not visible to the eye, at the top of the poles."

indicate that if Joe says that he sees something at a target site, it will be there three-quarters of the time. Since the targets in this series were very diverse — indoors and out, pastoral as well as technical — the results he obtained were both excellent and conclusive.

The events we are evaluating are themselves so improbable scientifically that their percentage of reliability is not the appropriate measure. It is as though Joe had been asked to walk across San Francisco Bay a hundred times without getting his feet wet, and we found that he could do that 75 percent of the time! What Joe demonstrated was an innate human capability rivaling the nation's most sophisticated technical assets in accuracy. It is clear why the government might be interested in ESP!

With regard to possible applications, we favor the government being as well informed as possible about what is happening in the world. We think this is one of the best ways to prevent war. However, during my decade at SRI, I felt that there was far too much emphasis placed on looking for ways to apply remote viewing, and not enough attention directed to the understanding of the phenomenology. I once expressed this concern directly to our on-site government contract monitor. He explained to me his view of his job, saying, "I am not paid to think, I am paid to make sure that you do the work my boss is paying you to do." I left SRI shortly after that conversation.

Although there are still many fascinating government files on our experiments waiting to be opened, they will not contain any great new surprises about the nature of remote viewing. The examples described in this chapter reflect all the dimensions of our larger body of work. We believe they demonstrate beyond any doubt the human mind's potential to transcend its conventional "local" restrictions by opening a window to a boundless universe, where we can explore our fundamental interconnectedness with everything that exists. Similar experimental work in psychic healing is still in its beginning stages, but it strongly supports the ability of our untrammeled, nonlocal minds not only to roam at will through time and space, but also to make mind-to-mind, mind-to-body connections that influence the healing process. We will explore this in much greater depth in later chapters.

Central Intelligence Agency

Washington, D.C. 20505

Mr. Russell Targ
1010 Harriet Street
Palo Alto, California   94301

Reference: P94-1192

Dear Mr. Targ:

   This is in response to your 20 September 1994 letter in which you presented an appeal of our lack of response to your 10 May 1994 Freedom of Information Act and Privacy Act request for reports with the approximate titles, "Perception Augmentation Techniques, Stanford Research Institute, Final Report, 1973, 1974, 1975." You stated that "[t]he authors are Harold E. Puthoff and Russell Targ" and "[t]here would be at least two reports from 1973/4 and 1974/5."

   Your appeal has been presented to the appropriate member of the Agency Release Panel, Mr. Anthony R. Frasketi, Information Review Officer for the Directorate of Science and Technology. Pursuant to the authority delegated under paragraphs 1900.51(a) and 1901.17(c) of Chapter XIX, Title 32 of the Code of Federal Regulations (C.F.R.), Mr. Frasketi has directed that a thorough search be conducted of those records systems which could reasonably be expected to contain documents responsive to your request. As a result of these searches, three responsive documents were located.
Mr. Frasketi has reviewed the documents and has determined that the documents, reports dated 31 October 1974, 1 December 1975 and one undated, can be released in their entirety. Further, in regard to your appeal and in accordance with CIA regulations appearing at 32 C.F.R. paragraph 1900.51(b), the Agency Release Panel, meeting as a committee of the whole, has affirmed this determination.

   A copy of the three documents as approved for release are enclosed. We appreciate your patience while your appeal was being considered.

                                        Sincerely,

                                        Edmund Cohen
                                        Chairman
                                        Agency Release Panel

Enclosures

What We Have Learned about *Remote Viewing*

Science is not simply a device for explaining away events and capacities hith-erto thought to be God-given. . . . All great scientists have understood this. But, those who hold a slavish belief in "scientific facts" and who do not understand uncertainties of modern science are likely to come to small con-clusions that are as trivializing as reducing "remote viewing" to repetitious "readings" of a pack of cards. As I understand contemporary trends of phys-ical science, there is increasing recognition of vast unknown areas which sci-ence may explore and assist in ordering, but to which it may never provide anything like complete answers.

— Margaret Mead
Preface to *Mind-Reach,* by Russell Targ and Harold Puthoff

HOW I WAS A PSYCHIC SPY FOR THE CIA AND FOUND GOD

What are these *"vast unknown areas"* of science that Margaret Mead *refers to,* for which we may never have "anything like complete answers"? One thoughtful person working on this problem is physicist Roger Penrose. He contends that our consciousness is one of the areas for which we will find no present-day scientific explanation. He tells us that "the mind cannot be explained at all in terms of the science of the physical world," echoing Aus-trian mathematician Kurt Gödel, who declared that no self-consistent model can be entirely self-explanatory.[1] In other words, consciousness may not be able to explain itself logically.

Psychic functioning is a step in the direction of consciousness becoming aware of itself. Remote viewing is the nonlocal mind revealing itself. Likewise, a spiritual healer would say that the experience of healing is a manifestation of nonlocal mind unfolding in the physical world. A spiritual healer's surrender of separateness, and willingness to be used as an instrument of healing, affects the world of form that we reside in. The physiology of the body responds to the caring attitudes within the community of spirit of our nonlocal mind. We now have solid experimental support of this fact.

I originally approached psi research from the point of view of a stage magician and a physicist, as related in Chapter I. The magician in me had experienced real ESP while doing conjuring tricks on the stage, leading me to realize that we do not have to *believe* in psi; we can experience it. Later I even had a psychic experience in the course of selling our remote-viewing program to NASA. I did a small card trick in which I asked the NASA contract monitor to shuffle a deck of cards, cut it, and choose a card. He put the deck back in the box, and I pulled out my pocket diary, and showed him that it said, "Today's card for George Pezdirtz was the eight of clubs" — the card that he thought he had freely chosen. The purpose was to demonstrate my awareness of the wily ways of magicians, and that we would not be deceived by tricksters in the course of our research. George then grabbed the deck and pulled out another card, and asked, "What's this one?" Since I had forced the first card, I didn't know what the second card might be. But as he asked the question, I got a clear mental picture of the three of diamonds (which I remember to this day). I asked him if that could be his card. Even with my poor vision, I could see his eyes grow large and his mouth fall open. It was the correct card. And NASA did eventually support our research.

So, the magician in me experienced psi regularly, but the physicist in me believed only in good experiments. As a follower of the logical positivist Alfred Ayer, I thought if an idea could not be directly demonstrated to the senses, it should be considered "non-sense." Since the concept of God could be neither demonstrated nor falsified, this too had to be rejected.

After twenty years of psi research, however, my view has been expanded. I have learned that God does not have to be a matter of belief: God may actually be experienced. I have sat in a darkened interview room with hundreds of remote viewers and shared their mental pictures with them. It is a fact that people can experience a mind-to-mind connection with each other. Fifty years of published data from all over the world attest to this. The mind-to-mind connection we experience in the laboratory feels the same to me as the oceanic feelings of love and connection that I experience when I am in meditation. I believe that these feelings of connections to our community of spirit are the feelings experienced by every mystic who ever sat peacefully on a rock and quieted his mind — from Buddha, to Jesus, to William Blake. Quieting our minds and stopping our chattering thoughts is the key for both psi and other experiences of the mystical domain.

The purpose of remote viewing is not to spy on the Russians or make money in the silver futures market. These are just attention-getting devices, serving to puff up our egos. A more important implication of psychic experiences is to reveal to us our nonlocal mind and connections to our community of spirit. Everything else is just a fancy magic trick.

It is not necessary to hold any particular religious belief in order to do remote viewing. After working on quieting your mind, however, there's no telling what might happen. Even to a physicist.

In the Sutras of Patanjali, the first line says that "Yoga is mind-wave quieting." In this great work, his guidebook to omniscience and the other Yogic gifts, Patanjali says that in order to psychically see the world, or the moon reflected in a pool of water, we must wait until every ripple is stilled. Then the clear image will appear. This is exactly the way it is with remote viewing.

The physicist and the mystic make their life's decisions based on data. For the physicist, this data comes from the laboratory, or observation of the physical world. For the mystic, it is derived from oceanic feelings of love and his or her spiritual community. Neither of them is bound by either belief in, or adherence to, any preferred theology — although these days the physicist is more likely to wonder about the creator of the universe than is the mystic.

We now know that an important ingredient of our remote-viewing success derives from the rapport between the remote viewer and interviewer, acting together as a single information-gathering team. The remote viewer's role is that of perceiver and information channel. The interviewer's role is designed to be that of an analytical control — from my point of view — a kind of psychic travel agent. This division of labor mirrors the two primary modes of cerebral functioning as we understand them. The *nonanalytic* thinking style predominates in spatial pattern recognition and other holistic processing (which is thought to predominate in psi functioning). The *analytical* cognitive style characterizes verbal and other goal-oriented reasoning processes. Only very experienced remote viewers appear to have the ability to handle both cognitive styles simultaneously.

The remote viewer is told that mental analysis, memory, and imagination constitute a kind of mental noise in the channel. Therefore, the closer the viewer can get to raw, uninterpreted imagery, the better. He or she is encouraged to report spontaneous perceptions — "What are you experiencing now? What are you seeing that makes you say 'such and such?'" — rather than analysis, since the former tends to be "on target," while the latter is often incorrect.

Since remote viewing is a challenging task, apparently similar to the perception of subliminal or hidden stimuli, it requires the full attentive powers of the remote viewer. The environment and procedures are designed to be as natural and comfortable as possible, in order to minimize the diversion of attention to anything other than the task at hand.[2] No hypnosis, strobe lights, sensory-deprivation procedures, or drugs are used, since in our view such novel environmental factors would only serve to divert some of the subject's much-needed attention. Our experience suggests that novice viewers following these simple procedures should be able to develop their psychic abilities without losing their mind or having to eat porridge at the feet of a guru.

When the agreed-upon time for the experiment arrives, the interviewer simply asks the viewer, "Describe the impressions that come to your mind with regard to where the target person is." The interviewer does not pressure the remote viewer to verbalize continuously, because the viewer might tend to embroider the descriptions to please the interviewer. This is a well-known problem in behavioral studies of this type. If the remote viewer becomes analytical in reporting the data she perceives — "I see arches...it must be McDonald's" — the interviewer gently leads her into description, rather than analysis — "You don't have to tell me where it is, just describe what you see." This is the most important and difficult task of the interviewer, but it is apparently necessary for good results with inexperienced remote viewers.

It is also useful for the interviewer to "surprise" the remote viewer by the introduction of alternative viewpoints — "Go above the scene and look down. What do you see? If you look to the left, what do you see?" The remote viewer's perception appears to be mobile, and can shift rapidly with such questions. It is as though the data comes through before the viewer's defenses can activate to block it out. Some shifting of viewpoint also gets around the potential problem of the remote viewer's tendency to spend the entire session giving meticulous detail of a relatively trivial item, such as a flower at the base of the Washington Monument. Even if correct, a clear description of a trivial item will generally fail to convey the essence of the target. Once a remote viewer feels that he sees something, he tends to hang on to this perception rather than let it go and focus on a new viewpoint.

It is important to recognize again that remote viewing involves a division of labor. It is the *interviewer's* (not the remote viewer's) responsibility to see that the necessary information is generated to permit an impartial judge to discriminate among the target descriptions. The remote viewer's responsibility is confined to exercising the remote-viewing faculty. He must describe and experience his mental pictures: he must not judge or analyze them. We have learned that analysis is the enemy of psi.

There is a door in the mind that opens with acceptance, and closes with judgment of any kind.

There is a door in the heart that opens with trust and closes when fear of any kind is felt.
— *Paul Ferrini* [3]

Sometimes the viewer draws a mental blank, and does not have any pictures to describe. He says, "I close my eyes, and it's dark." In this situation, an intrepid interviewer might say something like the following: "In 45 minutes we will take you to the target site. Can you look into your future, and tell me now what you will be experiencing then?" We have found that this approach is often surprisingly successful. It corresponds to our data suggesting that psi has a nonlocal nature, and that there are no known space-time limits to psi abilities. In this case it would appear that the viewer's feedback experience is the actual source of his psi.

Often, a viewer will say, "I see something *like* a fire hydrant." What he is conveying to the interviewer is that he is *not* seeing a fire hydrant. It is then a good time for the interviewer to ask the viewer, "What are you experiencing (or seeing) that makes you think of a fire hydrant?" The remote viewer is encouraged to sketch and write down everything he sees, even over his objections that he is not an artist, cannot sketch, etc. He may record impressions throughout, or wait until the end of the session, if intermittent drawing would distract his concentration. Since drawings tend to be more accurate than verbalizations, this is an extremely important factor for generating positive results.

Georgia O'Keeffe, the painter, once described her approach to painting in very similar terms. She said, "It's as if my mind creates shapes that I don't know about. I can't say it any other way. I get this shape in my head, and sometimes I know what it comes from, and sometimes I don't." That is the situation experienced by a remote viewer. The process resembles that of memory: we are familiar with its use, but we don't know much about how it works. Remembering what your childhood home looked like is experientially similar to viewing it psychically.

NO EXPERIENCE NECESSARY

As a psi researcher, it was my (Russell's) good fortune to have a lovely and wise lady as my psychic accomplice. SRI's great success with Pat Price and Ingo Swann caused our government sponsors to ask us to find someone to work with who was not an experienced psychic. They wanted a "control" subject.

We selected photographer Hella Hammid, whose passions were blue glass, beauty in the world, and egg custard soufflé. She had spent most of her life looking at the world through the viewfinder of her Leica, so for her to become an accomplished remote viewer was a completely apropos extension of her experiences. Hella was a longtime friend from New York, and she promised that she had no previous psi experience, although she was very excited about the challenge. So, Hella came to us as a "control," and she became our most reliable remote viewer for more than a decade.

The reason Hella was so appreciated at SRI is that she brought warmth and grace that permeated the entire laboratory. Hella was charming as well as astute, as you might be able to ascertain from her photograph in **Figure 12**. Since the 1950s she had been a regular contributor to *Life* magazine, and in 1974 she began her career as a psychic superstar. It was a label she thought hysterically funny, because she had no more idea than we did how psi worked. Hella died in 1992, but she is often in my thoughts as I continue the work that we did together.

FIGURE 12. PHOTOGRAPHER HELLA HAMMID began working at SRI as a control subject because she had never done anything psychic before. It turned out that she was an outstanding remote viewer and was with our team from 1973 to 1982.

Pat Price and Ingo Swann had both been experienced in the psychic world long before they came to SRI, but Hella and I had to figure it out for ourselves from scratch. In the initial trial of the first formal series, I remember sitting on the floor of our laboratory while Hella settled on the couch and asked me, "What do I do now?" My partner Hal Puthoff had already driven off to an unknown target location, and our job was to describe where he had gone to hide. I didn't know what to tell Hella at that time, but now we can answer that question by writing this book. (Jane likes to think that Hella is helping us to complete the project.)

Hella taught us much of what we understand about the potential of remote viewing. During her nine trials of viewing distant geographical targets, she achieved a rating in which the odds of her seeing what she saw were almost one in a million — even more successful than Pat Price had been in a similar series. We conducted successive studies in which Hella accurately described objects hidden in wooden boxes, small objects hidden in aluminum film cans, and even microscopic targets the size of a dot, such as those used by spies to conceal messages in letters. All these viewings were carefully judged, and found to be statistically significant. So in the end, our control subject became our most extensively published SRI psychic.

Hella was a cautious viewer, in that she did not elaborate on her descriptions beyond what she actually saw psychically. Pat Price, on the other hand, would go to extremes to give highly detailed descriptions of target sites. These were usually correct, but sometimes they were entirely off the mark. We would not say that one viewer was more psychic than the other. Rather, we would say that they had different styles. If a terrorist had planted a bomb somewhere in the city, I would probably call Pat to try and find it. If I had lost my keys somewhere in the house, I would call Hella to describe what piece of furniture they had fallen behind.

Hella's descriptions tended to be quite parsimonious. One day we did an experiment that did not have a person at the target, but instead provided geographical coordinates of the site. I showed her the coordinates of latitude and longitude, which were in binary form — 1s and 0s instead of the usual degrees, minutes, and seconds. Hella got to see a card showing something like the following: 10010100110-N and 11001001101-W. This gave the location of the target in degrees, minutes, and seconds. Hella commented, "That's an interesting-looking pattern." Then she closed her eyes, gave a great sigh (which was always a sign of good psi for her), and said, "I see some kind of round structure." She laughed, and continued, "It looks like a belly-button-shaped energy expander. There are three rays coming out of it."

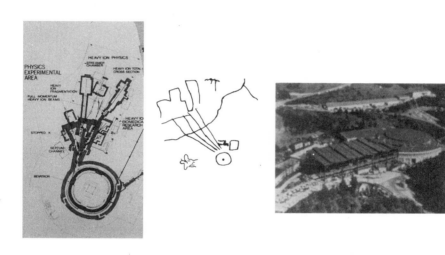

FIGURE 13. ABOVE ARE THE PLAN VIEW and photo of the Berkeley Bevatron, a particle accelerator, together with a sketch by Hella Hammid showing the four beam tubes. To the right is the clay model of the Berkeley Bevatron made by Hammid. She described it as a "belly-button-shaped energy expander."

Then she requested some clay to make a model of what she saw. She felt that the new medium would allow her an additional mode to express what she was experiencing. The target was the Berkeley University Bevatron. It is a hollow, circular particle accelerator that is, indeed, an "energy expander," and has four beam tubes leading to the experimental labs. The illustration in **Figure 13** shows the remarkable similarity between her drawing, her clay model showing the beam tubes, and the accelerator fifty miles away. With Hella, we often saw this kind of almost-magical connection between the function and form of the place. One day when the target was the Stanford Linear Accelerator, she saw "polished metal tubes or cylinders. . . . This has something to do with a trajectory," she said. Such a description is, of course, entirely appropriate for an electron accelerator.

In a 1983 BBC television program on ESP, producer Tony Edwards asked Hella how she did remote viewing. Her answer was that "We've been doing it all these years. We still don't know how it works. It would be wonderful if we did. But we still don't know." That program became the NOVA presentation entitled "The Case for ESP," and it continues to be one of their most popular reruns.

WHAT RESEARCH HAS TAUGHT US ABOUT REMOTE VIEWING

For a phenomenon thought in many circles not to exist, we certainly know a great deal about how to increase and decrease the accuracy and reliability of remote viewing. In the remainder of this chapter we will share with you what we know about the process.

ACCURACY AND RELIABILITY OF REMOTE VIEWING

Remote viewers can often contact, experience, and describe a hidden object, or a remote natural or architectural site. They can do this based on the presence of a cooperative person at the location, geographical coordinates, or some other target demarcation, which we call an address. We know that remote viewing is not mind reading, because viewers have often correctly visualized things that were totally unknown to anyone else at the time.

TARGET ATTRIBUTES MOST OFTEN SENSED

Shape, form, and color are described much more reliably by inexperienced viewers than the target's function, or other analytical information. In addition to visual imagery, viewers sometimes describe associated feelings, sounds, smells, and even electrical or magnetic fields. As a viewer, I (Russell) have learned that if I see a color clearly and brightly, or something metallic and shiny, it is the aspect of the target that I am most likely to describe correctly. It is even possible for viewers to experience aspects of a target which are not actually manifested. For example, some viewers can reliably describe the color of an object which is inside an opaque box, where there is no light to give it color.

TEMPORAL SENSING

Viewers can sense present, past, and future activities at target sites. Hundreds of successful present time as well as precognitive remote viewing experiments have been done at the Princeton psi research laboratory in the past decade. There is not a drop of evidence to indicate that it is more difficult to look slightly into the future than it is to describe an object in a box in front of you. Actually, it's better not to look at a box when you are doing remote viewing, because you may be tempted to see the target by pretending that you have x-ray vision, which, in our experience, does not work.

It is not proven, but I believe that it is easier to describe a target that you will see in the near future than one you will see many days in the future. It may be a purely psychological effect. If my feedback is delayed by a week or more, then I have somewhat forgotten what my description *felt like* to me. As a result, the feedback, which is supposed to be the source of that earlier perception, will have less of an impact on me, thereby decreasing the quality of the viewing. The idea that a later event is the cause of an earlier perception is a confusing though very important concept, and we discuss it further in Chapter 5.

ACCURACY AND RELIABILITY

Blueprint accuracy can sometimes be achieved in remote viewing, and reliability in a series can be as high as 80 percent. Unlike card-guessing or other forced-choice experiments, more than two decades of research have shown no decline in people's remote-viewing performance over time. With practice, people become increasingly able to separate out the psychic signal from the mental noise of memory, imagination, and analysis.

SPATIAL ACCURACY

Targets and target details as small as 1 millimeter can be sensed. Hella Hammid successfully described microscopic picture targets as small as one millimeter square in an experimental series at SRI in 1979.[4] She also correctly identified a silver pin and a spool of thread inside an aluminum film can.

In the 1890s, Annie Besant worked with psychic C.W. Leadbeater in an imaginative study to describe the structure of atoms. We believe that in this early research at the English Theosophical Society, Leadbeater was the first person in the world to describe the distinctive nuclear structure of the three isotopes of hydrogen. In his book *Occult Chemistry*, published in 1898, he wrote that he clairvoyantly saw that a given atom of hydrogen could have one, two, or three particles in its nucleus, and still be hydrogen. Isotopes had not yet been discovered by chemists. Leadbeater reported that atoms of different atomic weights could still retain their chemical identity.[5]

DISTANCE EFFECTS

Again and again we have seen that accuracy and resolution of remote-viewing targets are not sensitive to variations in distance of up to 10,000 miles. An example of such long-distance viewing is described in Chapter 2 with Djuna Davitashvili in the 1984 Moscow-to-San Francisco remote viewing.

ELECTRICAL SHIELDING

Faraday-cage screen rooms and underwater shielding have no negative effects on remote viewing. In fact, some viewers very much like to work in an electrically shielded environment. The well-known psychic Eileen Garrett showed me such a room that she had built for her own use, in her offices at the Parapsychology Foundation on 57th Street in New York City. Pat Price did his fine work from inside SRI's shielded room. In fact, recent findings from physicist James Spottiswoode suggest that both electromagnetic radiation from our Milky Way galaxy and the electromagnetic effects of solar flares degrade psychic functioning.[6] Electrical shielding seems to help performance, and so does carrying out experiments when the galactic radiation is at a minimum at your location. When the Milky Way is below your position on the earth, rather than above your head, it appears that you have a two-hour window of opportunity. It is still possible, however, to be abundantly psychic any time of the day or night.

In 1978, Hella Hammid and Ingo Swann successfully received messages sent from Palo Alto while they were inside a submarine submerged in 500 feet of seawater, 500 miles away.[7] Hella and Ingo each had five file cards to look at later. Each card had a target location description written on one side, and a message to instruct the submarine to do some type of activity on the other, as a sort of code device. For example, the five targets were a large oak tree, an indoor shopping plaza, etc., and the messages were the kind of things you might communicate to a submerged sub that was out of radio contact because of the salt water, such as, "Remain submerged," or "Return to port," or "Fire at priority targets," etc. In each case my colleague and I would hide ourselves in Palo Alto at a specified time, and the viewers in the sub would have to describe our location. They would then look at each of the five cards to see which one best matched their remote-viewing experience, and the message to be sent was found on the back of the card. Both trials in this experiment were successful. (The statistical significance would be found by multiplying together the two 1-in-5 events, to give a probability of $p = 0.04$, or less than four times in one hundred occurring by chance, which many would consider a significant result.)

FACTORS THAT INHIBIT REMOTE VIEWING

A prior knowledge of target possibilities, absence of feedback, and use of mental analysis all inhibit remote viewing. Any visual or audio distractions, or anything novel in the working environment will tend to show up in the viewer's pictures in the remote-viewing session. Numbers are much more difficult to perceive than pictorial targets. For example, it is much more difficult to guess a number from one to ten than it is to describe a location chosen from an infinitude of planetary locations that you have never seen before. In looking for the geographical target, you apparently search your interior mental landscape for a surprise, and that will usually be the correct answer. With a number target, there are no surprises, since you are already familiar with all the possibilities, and so you are apt to use analysis to rule out the various choices.

FACTORS THAT ENHANCE REMOTE VIEWING

Seriousness of purpose, feedback, heart-to-heart trust among participants, and acceptance of psi all enhance remote viewing. So does the pressure of performing in front of television cameras, as we saw earlier in the Moscow-to-San Francisco experiment. Experienced viewers learn to improve their performance by becoming aware of their mental noise from memory and imagination, and filtering it out; and by writing down their impressions, and drawing their mental pictures. Drawing is especially important because it gives you direct access to your unconscious processes.

MULTIPLE VIEWERS TO IMPROVE PERFORMANCE

The use of several remote viewers can sometimes bring additional information or different points of view. However, it is more likely that the viewers will all describe the same wrong target. If individual viewers each have their own target set, this problem can very likely be overcome. The experiment we describe in Chapter 5 successfully demonstrates this.

TECHNOLOGICAL CONSIDERATIONS

There are more than a hundred published reports suggesting that people are able to psychically affect the normally equal distribution of 1s and 0s from a random number generator. We believe that it is unclear, from the present data, whether viewers can perturb the electronic equipment by their mental processes, or whether they use their ESP abilities to choose an optimal moment to start an experiment or turn on the random number generator.

Edwin May and James Spottiswoode have written extensively on this subject, and throw into question the existence of any psychokinetic (i.e., mind affecting matter) phenomena that are part of a repetitive experimental series. Abraham Maslow, the famous psychologist, would call this optimal starting, "good choosing." May and Spottiswoode call it "decision augmentation."[8]

THEORETICAL CONSIDERATIONS

It appears clear to us that viewers can focus their attention on distant points in space-time and then describe and experience that distant location. Feedback is essential for learning, but is not necessary for psi functioning. It is as though the viewer is examining his or her own small, low-resolution, local piece of the four-dimensional space-time hologram in which he or she is embedded. We discuss this concept, which is based on the work of physicist David Bohm, in Chapter 12.

INGO SWANN'S STAGES OF REMOTE VIEWING

We have already mentioned that it was Ingo Swann who introduced us all to the great potential of remote viewing. He spent many years of his life developing an ontology of this ability. Swann feels that there are distinct stages that one passes through in a remote-viewing session, as one accesses increasingly detailed and analytical information. The first stage of remote viewing consists primarily of initial fragmentary images which can be sketched, as well as kinesthetic sensations. Stage two experiences contain basic emotional and aesthetic sensations of the target, such as fear, beauty, or loneliness.

Dimensional descriptions, such as "large," "heavy," or "thin," define the transition to stage three. At this point viewers often get strong urges to make unconscious free-form sketches whose meaning may not be apparent to them. Viewers in this stage frequently are tempted to make analytic guesses about the name or function of the target. Swann calls these labels analytical overlay, or AOL, and he encourages viewers to develop an awareness of this mental noise, and avoid such intellectualization. Information that actually describes the target's function or purpose forms the basis of stage four, during which Swann teaches his viewers to write detailed lists of their perceptions. The last bits of physical and functional descriptors are combined in a final sketch that can allow the target to be identified.

The above formulation was described by Jim Schnabel, a recent student of Swann's, and the author of a book entitled *Remote Viewers: The Secret History of America's Psychic Spies.*[9] We believe that anyone who takes the time to follow the exercises described in the next section below can learn to successfully pass through each of these stages of remote viewing, and has the opportunity to include these abilities in his or her daily life.

HOW YOU CAN DO REMOTE VIEWING

The mystery has been revealed, and, with a friend, you should now be able to practice remote viewing and learn to come into contact with the part of yourself that is psychic. The easiest way to practice remote viewing is to have a friend choose some interesting object from around the house, and put it into a bag on a table in another room. This will be your target object. The object should be bigger than a matchbox and smaller than a bread box. It should be visually interesting, and have describable parts rather than being compact. For instance, a Raggedy Ann doll is easier to describe than an ivory Buddha figurine. A pineapple is easier to describe than a peach. A hairbrush is better than a nail file. A remote-viewing object should be attractive and worth describing: no lumps of coal or ordinary pencils;

nothing that might be perceived as frightening or distasteful to the viewer. This is an important point, since you would not want to violate your viewer's unconditional trust of you or the process.

Write your name on the top of your page together with, "Target for today's date xx/yy/zz. I can do remote viewing." This is your affirmation for success. After twenty or thirty remote viewings, you can think about skipping this if you want to, but always write "Target for today's date," as an indication of your seriousness of purpose.

Your friend can then sit with you in a dimly lit room, with pen and paper, and tell you that she has "an object that needs a description." You should then close your eyes, relax for a couple of minutes, and tell her about your mental pictures relating to the object, *starting with the very first fragmentary shapes or forms.* These first psychic bits are the most important shapes that you will see. You should make little sketches of these images as they come to view, even though they don't make sense, and are not objects. Your hand may make little movements in the air over the paper — notice them and describe what your subliminal mind is trying to tell you. Take a break, and remember to breathe after each new picture comes into view. You should then look again, and hopefully you will be given another bit, or perhaps the same one again. You should continue this process until no new bits come to you. The whole process should not take more than ten to fifteen minutes. Remember: To be right, you have to be willing to be wrong. This is where the issue of trust is so important.

Since your interviewer in these beginning exercises already knows what the target is, she is very limited in what she can say to you. However, if you say that the object is like a tube of lipstick, for example, she can ask you, "Why is it like a tube of lipstick? What are you seeing that makes you think of lipstick?" She, of course, shouldn't give you any suggestions. Basically, all the interviewer can say in this situation is, "Tell me more." In a laboratory trial, of course, the interviewer has no knowledge of either the chosen target, or other items in the target pool. Often before I end a session, I will ask a viewer, "What is that recurrent thing that you are seeing, but not telling me about?"

As a viewer, you are looking for surprising and novel images that do not belong to your normal repertoire of mental images. After you have described a number of different images, it is good to make a summary of all the things you have said. Try to specify which images you feel most strongly about, and which ones are more likely from memory or imagination, or things you saw earlier in the day. That is, you must go through your notes and separate out the psychic bits from the analytical noise. The remaining collection of bits will then be your description of the target.

If you are told in advance that your target will be one of two objects that were named for you, the difficulty of describing the correct target is greatly increased, since you have a perfect mental picture of both items in your mind. To separate out the psychic bits of information from the analytic overlay (mental noise), you have to go through the bit-collecting process many times. So, we recommend that you don't do this.

After you have made your sketches and written down your impressions, your friend will show you the object. Your interviewer should review with you the correct things you saw in your description. You can then have the experience of saying, "I saw one of those, but I didn't mention it!" The rule in the remote-viewing game is that if it didn't get written on the paper, it didn't happen. So, it is important to write everything, and eventually you will learn to separate the signal from the noise.

There is no substitute for practice. If all this sounds very simple, it is. Our contribution here is to tell you how to get started, and most importantly, to give you permission to express and use your innate abilities and gifts. From two decades of experience, I have no doubt that you can do remote viewing if you follow these instructions. No secret ingredient has been omitted. We wish you success and the feelings of excitement and awe that accompany it.

After you have demonstrated for yourself that these intuitive abilities are, indeed, available, you may begin to wonder about other aspects of our nonlocal mind that can be explored. The true value of remote viewing lies in the fact that it puts us in contact with the part of our consciousness that is unbounded by distance or time. Remote viewing allows us to become aware of our connected and interdependent nature. Its importance becomes particularly apparent when we share our knowledge with our friends. We are here to help each other expand our awareness, so that we enable each other to come in contact with our greater spiritual community.

PROPOSED GUIDELINES FOR REMOTE VIEWING

Based on our experience, we offer the following suggestions and reservations to anyone wishing to carry out remote-viewing experiments of the type we have described here:

- Use viewers who are open to, and even excited about, the prospect of psychic experiences.
- Pay attention to each viewer by giving consideration to his or her mental state at the time of the experiment.
- Provide trial-by-trial feedback of only the correct target, and do it as soon as feasible.
- Create trust by full disclosure, and no hidden agendas.
- Psi is a partnership, not a master/slave relationship.
- Seriousness of purpose provides motivation to both the viewer and the experimenter.
- Targets should be physically and emotionally attractive, and uniquely different. No tarantulas for those who don't want to experience them.
- Do not create large target pools. Have two to four items at most.
- Take enough time to achieve rapport, plus ten to thirty minutes for each trial. One trial per day is plenty. One trial per week is better, to maintain seriousness of purpose.
- Practice allows viewers the opportunity to recognize mental noise and separate it from the psi signal.

We believe that this humanistic approach, which emphasizes rapport, is what makes this remote-viewing protocol the most reliable (with the largest effect size) of the various parapsychological paradigms being examined today. We consider the maintenance of rapport among experimenters to be paramount throughout the process. When necessary, we took the time to debrief discordant moods of participants in an honest and intimate fashion, and through it all, an enduring community of spirit prevailed.

We believe that such commonality of purpose and mutual trust are essential prerequisites for the appearance of psi. Such agreement and coherence among individuals is often difficult to achieve and maintain. However, in a situation where no personal gain and no specific outcome is sought, a meeting of minds, or resonance, may easily occur. Jazz musicians playing together, with the mutual understanding that the music produced is an ad-libbed group creation, often experience such psychic cohesion. Group meditation or prayer for the purpose of healing are other examples where the merging of individuals' consciousness is easily attained, because there is no consideration of personal profit involved. Einstein believed that:

> The true value of a human being is determined primarily by the measure and the sense in which he has attained liberation from the self.[10]

When doing remote viewing, our consciousness becomes liberated in space and time, and is directed by our intention to *acquire or access information*. Such liberation from self-consciousness can also be attained whenever people surrender their individual identities and join their minds together, focusing their attention on creating a common goal, or being of service to others. The trust and rapport that we have been talking about can then be quickly achieved.

chapter four

The Masters
of the Universe
and the Mystery of Psi

The most beautiful experience we can have is the mysterious. It is the fundamental emotion which stands at the cradle of true art and true science.

— Albert Einstein, *Ideas and Opinions*

AGELESS WISDOM, TIMELESS MIND:
THE PERENNIAL PHILOSOPHY AND OUR NONLOCAL AWARENESS

This chapter is about extrasensory perception and our untapped capacities for expanded awareness. Research data from laboratories around the world show that these abilities are available and can be put to use in our lives. The idea that we are able to tap into an omnipresent nonlocal mind that transcends space and time extends from Buddhist teachings as early as 400 B.C. The Diamond Sutras of Buddha, which were the essence of his teachings, portray our consciousness as unconstrained by the apparent limits of space and time. (Ironically, as we have seen, this same insight about our nature makes possible psychic spying into the depths of a Soviet weapons laboratory by the CIA.) The *Vedas*, which are the oldest records of Eastern wisdom, reaching back at least 3,500 years, also teach that separation of individual minds is an illusion. This concept was described by Jesus of Nazareth, who taught of a universal love as a manifestation of our interconnectedness. Today we speak of mind-to-mind connections and nonlocality of mind, unlimited by distance or time. Recent experiments in modern physics shed a new light on classical spiritual teachings, indicating yet again that the world appears more like a great thought than a great machine. Psychologist William Braud, preeminent researcher in remote mental influence, describes the essence of psi as best characterized as the experience of direct knowing.

Many people are concerned that this mind-to-mind connection presents a threat of unlimited or uncontrolled intimacy among people, creating fear of our unlimited potential for expanded awareness. However, if we are able to overcome this fear of our natural psychic abilities, we can take steps toward claiming our heritage of spiritual community, and accessing the omniscience described in the Vedas. After all, the core teaching of Buddhism is of joy, direct experience, and no boundaries of mind; and Jesus spoke of the kingdom of God within each one of us as being peaceful and loving. Enlightened teachers throughout the world have taught that direct participation in the universe is available to the quiet receptive mind. Such participation allows individuals to tune into a greater nonlocal mind, and that experience is transforming as well as enlightening.

Spiritual healing is also about the experience of mind-to-mind connection between people. Healing occurs through a transcendent nonlocal mind expressing itself through a spiritual healer's state of consciousness, rather than from the sending of healing energy from healer to patient. Healing, like ESP, appears to be unbounded by space and time, and appears to involve an exchange of information.

THE SMARTEST PEOPLE IN THE WORLD

It happens over and over again: A recognized expert in the field of medicine, physics, mathematics, etc., stands up and says, "We finally understand it all" — at which point, an unrecognized, nonexpert publishes a paper showing that without a doubt, the expert not only didn't understand *everything*, but in fact, had it entirely wrong.

Physics is at that point today. Several Nobel laureates have written books declaring that the Grand Unified Theory explains everything (or almost everything) that can be observed in the physical universe. In the light of history, this is a very risky proposition. The U.S. Congress turned down a multibillion dollar request from the high-energy physics community for a Superconducting Supercollider Accelerator. The scientists had argued that with the new accelerator, they would be able to find the Higgs particle, postulated to be the last particle needed to complete the Grand Unified Theory. Some even called it "the God particle," but Congress didn't buy it.

In an inaugural lecture at Cambridge University in 1980, the distinguished astrophysicist Stephen Hawking said:

> I want to discuss the possibility that the goal of theoretical physics might be achieved in the not-too-distant future: say by the end of the century. By this I mean that we might have a complete, consistent, and unified theory of the physical interactions that would describe *all possible observations* [emphasis added].

We consider this to be an extraordinarily optimistic view. If psychic abilities are to be considered as part of this program, he had better get cranking on his theory. After twenty-five hundred years of scientific inquiry, we have learned that there is, in general, no one answer to anything — only successive approximations, and a handful of good-looking metaphors. Some lessons from history:

Zeno of Elea — The ancient Egyptians and Greeks knew a great deal about the way the world works. They correctly calculated the diameter of the earth, and they knew that it was spherical. They knew the sun was the center of the solar system, and they calculated the times of eclipses. The Greek scholar Pythagoras was a master of geometry and could calculate the areas of regions, and predict the effects of floods. He felt, with some justification, that he understood all that the eye could survey. He was also the head of a large and powerful mystery school in Athens. At about that same time, 450 B.C., the philosopher Zeno came upon the scene to challenge Pythagoras. Working with his teacher Parmenides, this great intuitive genius discovered some of the mysteries of the very large and very small — what we would call the infinite and the infinitesimal.

The young Zeno had a number of simple questions to ask the school of Pythagoras. The questions all dealt with infinite collections of very small things. How can an object be made of an infinite number of small parts, and still be finite in size? A specific form of the question dealt with the infinite number of parts making up any finite motion: If you walk one mile on the first day, and a half mile on the second day, a quarter mile on the third day, etc., how far will you have walked after walking for an infinite number of days? The answer is two miles, but Pythagoras had no way of beginning to solve this problem, or the others presented by Zeno. Pythagoras' followers solved the problem by having Zeno executed a few years later, for both his ideas and his politics.

The Greeks obviously took their philosophy seriously. Psychologist Dr. Charles Tart says that when an audience is presented with a theory that is one level above their understanding, they find it inspiring. When the information is two levels above their comprehension, they fall asleep. At three levels, they become angry; and when the data reaches four levels above the level of the audience, they want to kill the presenter.

This humorous observation from Dr. Tart confirms my experience of seeing highly intelligent scientists become enraged at the very mention of ESP. Then again, I've been there myself — but I will only admit to falling asleep.

Albert Einstein — In the 1800s, the greatest scientist of the time, Pierre-Simon Laplace, had said that the world is like a great machine: "Give me the initial conditions, and I can tell you what all the final states will be." At the end of the nineteenth century, Lord Kelvin and many other scientists believed, and said openly, that although there were some loose ends, all that remained for physics to accomplish was to calculate additional decimal places for the physical constants. At that time, so-called classical physics considered itself in a wonderful state: James Clerk Maxwell had created a unified theory for electromagnetic waves and visible light waves. Through the work of Kelvin, mechanics, heat, energy, and thermodynamics were well understood. Then in 1905, Einstein, an unknown patent clerk working by himself, published four papers showing that these models were entirely incorrect. One paper dealt with the photoelectric effect of light, and showed that light does not always behave like a wave. Another paper presented the theory of relativity, demonstrating that all motion is relative, and that matter and energy are equivalent. Specifically, Einstein showed that physics was a wide-open field, nowhere near complete.

Kurt Gödel — Ten years after Einstein published his breathtaking physics papers, Bertrand Russell and Alfred North Whitehead, the leading mathematicians of their day, published their monumental contribution to symbolic logic, *Principia Mathematica*.[1] The perfection of mathematics had been Russell's passion for more than a decade. He sought to organize all mathematics into a complete axiomatic framework. In 1931, Kurt Gödel published his now famous "Incompleteness Theorem," which shows that any system of postulates and axioms (such as mathematics, and probably physics) will contain propositions, which although they may be true, cannot be proven. Gödel proved that what Russell and Whitehead had considered accomplished, not only had *not* been accomplished, but was impossible!

BELIEF VS. EXPERIENCE

For the past several years, many distinguished Nobel Prize-winning physicists have written books and publicly declared that all physics is solvable in terms of what we know today. They seem to believe that there are no outstanding problems that cannot be handled within the Grand Unified Theory, the "Theory of Everything." I do not believe that this is true for physics, and I *know* it isn't true for the phenomena of parapsychology.

In this chapter we describe groundbreaking experiments which show that mild-mannered researchers sitting in the laboratory, or you in your living room, can experience and describe distant events and locations blocked from ordinary perception. These data demonstrate that our perception can, and does, transcend the current physical description of the space and time in which we live. The experiments show that we misapprehend the nature of the apparent separation between things and people, challenging the space-time metric commonly used by physicists to measure distance.

The illusory nature of this distance and the separate self are cornerstones of the mystic teachings of many major faiths — Zen Buddhists, Hindu Yogis, Kabbalistic Jews, Islamic Sufis, and Christian mystics. The idea that there are levels of existence forming a continuum from mud to mysticism has been described by writers and philosophers for more than three thousand years. In more recent times, William James, Carl Jung, Krishnamurti, and Ken Wilber have written of our inherent connected nature, and that our experience of personal separateness is an illusion. This has been a fundamental idea of the "Perennial Philosophy," a term coined by philosopher Aldous Huxley to describe the unifying threads of Eastern and Western spiritual thought. These principles were most cogently recorded by Patanjali in the *Yoga Sutras* (aphorisms) sometime around 400 B.C.[2] The same concepts are described beautifully and clearly in Ken Wilber's thoughtful books *Spectrum of Consciousness* and *No Boundary*, as well as in the seventh-century Hindu classic, *The Crest Jewel of Discrimination*, by Shankara.[3]

In Wilber's model of levels of awareness he includes: the objective external world, the five senses, the subjective Ego level in which we identify who we are, the Transpersonal level which is the subject of this book, and the infinite and eternal. The idea that our ego can and does experience levels of awareness integrated into a larger transpersonal and all-encompassing spiritual entity has been described by Ralph Waldo Emerson in his description of the Oversoul, by Jung in his writing of the collective unconscious, and by physicist David Bohm as quantum interconnectedness. We have called this transpersonal connection our community of spirit. The spectrum of consciousness is a metaphor, but the interconnectedness we are writing about is not metaphorical: It is real, and can be experienced and demonstrated.

Modern physics is, of course, not wrong, by any means. It is very successful, but it is significantly incomplete with regard to the phenomena we are discussing. Einstein's theory of relativity didn't make Newton wrong. It just showed that more is going on than is described by Newton's formulation. There is far more in heaven and earth than was dreamt of in his philosophy — and, I suspect, in our philosophy and science as well.

WE DO NOT *BELIEVE* IN ESP

I (Russell) am a physicist, and have worked in the field of laser research for more than thirty years. People do not ask me if I "believe" in lasers, even though they may never have seen one for themselves. Before there were any lasers, some physicists believed they could be built, and others felt that there were theoretical reasons why one could never be constructed. This latter group was, of course, wrong.

Still, I would not say today that I *believe* in lasers. I would say I have data that show their behavior and properties. Similarly, I would not say I believe in ESP. I would say that there are strong and consistent data from more than fifty years of research that demonstrate the existence of the phenomena that we have classified as "psi" or "psychic." In this chapter we will outline some of these experiments that have endured the test of time and critical scientific scrutiny, and that inform us of the range and power of psychic abilities.

In 1972, just before Bobby Fischer decisively won the World Chess Championship in Reykjavík, Iceland, he was asked by an interviewer what psychological strategies he thought his Russian opponent, Boris Spasky, might use in the match. Fischer, never one to mince words, said, "I don't believe in psychology. I only believe in good moves." As a physicist, I like to think that I don't believe in psi; I only believe in good experiments, and my own experience.

THE GOLDEN EXPERIMENTS

In this book we are concerned with a wide variety of psi abilities that are available to us. The groundbreaking experiments that we describe here present data that have brought reliability and respectability to a phenomenon that had occurred previously only in the drawing room and meditation center. These pioneering studies have stood the test of time, and have provided the inspiration that has drawn generations of researchers to devote their lives to the exploration of mind-to-mind connections. We have organized our discussion of psychic abilities into three general classes of investigations: "forced-choice" ESP experiments, in which subjects have a limited number of possibilities to choose from that they are aware of beforehand; "free-response" ESP experiments, in which subjects are free to describe anything that comes to mind; and "healing analog" studies, which we will explore in depth later. Most of these experiments were conducted by researchers known personally to us. The first category of mind-to-mind studies includes examples of "forced-choice" ESP experiments, consisting of highly successful card-guessing in the 1930s with a divinity student at Duke University. Other series of this type were carried out with *perfect* accuracy: One used hypnosis during the sixties in Czechoslovakia, and the other, in 1975, used a "majority-vote protocol" with inexperienced psychology students as subjects.

We next describe what are called "free-response" experiments, where the psi target is a picture whose subject matter could be, literally, anything. The free-response studies include: dream telepathy experiments, in which subjects were asked to try and dream about the events that they would experience the next day after awaking; ganzfeld (meaning "total field") experiments, in which a person in a sensory isolation chamber was asked to describe the video segment that another person was observing in a distant room; and finally, remote-viewing experiments, in which a woman in Detroit was repeatedly able to describe the location and activities of a distant person in randomly chosen hiding places in Rome, Italy. The results of these studies document the increasing success of psi researchers in harnessing ESP abilities, and making them available for broader and broader applications. We will look at six experiments that comprise the mind-to-mind and mind-to-universe investigations. The final studies deal with the mind-to-body connection: They describe the healing of blood cells in a toxic environment, and the paranormal healing of injured animals.

CARD-GUESSING EXPERIMENTS AND
THE SEARCH FOR PERFECT PSI

In the summer of 1933 at Duke University, Dr. J.B. Rhine, who is considered "the father" of laboratory psychical research, began a card-guessing experiment that he considered definitive in demonstrating the existence of ESP. General ESP (GESP) includes *telepathy*, which is a mind-to-mind connection, as well as *clairvoyance*, in which a person appears to make direct contact with an object unknown at that time to any person. Rhine went on to do many years of highly successful pioneering research involving the psychokinetic (mind affecting movement of matter) control of dice, as well as card guessing. He thought that ESP was a naturally occurring ability that a person either did or did not have. When Rhine came to visit the Palo Alto-based Parapsychology Research Group, which Charles Tart and I had founded, he told us that he thought we were on the wrong track in trying to build an ESP-teaching machine. In his experience, psi performance flourished in people's lives, but always declined in the laboratory, and he did not think that we would be able to teach people to improve their psi ability. (In actuality, Charley and I were both able to help people measurably improve their scores with our various ESP-teaching machines.) Rhine also told us that he believed that psi was part of man's spiritual nature, and that he did not expect to find a physical description of its mechanisms.

In Rhine's experiments, a special deck of cards was used for testing subjects in the laboratory. These decks, called Zener cards, were of 25 cards each, and consisted of 5 types of symbols: Printed on each card was either a square, a circle, a cross, a star, or three wavy lines. After the deck was shuffled, the subject was asked to identify which symbol was on each card, shown to him facedown. With 5 different symbols, a subject would be expected to get 5 out of 25 correct by chance alone.

In Rhine's lab, experiments were carried out to determine the existence of telepathy as distinct from clairvoyance. In these series, the sender would sometimes look at the card that she was trying to send to the receiver, and at other times the card would simply be removed from the top of the deck, unseen by anyone. The first case would be general ESP, and the latter would be clairvoyance. Although both types of experiments often gave statistical significance, the results showed that better scores were achieved when the sender looked at the card, giving evidence for the helpfulness of the mind-to-mind connection. Experiments of this type, along with the distant hypnosis experiments of L.L. Vasiliev (described in Chapter 9) are among the best laboratory data we have for purely telepathic connections between people.

One particularly gifted subject was Hubert Pearce, who was a divinity student at Duke when he offered himself as a potential subject to Rhine. He scored a 32 percent hit rate (8 out of 25), when only 20 percent was expected. This might not seem so exciting, but when he showed that he could continue this hit rate for hundreds of trials, the results were highly statistically significant. Pearce told Rhine that he believed he had inherited his psychic ability from his mother, who had a similar talent.

In a famous and much scrutinized experiment, Pearce was sequestered on the top floor of the Social Sciences building at Duke, and the experimenter, Gaither Pratt, was in the college library 100 meters away.[4] At the rate of one trial per minute, Pratt would remove the top card, facedown, from a shuffled deck, and without looking at it, place it, facedown, on his record book. This was a clairvoyance experiment, since no person knew what the card was at the time of the trial. If someone had known the card's identity, then there would have been a possibility of a mind-to-mind telepathic connection as well as a direct connection to the card. In the experimental cubicle, Pearce would record each of his guesses, trial by trial, until he had completed 25 calls. He would then have a five-minute rest, and write down his impressions of the next 25 cards.

Over a six-month period, Pearce carried out 74 runs of this type. He scored correctly on 558 trials, where only 370 would be expected by chance. The probability of these extra 188 hits occurring by chance is less than one in 10^{20}, or one in a hundred billion billion. Pearce did not receive any feedback on his trials, and he obviously didn't need it. He probably had some internal method of cleaning his mental slate from the residue of each previous trial.

In our experience, feedback is an essential ingredient for improving psi ability, although it is not necessary for psi to occur. Most people like feedback, so that they can achieve a degree of closure from the previous trial. This amazing landmark experiment achieved its dual goals: It demonstrated for the first time that increasing the distance from across the room to across the campus did not decrease the ESP scoring rate, and showed conclusively that it was not necessary for anyone to see a target card for a viewer to identify it correctly through psychic means.

TRANSMITTING MESSAGES WITH PSI

Milan Ryzl was a chemical engineer in Czechoslovakia when he started doing psychic research in the 1960s. Ryzl wanted to find a way to achieve error-free communication with psi. He felt that through the use of hypnosis, he could create a psi-conducive state in which people could greatly increase their psychic ability. Instead of "running" his subjects impersonally, which is so often done, Ryzl worked with people one at a time, on a personal basis, initially using free-response pictorial targets, and household objects. He also provided supportive feedback to help his subjects identify *what it felt like* to be functioning psychically.

In Ryzl's most famous experiment, a talented subject was able to determine a fifteen-digit number by psi, using an ingenious and complicated system.[5] Our government is spending billions of dollars trying to achieve this kind of accuracy in its efforts to communicate with submerged submarines that cannot be contacted by ordinary radio. To accomplish his goal of perfect message-sending, Ryzl had an assistant randomly select five groups of numbers of three digits each. The fifteen digits were then encoded into binary form (1s and 0s) and translated into a sequence of green and white cards, which were placed into opaque, sealed envelopes. Ryzl was working with an excellent hypnotic subject, Pavel Stepanek, in this experiment, which is one of the most striking in the annals of psi research because of its unparalleled accuracy.

We explain Ryzl's message-sending system in the paragraphs below for readers who are especially interested in cryptography. For those who are less interested in these details, please skip ahead a few paragraphs.

As previously noted, Ryzl had an assistant draw up five groups of three decimal numbers, and then change each number into binary digits of ones and zeros. Each binary number was then translated into a series of green and white cards that were put into sealed envelopes. For example, using green for "one" and white for "zero," the digit 7 would read III in its binary form (I for 2^0, plus I for 2^1, plus I for 2^2, [remembering that I plus 2 plus 4 = 7], and green green green in the color form). Ryzl had Stepanek, the subject, repeat his calls for each envelope many times. Then he used an elaborate majority-vote protocol to decide if a given envelope was to be called green or white in the final tally. He was able, after 19,350 trials, to have the confidence that there was enough consistency in the calls for each of the binary digits.

Stepanek averaged nine seconds per call, over many weeks of work. The astounding result was that he had, in fact, correctly identified each of the numbers. Calling his cards one by one, Stepanek's hit rate for the series was 61.9 percent, where 50 percent was to be expected (since the only choice was either green or white on each call). The probability of identifying all fifteen decimal digits correctly is one in 10^{15}, or one in a million billion.

Stepanek was an indefatigable card guesser, and he continued with this remarkably boring task for more than a decade after Ryzl's first highly significant experiments. Stepanek went on to produce highly significant ESP results with researchers from all over the world, including Pratt, who went to Prague to work with him. Pratt discovered that Stepanek demonstrated an inexplicable "focusing effect," in that he had a significantly higher scoring rate over and over with particular cards. In Ryzl's work the cards had been in opaque envelopes. Pratt put the cards and envelopes into ice cream jiffy bags to further isolate them, but the rate of Stepanek's success was not at all affected.[6]

A similarly successful experiment in message-sending was carried out by Dr. James Carpenter, working with college students at the University of North Carolina in 1975.[7] Carpenter felt that hypnosis was not necessary for successful psi, so he encoded the word "PEACE" into Morse code, using a series of binary dots and dashes, and had a class of psychology students make repeated calls for each of the twelve bits. Then, like Ryzl, he had the students continue to guess, without feedback, until he had a solid majority vote for the identity of each of the twelve bits. Carpenter was successful in transmitting each bit of his message perfectly, using untrained college students as messengers.

Although highly successful experiments like these were carried out for more than forty years, the participants never improved their ability. Some, like Stepanek, held on to their scoring ability for years, but the performance of many declined to chance odds in a relatively short time. It's as though the most reliable phenomena in psi research at that time was the experimenters' ability to eventually extinguish the participants' natural ESP in the laboratory.

This so-called decline effect appeared to be the inevitable result of lengthy card-guessing experiments. In an effort to make the experiments less boring to the subjects, researchers began to use pictures of interesting scenes, and three-dimensional objects as targets. In this way, a subject could freely describe his mental pictures, instead of searching through his memory for a small set of possible targets, all known beforehand. The use of free-response target material was a great advance in psi research, because it gave the subject a task that actually corresponds to the way psi ability works. It allows the subject to use his psi, rather than his analytic abilities.

One of the most important things that we have learned is that analysis of target possibilities is the enemy of psi. If your only criterion for the existence of psi is how accurately a person can psychically read the serial number on your dollar bill, then you'll conclude that there is no psychic functioning.

This concept was understood by writer Upton Sinclair, who, in his 1930 book *Mental Radio*, thoughtfully describes years of successful telepathic picture-drawing experiments that he carried out with his wife, Mary Craig.[8] Craig was a heartful and spiritual woman who had a deep understanding, both intuitive and analytical, of the process of psychic perception. Einstein himself wrote in the book's introduction that the Sinclairs' work deserved "the most earnest consideration." The following paragraphs contain her instructions for "the art of conscious mind reading," condensed from a lengthy chapter in *Mental Radio*:

> The first thing you have to do is learn the trick of undivided attention, or concentration...putting the attention on *one* object.... It isn't thinking; it is inhibiting thought....
>
> You have to inhibit the impulse to think things about the object, to examine it, or appraise it, or to allow memory-trains to attach themselves to it.... Simultaneously, [you] must learn to relax, for strangely enough, a part of concentration is complete relaxation...under specified control....
>
> Also, there is something else to it — the power of supervising the condition. You succeed presently in establishing a blank state of consciousness, yet you have the power to become instantly conscious.... Also, you control, to a certain degree, what is to be presented to consciousness when you are ready to become conscious.[9]

Engineer René Warcollier also presents both theory and experiments of psi communication in his 1939 book, *Mind to Mind*.[10] He describes in detail why free-response experiments are almost always greatly superior to forced-choice trials, because they free the viewer from the mental noise of memory and imagination. Unfortunately, it took another twenty years for ESP researchers to take the ideas of these brilliant amateurs into account when designing their experiments.

The next three experiments described here all gave the subject something much more interesting than cards to look at psychically. The researchers also carried out their experiments in environments that were much more psi-conducive than classrooms or laboratories.

DREAM TELEPATHY

Psychic dreams have been with us since the days of Cassandra in ancient Greece, and Joseph and the Pharaoh in the Old Testament. From the data collected by Louisa Rhine, it appears that more than half of all spontaneous ESP experiences take place in dreams.[11] Sigmund Freud wrote about the telepathic content of dreams.[12] And psychiatrist Jule Eisenbud has spoken and written widely about patients who have dreamt about events in Eisenbud's own life.[13]

Based on the idea that dreams might be a good source of ESP, researchers at Maimonides Hospital in Brooklyn, New York undertook a decade-long study in the 1960s of the occurrence of psychic events in dreams. This pioneering team included psychiatrist Dr. Montague Ullman, who was research director for the hospital, psychologist Dr. Stanley Krippner, and writer and researcher Alan Vaughan. Krippner went on to found Saybrook College, and to become a distinguished researcher of psychic healing around the world, and Vaughan became a highly regarded author, healer, and psychic. This team carried out many successful, innovative experiments in which a subject was asked to go to sleep and dream about a randomly chosen painting that a sender would look at throughout the night.

The sleepers had electrodes attached to their heads so that the experimenters would know from their brain waves and rapid eye movements (REM) when they had entered dreaming sleep. In 1953, Nathaniel Kleitman and his colleagues at the University of Chicago showed that REM sleep is very reliably associated with the dreaming state.

In the Maimonides experiments, the researchers would, at the first signs of REM activity, alert the sender — who was 98 feet away in another part of the hospital — to pay particular attention to the picture he or she was viewing. At the end of each dream period throughout the night, the experimenters would awaken the sleeper and tell him or her, "We know you have just been dreaming. Please tell us about it." The results were remarkable. As described in their book *Dream Telepathy*, the sleeper was able to relate dream experiences that were strongly correlated with the pictures viewed by the sender. These statistically significant correlations were made by "blind" judges who had to match each of the eight dream reports against the eight pictures used for that series.[14]

Two series of particularly successful trials were carried out with psychologist William Erwin as the sleeping subject. "Multisensory" materials were given to the sender to help him or her experience and empathize with the picture that they were to send. For example, when the target picture was *Descent from the Cross*, the materials contained a small wooden crucifix, some thumbtacks, and a red felt-tipped marker. The instructions read, "Using these tacks, nail Christ to the cross; using the marker, color his body with blood." (This is the sort of thing that gives psychologists a bad name.) Nonetheless, excerpts from Erwin's dream that night included:

> We were going to be sacrificed, or something, and there were political overtones...what we would do is pretend that we were gods...in looking at the so-called king, chief, or whatever the native was...it would be almost like...looking at one of those totem pole gods.

The results of this study were significant at 10,000 to one odds when evaluated by outside judges, who were successfully able to match each of the eight dream descriptions with the correct picture.

In another trial, the target picture was *Downpour at Shono*, showing a Japanese man with an umbrella in the rain. The sender was given a small umbrella, and told to take a shower in the adjoining washroom. Selections from Erwin's dreams include:

> ...something about an Asian man who was ill....The part I remember — it sort of faded away — had to do with fountains, a big fountain. It would be like you see in Italy. Two images, and water spray that would shoot up.

One last example gives Erwin's description of his dream in response to *Both Members of the Club*, showing two boxers in a savage fight. The sender's materials this time included a dark leather, laced boxing glove.

> There were a lot of people....There was a lot of activity going on....I was watching some cars parked on the beach being pounded by the waves. One was smashed so hard it hit another car and completely broke it to pieces.
> (In a later dream): The only thing I can remember was cleaning a

shoe. It was a black leather shoe. The process was cleaning a dirty shoe. Just a man's shoe. A lace shoe....

These experiments were important to psi research for two reasons: First, they were successful year after year for a decade, giving researchers a stable phenomenon to investigate. Even more important, this approach provided a valuable insight into the pictorial and non-analytic processes underlying psi functioning. In the 1960s, researchers considered psi to be a weak perceptual ability, often masked by internal and external mental and somatic sensory noise. These experiments led researchers to ask, "Can we find a way to let subjects rest in a dream-like state, but still be awake enough to tell us what they are experiencing?"

THE GANZFELD

The ganzfeld, meaning "whole field," is a controlled environment used in ESP research, in which all ordinary inputs to the psi subject are limited by sensory isolation. The ganzfeld idea came out of the 1960s, when it was thought that altered states of consciousness would lead to more effective psychic functioning. (Earlier attempts at creating a psi-conducive state had used sensory bombardment.)[15] The receiving person is located in a soundproof room that has a uniform and featureless visual field. This is accomplished in a simple manner by taping Ping-Pong ball halves over the eyes of the viewer and bathing them in uniform red light, while "white" noise is provided by earphones.

Like the dream telepathy experiments, the ganzfeld studies investigated telepathic communication between an ostensible sending person and a receiving person. This approach was pioneered and investigated for more than fifteen years by Charles Honorton, who was Krippner's successor at the Maimonides Hospital Research Center.[16] Honorton was an outstanding theoretician in psi research, as well as a funny and congenial researcher. As a result of his affable rapport with subjects, he was one of the most consistently successful experimenters in the field.

Chuck Honorton confided to me that he was concerned about the fact that his lab was in the basement of a mental hospital. The mental patients were never used as viewers in his research, but he and his staff always wore white lab coats when at work, to enable the doctors to distinguish the psi researchers from the mental patients. After Chuck would describe the ganzfeld protocol to the next day's subjects, he was known to advise them to "Take two Ping-Pong balls, and call me in the morning." Regrettably, Chuck died in 1992 at the early age of 46, depriving us of a great and compassionate seeker who devoted his entire career to the field of psychic research. We miss him.

Throughout his career, Honorton made consistent efforts to address the attacks of the skeptics and critics of his work in as positive a way as possible. Many psi researchers view their critics as being not particularly well-intentioned. Therefore, they consider the attention given to dealing with their nonconstructive criticism to be a waste of precious time. Honorton, however, continually modified his experiments to meet skeptics' criticisms.

In 1994, after his death, a fifteen-page paper was published that was co-authored by Honorton with psychologist Dr. Daryl Bem, a professor from Cornell University and a former skeptic. The publication signified a landmark accomplishment in the field of psi research because it appeared in the prestigious *Psychological Bulletin*.[17] The experiments described in that paper were called "the auto-ganzfeld," because the researcher, sender, and receiver were all isolated from each other, and the researcher was isolated from the selection of the target videotapes, which were chosen and shown to the viewer automatically by a computer.

In these experiments, the receiving person was generally a volunteer from the community. Receivers were seated comfortably in reclining chairs, in a soundproof room, with the Ping-Pong balls over their eyes and white noise fed into their earphones. (They might have appeared to an outsider to be bug-eyed monsters from a science fiction novel of the 1950s.) The receiver's task was to remain awake, and to describe into a tape recorder all the impressions that passed through his or her mind during a thirty-minute session. Meanwhile, an ostensible sender would be looking at a randomly chosen videotape selection that would be repeated over and over during the session. In some of these trials, the receiver's narration was so accurate that it sounded as if the receiver were psychically watching the target videotape just as it was being shown to the sender.

At the end of each trial, the computer controlling the experiment would show the receiver the chosen segment and three other video segments, in random order. The receiver's task was then to decide which of the four mini-movies the sender had been watching. By chance, one would expect a 25 percent success rate in this process. In the entire series of eleven experiments, which involved 240 people in 354 sessions, the hit rate was 32 percent, which departs from chance expectation by 500 to 1.

The most successful of the auto-ganzfeld studies was conducted by Honorton in conjunction with Dr. Marilyn Schlitz, who went on to become the Research Director at the Institute of Noetic Sciences (IONS) in Sausalito, California.

In 1991, Schlitz was working on a creativity research project with students at the Julliard School in New York. As part of this work, she enlisted twenty classical music and modern dance students to take part in a ganzfeld study.[18] Each day they would take the train from their urban campus on Broadway out to the pastoral setting of the laboratory in Princeton. Climbing off the railroad car into the grassy surroundings would already initiate the New York City students' altered state. These talented and practiced artists, working in pairs with their friends, scored at a 50 percent rate in choosing the correct target from four possibilities. This is twice the rate that you would expect by chance, and was the highest result in all of the published ganzfeld research.

We often say that psi is like musical ability: It is widely distributed in the population, and everyone has some ability, and can participate to some extent — even as the most nonmusical person can learn to play a little Mozart on the piano. On the other hand, there is no substitute for innate talent or practice.

We believe the reason these young artists turned out to be the most successful participants in the entire ganzfeld series is that, although they left their violins and leotards behind, they brought with them to the lab a good friend or study partner, and their heart-to-heart and trusting connection is what contributed to the free flow of psi between them. We also think that the fact that the participants were creative artists made them less inhibited in sharing their psychic impressions.

In our society, psychic functioning is to some extent forbidden, or even considered as evidence of mental illness. The ganzfeld ritual of the Ping-Pong balls, the red lights, the white noise in the earphones, and the slamming of the heavy door of the electrically shielded, soundproof booth had a powerful permission-giving effect on the viewer.

The earlier Maimonides ganzfeld experiments had used "View Master" stereo slides instead of videotapes, but the results were quite similar. The viewers didn't know if the senders would be looking at Doris Day, Donald Duck, or downtown Las Vegas. For example, when the target episode was from *The Flying Nun*, the illustration showed a nun leaping off the roof of a two-story building. The viewer described:

> ...the archbishop's hat.... Tiny people far away.... Floating, a lot of clouds and a skyline... arches. A church... an aerial view moving to the ground fast. A road with bridges and towers... a church and columns. A window up high in a stone wall, more bells, a peaked roof.[19]

This segment of transcript shows how a viewer will often experience icons and associations that are related to the target material, but are not actually present in the picture. Another example of this that comes to mind took place in an experiment with Israel-born Uri Geller at SRI. I was in a shielded room with a target picture of a devil with a pitchfork; Geller, outside in the laboratory, drew a picture of The Ten Commandments tablets as his first response. After he saw the target, he objected to it, saying that there is no devil in Israeli culture, so how could he be expected to draw such a thing?

In a second trial from the Maimonides View Master series, the viewer was trying to describe a series of pictures set around the television western show, *Gun Smoke*. The target picture showed a cowboy holding a gun. The viewer described the following scene:

...now a desert, probably because I am thirsty. There is a skull of a longhorn cow...a pool of water, buzzards flying over it...a gray horse and rider...a teepee and two Indians...handgun from around 1860 or 1870, like from the Westerns...[20]

There is, very likely, other material in the original transcript of the published reports which is less correlated with the View Master slides. What we are illustrating here is the uniquely pictorial quality of the transcripts, which leads a blind judge to correctly separate the nuns from the guns, and to match the "gun" transcript to the "cowboy with gun" target, and the "archbishop and church" transcript to the "nun" target.

These ganzfeld experiments were so successful, year after year, that they captured the attention of researchers all over the world. They also attracted the attention of local skeptics, many of whom have created careers based on trashing the work of researchers. Skeptical psychologist Dr. Ray Hyman from the University of Oregon conducted a meta-analysis of 42 ganzfeld studies carried out in laboratories all over the world. In his investigation, he chose 28 experiments as having common evaluation approaches, and found that 82 percent of these had positive outcomes. Much to his surprise, he found himself co-authoring a paper with Chuck Honorton, in which Hyman concluded that this result could not be explained by errors in protocol, and that the ganzfeld work was worthy of further research.[21]

The downside of the ganzfeld research is that such a significant outcome required 354 trials, involving at least three people for two hours for each trial. We believe that part of the cause of this inefficiency is that a new and inexperienced viewer was used for each trial. In our remote-viewing work we try to *train* a viewer to separate the psychic signal from the mental noise, and then we continue to work with him or her. We have found that with practice, any viewer is able to greatly improve his or her performance, and it is desirable to work with these experienced subjects.

INTERCONTINENTAL REMOTE VIEWING

One such experienced viewer is anthropologist Dr. Marilyn Schlitz, the researcher in the study with the musicians and dancers. In 1979, she took part in an intercontinental remote-viewing experiment that illustrates the advantages of the one-talented-subject approach.

Remote viewing is an extension of the free-response protocol; it goes beyond pictures in the laboratory to the whole world of living, outdoor geographic and architectural targets. Schlitz hoped to replicate the new SRI remote-viewing experiments that we were conducting at that time. She wanted to do remote viewing at much greater distances than had been published in any of the SRI papers. To carry out this experiment she enlisted the help of her friend Elmar Gruber, a European parapsychologist who was traveling in Italy.

Each day for ten days in November of 1979, Schlitz, at home in rainy Detroit, Michigan, would try to experience and describe the place in Rome where Gruber was located at 11:00 a.m. Michigan time. Gruber, for his part, had made a list of forty different target locations in Rome. These included both indoor and outdoor sites at parks, churches, the airport, museums, the sports arena, the Spanish Steps, etc. Could Marilyn, 3,000 miles away, describe each day's target place with enough accuracy to allow a future judge to match each day's description with that day's target? In addition, could she do it without receiving any feedback as she attempted this psychic investigation?

An example extracted from one of Marilyn's successfully matched remote-viewing transcripts is as follows:

> Flight path? Red lights. Strong depth of field. Elmar seems detached, cold . . . outdoors. See sky dark. Windy and cold. Something shooting upward. . . . Not a private home or anything like that — something — a public facility. . . . He was standing away from the main structure, although he could see it. He might have been in a parking lot or field connected to the structure, that identifies the place. I want to say an airport, but that just seems too specific. There was activity and people, but no one real close to Elmar.[22]

In fact, the target site was the Rome International Airport, where Elmar had been standing on a hill to the side of the terminal building. Marilyn's transcripts and Elmar's descriptions of his hiding places were sent to Dr. Hans Bender, a German researcher who arranged the judging for the experiment. Five judges looked at the material. Their job was to go to each of the ten target sites, read Gruber's comments about what he had been doing at the site, and while there, to decide which of Marilyn's ten transcripts was the best match for that site, which was the second best, etc. It turned out that of Marilyn's ten transcripts, six were matched correctly (first place) to the target that Elmar was visiting on the day the transcript was created. The likelihood of that happening by chance is less than 6 in 10,000.

This experiment received a great deal of examination by the critical scientific community. It was suggested that because Marilyn and Elmar were friends, they may have been similarly affected by world events, even though they did not communicate during the experiment. It was proposed that Elmar's comments about each place he visited might contain words or ideas, based on world events or the weather, for instance, which might have contaminated Marilyn's transcripts. As a result of this far-fetched but not totally invalid criticism, the entire judging process was repeated, omitting Elmar's comments about what he had done at each site. The overall significance of the experiment was calculated, and the likelihood of it happening by chance was less than 1 in 1,000 — still remarkable for an experiment with only ten trials.

This experiment, along with most of the others in this chapter, made it into K. Ramakrishna Rao's 1984 book, *The Basic Experiments in Parapsychology*, which I consider to be in the ESP Hall of Fame.[23] Since our first publication of the remote-viewing protocol, in *Nature*, in 1974, there have been at least twenty-three successful replications of the work, and this is one of them.[24] Taken together, the data from the ganzfeld and remote-viewing experiments have contributed giant steps toward substantiating the claims for clairvoyance that have been reported throughout history.

By now you may wonder, what is a reasonable person to believe about his or her own psychic abilities? We have offered a glimpse into the experimental evidence for mind-to-mind and mind-to-universe connections. As a physicist, I find it impossible to write about these experiments without again feeling the sense of awe and wonder that I have felt since I first experienced psychic events as a teenager doing magic on the stage. We haven't dealt with precognition yet, but it's clear from our experiments that our consciousness has access to information unlimited by our ordinary understanding of spatial separation. We must conclude that physicists have a lot to learn before a "Theory of Everything" is on the horizon. Indeed, as I write this, today's *New York Times* has a story describing recent discoveries by the Hubble space telescope, showing that the age of the universe appears to be less than the age of some of its best-known globular star clusters! Here we are faced with an obvious contradiction regarding something we thought we really understood. This is, of course, what makes science so exciting.

One of the great puzzles for medically oriented psi researchers is to separate the data for mind-to-mind connections from experiments in the mind-to-body arena. For instance, when considering the case of a person who has been treated by a healer, how can we tell whether his health has been enhanced by a mind-to-mind interaction, or a mind-to-body treatment? What do healers really do? How many different kinds of healing are there?

MIND-TO-BODY INVESTIGATIONS: MIND-TO-CELLS

In Unity Church, the children sing (to the tune of "Shortnin' Bread"), "Every little cell in my body is healthy, every little cell in my body is well!" In physician-free Christian Science doctrine, Mary Baker Eddy teaches in *Science and Health* that "destroying through the power of God, the *belief* that sickness could be happening, also destroys — and actually heals — the sickness in human experience."[25] She reached the conclusion "that all causation rests with the Mind, and that every effect is a mental phenomenon." Daily affirmations to promote health are aspects of many religious philosophies today. The idea that stressful thoughts can contribute to illness is not a surprising concept to an audience in the 1990s. The healthful results of relaxation and meditation are widely accepted, from the work of Herbert Benson, M.D., concerning the Relaxation Response, and from Dr. Dean Ornish's heart-healthy program, involving meditation and healing imagery.[26] Sir John Eccles, Nobel laureate, maintains that one's mind routinely exerts a true psychokinetic influence upon one's own brain through "cognitive caresses" of the synapses of cortical neurons.[27] For all practical purposes, we can view our own nonphysical thoughts as the agency that allows us to extend an arm, by interacting with our own muscles through psychokinesis. What is still surprising, however, is the idea that we can affect or consider healing *someone else's* body with our thoughts.

According to the remote-viewing data, it is clear that people can experience the thoughts and images held by another person in a distant place. So, just as I am able to send you the mental picture of a flying nun, I could send you positive and healing affirmations. I can imagine that these could stimulate in you the same healthful psychoneuroimmunological effect that they have for me. We believe that a doctor's acts of compassion and sending positive loving thoughts to his or her patients is an important part of the healing process.

Dr. William Braud, at the Mind Science Foundation in San Antonio, Texas, took great steps toward answering that question. Over a period of almost fifteen years ending in 1992, psychologist Braud carried out dozens of experiments investigating the ability of a person to directly influence the behavior of remote living systems, using mental means alone. These experiments, often in collaboration with Marilyn Schlitz, included efforts to remotely influence a person's state of relaxation, as measured by his galvanic skin response (GSR), and blood pressure. Other studies involved trying to increase the rate of activity of gerbils running on a wheel, and influencing the spontaneous swimming behavior of small knife fish (a kind of carp).[28] All of these experiments in mental-influence-at-a-distance were successful, and most important, they were repeatable.

Braud's theory is that labile systems — living things that already exhibit some level of activity — are easier to move or affect than systems at rest.[29] This is a kind of psychological statement of Newton's third law, which says that objects in motion tend to stay in motion, and objects at rest tend to remain at rest. In his efforts to demonstrate mental influence, Dr. J.B. Rhine recognized that it is easier to affect the trajectory of falling dice than it is to levitate dice that are resting on the table.

Braud was very selective in the systems he studied. If the creatures are not labile enough, or too sluggish, it is often too difficult to get them started. If the animal's behavior is very near the activity ceiling, it may be exhibiting all the action you can expect from it. For instance, a gerbil would be a better target than a snail or a slug, or a hummingbird or a bee. It would be very hard to get the snail's attention, and similarly difficult to increase the activity level of the hummingbird.

Although most of Braud's highly successful work involved increasing and decreasing the degree of relaxation of people at a distant location, our concern is with the experiments he did to psychically come to the aid of threatened red blood cells. In all the other experiments he did with living systems, the creature (even the goldfish) had a level of consciousness which could, in principle, be affected by a distant person. In the experiments we are now going to describe, subjects in the laboratory were asked to influence the behavior of red blood cells, which to the best of our knowledge have not shown any independent consciousness.

In these studies, the cells were put into test tubes of distilled water, which is a toxic environment for them. If the salt content of their solution deviates too much from that of blood plasma, the cell wall weakens, and the contents of the cell go into solution. This unfortunate situation is dispassionately called *hemolysis*. The degree of hemolysis is easily measured, since the transmission of light through a solution containing intact blood cells is much less than through a solution of dissolved cells. A spectrophotometer is used to measure the light transmission over the duration of the experiment. In each series, twenty tubes of blood were compared for each of thirty-two different subjects. The subjects, situated in a distant room, had the task of attempting to save the little sanguinous corpuscles from destruction from too little salt in their ten target test tubes. The blood cells in the ten control tubes had to fend for themselves. Braud found that the people working as remote healers were able to significantly retard the hemolysis of the blood in the tubes they were trying to protect.[30]

These experiments are important because each is a case where the mind of the subject/healer was able to directly interact with a living system, and where one could not reasonably say that it was due to the placebo effect, or a charming bedside manner, because the blood cells ostensibly had no expectations. Another striking finding in these experiments was the fact that the participants who produced the most statistically significant results were slightly more successful in protecting their own blood cells than they were at preserving the life of cells that came from another person. This result is open to interpretation. It may be that if psychic functioning is viewed as a kind of resonance, it is as though one is more in resonance with a part of himself, than with a part of another person.

A similar experiment was carried out in the 1980s, in which a healer was able to prolong the life of bacteria that were challenged by antibiotics. Dr. Elizabeth Rauscher, a physicist, and Dr. Beverly Rubick, a biologist at the University of California, Berkeley, both worked with the legendary American healer Olga Worrall, whom we discuss in later chapters.[32] As a healer, Mrs. Worrall refused to consciously harm any living thing. However, she was willing to attempt to heal *E. coli* bacteria that had been poisoned with tetracycline. In well-controlled side-by-side comparison tests, the two researchers showed that Mrs. Worrall was able to keep alive the *E. coli* cells toward which she was directing her healing thoughts for a longer period of time than the controls. After four hours of exposure to the antibiotic, all of the control bacteria were dead, while a significant number of bacteria for whom she had been praying lived on. An important finding from this study was that the healer was not able to increase the reproduction rate of the healthy bacteria colony. Rather, she was able to aid the bacteria that were in need of healing, like the red blood cells in a toxic solution.

Bacteria are much smaller than red blood cells, but they have a nucleus and are able to reproduce, so they are more complex systems than blood cells. Both of these one-celled systems are alive, and we can therefore imagine them having interaction with human consciousness. However, similar experiments have been carried out with ordinary distilled water as the target for healing change. A mental influence over the state of a nonliving system, such as water, implies direct psychic interaction with a part of the physical universe, as the following studies demonstrate.

From 1957 to 1965, Dr. Bernard Grad at McGill University in Montreal had been investigating the ability of healer Oscar Estebany to affect distilled water in sealed containers (ampoules).[32] Sealed ampoules are the gold standard of sterile hygienic practice in hospital settings. If a doctor is about to give an injection of material drawn from a sealed ampoule, he does not want to have to ask if anyone has directed bad thoughts toward the solution. The implications of experiments on nonliving systems pose just such a question. In an early set of experiments, Dr. Grad grew some pots of barley seeds which he stressed by watering them with salty water (1 percent saline). Estebany agreed to treat some of the saline-filled ampoules before they were used for watering. The seeds that were watered with the psychically treated water grew significantly faster than the plants with the untreated water. To attempt to explain the outcome of this experiment, researchers went on to look at the physical changes in water that could be caused by a healer.

The results of this study led to experiments by Dr. Douglas Dean and Stephan Schwartz.[33] These experiments offer strong evidence that a healer can actually change some physical property of water that affects its spectroscopic absorption of infrared light. These studies concerned a healer's effect on distilled water, again, a target that is thought to have no consciousness, and is not even a living system. It is still undetermined whether the observed changes in the water were the result of an interaction between the mind of the healer and the water sample, or due to a change in the water's absorption of infrared light. Since the healer held his hands close to the water container, electrical polarization effects from the healer can't be ruled out.

MIND-TO-MAMMALS

After Estebany's successful experiments with water and plants, Dr. Grad went on to investigate the healer's ability with animals, using the practice known as "laying on of hands." In these trials, Estebany was able to significantly accelerate the healing of wounded mice.[34]

The protocol involved creating surgical wounds of about one-half inch in diameter on the backs of forty-eight mice. (The practice of creating wounds for healing research understandably makes us uncomfortable, but it is very hard to get informed consent from a mouse.) The mice were divided into three groups of equal size. Estebany was asked to hold the cages of one group for fifteen minutes, twice a day, for fourteen days. One group was warmed up with heating tapes to simulate the heat from being held, and the control group was simply transferred from one cage to another.

The results were remarkable. The incisions were photographed each day, and by the seventh day, there was a clear and striking difference between the size of the wounds in the two noncontrol groups. By day fourteen, most of the mice in the held cages were entirely healed, and none of the untreated mice were healed. Eventually, when the research was finished, all the mice in the control group received healing treatments and became healed as well. We hope that they will agree with us that it was all for a good cause.

The work with animals is very important in the study of psychic healing because we believe that there is no placebo effect with animals. That is, they have no expectation that any particular thing that is done to them is going to make them heal more quickly. The difficulty in doing healing research with humans is that researchers must obtain their informed consent, without creating expectations that could easily lead to the placebo effect. In Chapter 9, we discuss the significant experiments that have been done with humans that indicate mind-to-mind interactions can affect human physiological functioning from a distance.

An important recent book by researcher Dean Radin, Ph.D., called *The Conscious Universe*, evaluates the statistical significance of hundreds of ESP experiments of the type we have discussed in this chapter. Radin discusses his own pioneering work showing that peoples' galvanic skin response changes in the seconds *before* they are shown alarming or shocking pictures. We discuss such precognitive perception of the future, which Radin terms "presentiment," in the next chapter.[35]

chapter five

Precognition:
Time and Time Again

For us believing physicists, the distinction between past, present and future is only an illusion, even if a stubborn one.

— Albert Einstein,
To the children of his good friend
Michele Besso, after Besso's death

In this chapter we explore things that we understand even less than remote viewing; namely, how much or what can we know about events before they occur. We will examine how much of the future can be foretold. In the framework of *A Course in Miracles (ACIM)*, a spiritual path of teachings that we discuss in later chapters, a miracle is defined as a change in perception. One of the principles of *A Course in Miracles* states that:

Miracles are both beginnings and endings, and so they alter the temporal order. They are always affirmations of rebirth, which seem to go back, but really go forward. They undo the past in the present, and thus release the future.[1]

The idea here is that a miracle is a thought that recognizes the illusion of our separation, just as Einstein (above) says that time is an illusion. The data for both healing and precognition show us that our nonlocal mind transcends the boundaries of bodies in physical space, and is unlimited by time. The remote-viewing data provides evidence that our minds have access to events occurring in distant places, and into the future. The healing data that we review in Chapter 9 suggests that our minds are connected through space, and that mind-to-mind communication may be instantaneous. In the summary Chapter 12, we discuss the physics of these nonlocal connections.

When it comes to writing about time, we have a fundamental problem, because no one knows how to measure time. Rulers measure distance, but clocks do not measure time; they simply tick at the rate of one tick per second. They do not measure the "passage of time," or our supposed progress down the time line at a rate of one second per second. Today, a second is defined from the vibrational period of an excited cesium atom. Time is a mental construct, and cannot be measured by scientific instruments. According to author-physician Dr. Deepak Chopra, time is a continuity of memories. There is no instrument that allows us to watch time flow through it, like water past a paddle wheel, because time does not flow.

It has often been said that time was invented by God so that everything wouldn't happen at once. In that view, time is seen as the "distance" between events that occur at the same place. My birthday was celebrated in the same house this year as it was last year. The temporal distance separating the birthdays is one trip of the earth around the sun; one tick of the planetary clock. But, can next year's birthday be sensed from the previous year's party? It certainly can be. There is no doubt about it. The goal of this chapter is to try to make that assertion believable.

Einstein asserted that we live in a four-dimensional universe, which we have learned to call space-time. To represent this as a coordinate system, we can visualize a tall apartment house large enough to fill a city block. We can imagine the space axes of this system as being the cross streets at the base of the building. Forty-second Street goes from left to right, and Fifth Avenue goes from back to front. Time is the vertical dimension in this model, with each story of the building representing one year. This is a three-dimensional space-time coordinate system. As we sit quietly in our armchair on the first floor of this building, our whole universe rises up with us at the rate of one second per second along the vertical time line. Our travel along the time-line may be said to be through "block time." It carries the definite implication that the upper floors of our building are already occupied, and our consciousness simply moves into the new space-time location that is waiting for us. A person standing in his or her own frame of reference, in another building across the street and outside of our block universe, would have no trouble seeing our path into the future, which is what Einstein called our world line.

Precognitive dreams are probably the most common psychic event to appear in the life of the average person. These dreams give us a glimpse of events that we will experience the next day or in the near future. In fact, we believe that the precognitive dream is caused by the experience that we actually will have at a later time. If you dream about an elephant passing in front of your window, and wake up the next morning and find a circus parade led by an elephant going down your street, we would say that last night's dream was caused by your experience of seeing the elephant the next morning. This is an example of the future *affecting* the past. There is an enormous body of evidence for this kind of occurrence. What cannot happen, we believe, is a future event *changing* the already observed past.

Logical consistency requires us to believe that nothing in the future can cause something that has already happened, to have not happened. This is the so-called intervention paradox, illustrated by the example in which you kill your grandmother when she was a child, and you therefore cease to exist. That kind of thing is interesting to think about, but there is no evidence to make us take it seriously at this time. The Persian poet-astronomer Omar Khayyam described the immutability of past events beautifully in his timeless epic, *The Rubaiyat*:

> The moving Finger writes; and, having writ,
> Moves on: nor all your Piety nor Wit,
> Shall lure it back to cancel half a Line,
> Nor all your Tears wash out a Word of it.

To know that a dream is precognitive, you have to recognize that it is not caused by the previous day's mental residue, your wishes, or anxieties. We find, rather, that precognitive dreams have an unusual clarity, and often contain bizarre and unfamiliar material. Dream experts like to speak of their preternatural clarity. These are not wish fulfillment nor anxiety dreams. For example, if you are unprepared for an exam, and dream about failing it, we would not consider that to be precognition. On the other hand, if you have taken hundreds of plane trips, and then have a frightening dream about a crash, you might like to rethink your travel plans.

One of our CIA contract monitors was in Detroit with his colleague, overseeing another project. Although they had gotten to bed very late on their last night there, my friend had a hard time getting to sleep. When he finally did fall asleep, he had a frightening dream in which he was in a fiery airplane crash. Throughout the next day he was concerned about the dream, since he was scheduled to fly out of Detroit that evening. Because the dream had been so realistic, he tried to avoid having that experience in real life. He told his partner that he was going to stay over in Detroit for another day. Of course, he thought that it was very unlikely that his plane would actually crash, but, on the other hand, he had seen enough psychic events in our SRI laboratory to give him pause. Since he, like most of us, did not want to appear to be silly or superstitious, he didn't tell his buddy why he was delaying his departure. And in certain branches of the government, you are taught not to ask too many questions. Later that day, as our friend was driving away from the airport along the frontage road, he heard a muffled explosion. It was the crash of his airplane, killing many passengers, including his partner. Our friend was in shock for a week.

What can we conclude from this true story? First of all, everyone is probably a little anxious about flying, but I, for one, have never had a dream of being in a crash, and neither had my friend. In his business, he was a very frequent flyer. So, we can consider, without conducting a survey, that to dream of being in a plane crash is an unusual event. "But," I hear you saying, "he wasn't in a plane crash. He just witnessed one." This deals with one of the most interesting questions in all of psychic research: Can you use precognitive information to change a future that you perceive, but do not like? The problem comes, of course, from the idea that if you change the future so that the unpleasant thing doesn't happen to you, where did the dream come from? There are two fairly sensible answers to that question, both of which might be correct.

First of all, a precognitive dream is not a prophecy: It is a forecast, based on all presently available data (world lines). If I wish to make use of my newly received precognitively derived information, I can change the future. For example, if I am looking forward to having a dinner date with someone, and have a very clear dream about meeting her in a colorful and unusual restaurant, I will have a certain level of confidence that the event will come to pass, even though it might also be a wish-fulfillment dream. However, if I tell my prospective dinner companion about my dream, she may well say, "I was planning to meet you at that new and interesting restaurant, but I don't want you to get the idea that I am the slave of your dreams, so I'll see you next week instead." This is the vicious-circle type of paradox about self-referential statements that Bertrand Russell describes in his writing in *Theory of Types*.[2] The dream is a forecast of events to come about in the future, unless you do something to change them, based upon this new information. *Such an action does not falsify the forecast.* There is no paradox. To make this clear, since it is a cause of a lot of confusion, we can discuss another hypothetical example.

A messenger has information from a spy who has learned that an enemy is going to attack us. That's the message. Armed with this new data, we launch a surprise attack on the enemy, and chase him away. He then, of course, cannot and does not attack us. However, we do not fire the messenger or the spy as a result of this, because the information in their message didn't come to pass. Their message described the probable future, which would have come to pass without the intervention that was made possible by the message.

A second question asks, "How can I dream about being in a plane crash, if I don't actually get to experience it?" The answer here is quite different. You dream about the real crash, and then dramatize the events to include yourself in it. Our friend got to see a plane crash at quite close range, and since he was supposed to be on the plane, he had no trouble putting himself on the plane in his dream. We would say that the frightening crash that he experienced in the afternoon was the cause of his dream the previous night. He had a correct perception of an actual plane crash in the future, and armed with that information, chose not to put himself on the plane. This is called retro-causality, and it may be the basis of most pre-cognition, and the "presentiment" mentioned in the previous chapter.

In all of this, we are arguing against the existence of any implacable arrow of time. Rather, we would say that there are certain time-irreversible phenomena, such as heat conduction, diffusion, chemical reactions, and alas, aging. In all of these cases, a movie of the effect under consideration will quickly reveal whether it is being run forward or backwards. On the other hand, there are a wide variety of reversible effects that can be run either way. These include all of electromagnetism, wave propagation, and the laws of mechanics. So, it appears that the irreversibility of time is more in the observation than in the law. It all depends on the type of event being observed. A lawyer would say that this prohibition is more *de facto* than *de jure*. There cannot be a law against precognition, since under the right con-ditions, it is a common occurrence.

On the other hand, philosopher Stephen Braude and psychiatrist Jule Eisenbud believe that all of precognition is caused by psychokinesis — that is, mind affecting matter.[3] They would say that the mind of the psychic doing the precognitive remote viewing actually caused the random number generator to select the target he had previously described. They think that is a more attractive explanation than allowing a future event to retro-causally affect the mind of the viewer in the past. We think their explanation is unlikely, because data for precognitive remote viewing typically gives us a four out of six hit rate, where only one is expected; whereas psychokinesis experiments with dice-throwing or random event generators (REGs) give only about a one percent improvement above chance.[4] The reason that our experiments in precognitive remote viewing of the silver futures market (that we discuss later) are important for our understanding is that it is dif-ficult to believe that the entire silver market is susceptible to psychokinetic influence by a few researchers.

In a summary of research data for what we call paranormal foreknowl-edge of the future, from 1935 to 1987, Charles Honorton and Diane

Ferrari found that 309 precognition experiments had been carried out by 62 investigators.[5] More than 50,000 participants were involved in more than two million trials. Thirty percent of these studies were statistically significant in showing that people can describe future events, where only 5 percent would be expected by chance. This gave overall significance of greater than 10^{20} to one, which is akin to throwing seventy pennies in the air and having every one come down heads. This body of data offers very strong evidence for confirming the existence of foreknowledge of the future that cannot be ascribed to somebody's lucky day. There is no doubt that we have contact with the future in a way that shows unequivocally that we misunderstand our relationship to the dimension of time.

Before we discuss the laboratory data for precognition, we will offer one additional example of the slipperiness we experience as we slide up and down the dimension of time. In most of the research and our personal experiences with mental time travel, we believe we are deriving information from the future. However, we have described several examples of how the future appears to influence the past. Could we, by an act of our own will, affect the past, recognizing, of course, that we cannot change it?

WHAT IS A MIRACLE?

Consider the following hypothetical story: My best friend Brown has gone skiing in the Sierra Mountains for the weekend. On Sunday night I hear on the radio that there has been a devastating avalanche at the Squaw Valley ski resort where Brown had gone. No problem so far. I try to think of a way to help my friend, who may possibly already be buried in the snow. I decide to send him a helpful prayer. So, on Sunday night I say, "Dear God, this is Russell calling from Sunday night. Please don't let Brown have died in the avalanche." Notice that this is a retro-causal prayer, but there is still no problem. The next day, in the morning, I am happy to see Brown at work! I tell him that I was very worried about him. And he tells me the following: "As I was driving to Squaw Valley on Friday night, I thought I heard you, in my head, calling to me, something about an avalanche. I remembered that avalanches are often a problem there in late winter, so I decided to drive on to Homewood, a much less exciting but safer ski resort. In any case, I had a terrific weekend, and thanks for thinking about me." This is a case where the future may have been able to affect the past. However, if the radio had told us that Brown had been among the dead and buried, we could no longer pray to save his life, because past events cannot be undone.

We have personally conducted many series of experiments in which people have described and experienced events that didn't occur until two or three days in the future. One of these involved precognitive forecasting of changes in the silver commodity market, in which the authors were successful in eleven out of twelve individual calls.[6] We, therefore, have no doubt that the precognitive channel is available.

In our avalanche scenario, God was perceived as being the active agent. But we know from the experimental data of psi research that a viewer in the laboratory can focus his or her attention anywhere on the planet and reliably describe what is there. We know, also, that this same viewer is not bound by present time. From data of the past twenty years, we believe that an experienced viewer can answer any answerable question about events in the past, present, or future.

Physicist David Bohm thinks that we greatly misunderstand the illusion of separation in space and time. In his physics textbook, *The Undivided Universe*, he tries to defuse this illusion as he writes about the quantum-interconnectedness of all things.[7] As physicist Norman Friedman puts it, "It is as though events do not occur, they just are."[8] From what we have already described, it should be apparent that this nonlocal reservoir of consciousness has many of the omnipresent and omniscient properties that people customarily associate with God.

The familiar river-of-time model makes precognition seem less magical. *On the average*, we know that the river flows downstream, with causes preceding events. However, if we look closely at the fine structure of the stream, we will see some eddies in the flow. There may be a boulder that causes a wake downstream, with the cause clearly coming before the effect. But upstream we see a great whirlpool. Where does that come from? It comes, of course, from the boulder downstream. This is a case where the effect may be experienced *before* we see its cause. Physicists, these days, are calling this situation "stochastic (or probabilistic) causality," which is like a temporal uncertainty principle in the turbulent flow.

RETRO-CAUSAL HEALING: WHAT DOES PRECOGNITION HAVE TO DO WITH HEALING?

We have just described a hypothetical example in which we saved Brown from being trapped in an avalanche, by sending him information that could be useful to him, even though it was sent after the event occurred. This makes us ask, "Can we send healing thoughts into someone's past, to help them be less sick then they presently are?" Researcher William Braud and many others think that this is a possibility worth investigating. Surprisingly, there are data that suggest we can facilitate this healing, so long as no one knows how sick the patient really is. According to the Observational Theory of psi, an early and definitive diagnosis of an illness might serve to "lock in" the illness, thereby making it impossible to affect or cure it retro-causally. Whereas, if you see a healer when you are suffering only from vague, undifferentiated complaints, she might still be able to reach into your past and send you healing information that you can incorporate into your physiology in a health-promoting way. There are actually two groups of laboratory data that support this remarkable assertion.

We are all familiar with the idea of a premonition, in which one has inner knowledge of something that is going to happen in the future — usually something bad! There is also the experience of presentiment, where one has an inner sensation, a gut feeling that something strange is about to occur. An example would be for you to suddenly stop walking down the street because you felt "uneasy," only to have a flowerpot then fall off a window ledge and land at your feet — instead of on your head. That would be a useful presentiment.

In the laboratory, we know that if we show a frightening picture to a person, there will be a significant change in his or her physiology. Their blood pressure, heart rate, and skin resistance will change. This fight-or-flight reaction is called an "orienting response." Researcher Dean Radin has recently shown, at the University of Nevada, that this orienting response is also observed in a person's physiology, a few seconds *before* they see the scary picture.[9] In balanced, double-blind experiments, Radin has shown that if you are about to see scenes of violence and mayhem, your body will steel itself against the insult, but if you are about to see a picture of a flower garden, then there is no such strong anticipatory reaction. Fear is much easier to measure physiologically than bliss. We would say that this is a case in which your direct physical perception of the picture, when it occurs, causes you to have a unique physical response at an earlier time. Your future is affecting your past.

Experiments with a similar interpretation were carried out by Helmut Schmidt at the Mind Science Foundation in San Antonio, Texas. Schmidt was examining the behavior of electronic random number generators that produce long haphazard strings of 1s and 0s.[10] He had already shown, through a lifetime of work, that a person could mentally interact with the machine from a distance, to obtain more 1s or 0s just by paying attention to the desired outcome. This effort to affect the output of digits takes place at randomly selected times while the tape is being recorded. In his latest and most remarkable experiments, he has shown that even after the machine is run, and has generated a tape recording of its output of 1s and 0s, a person can still affect the outcome by paying attention to the tape, as long as no one has seen the data beforehand. The observable fact is that the tape in hand is found to have a statistically significant nonrandom distribution of 1s and 0s, where the control tapes all have balanced distributions. We do not believe that the person is actually changing the tape, which may be a punched-hole paper tape, but rather, Schmidt and others believe that the person with the tape in his hand is reaching back in time to affect the machine at the time of its operation.

Schmidt has even demonstrated that the prerecorded, but unobserved, *breathing rate* of a person in the past can be affected by the mental activity of a person at a later time![11] Both of these experiments suggest that a healer can similarly reach back in time far enough to affect her patient's — or even her own — physiology at a point early enough where it can still do some good, and achieve a healing outcome. We do not know what kind of physiology is most amenable to such treatment, or how long into the past the healer can reach. These are exciting questions that still remain to be answered.

PRECOGNITION IN THE LAB

For years, parapsychologists have been trying to find ways to encourage their subjects to demonstrate psychic glimpses of the future. Earlier in this chapter we mentioned a large retrospective analysis of 309 precognition experiments carried out over 50 years between 1935 and 1987. These were forced-choice experiments, in which subjects had to choose which of four colored buttons would be illuminated right after their choice, or which of five cards they would be shown at a later time. In all of these cases, a random number generator of some sort selected the targets, to which the researchers were blind. Participants had to try and guess what they would be shown in the future, from among known alternatives. In some cases they had to choose which target would be randomly chosen in the future, where they never received any feedback at all as to which target was actually selected.[12] There are two kinds of important information for us in this study.

We see that there is overwhelming evidence for the existence of precognition, but more importantly, we learn that there are more successful and less successful ways to do experiments. Four different factors were found to vary significantly with success or failure in these experiments. It is important to keep these ingredients in mind, if you want to experiment yourself, and want your experiments to succeed.

• Experiments are much more successful when they are carried out with subjects who are experienced and interested in the outcome. For example, running ESP experiments in a whole classroom of moderately bored students will rarely show any kind of ESP success. Participants who are enthusiastic about the experiment are the most successful in these precognition studies. The difference in scoring rate between these two kinds of tests, with experienced and inexperienced subjects, was significant at odds of 1,000 to 1.

• Tests with individual participants were much more successful than experiments with groups. Making the trials meaningful to each participant is important to success. The success level comparing individuals versus groups was statistically significant at 30 to 1 against chance.

• We have always felt that feedback is one of the very helpful channels in all psi functioning. In precognition, we feel that it is the experience the viewer has when shown the feedback at a later time that is often the source of the precognitive experience. This view is strongly supported in the forced-choice studies, but it is true that studies by Gertrude Schmeidler at City College of New York showed precognition in forced-choice trials of computer-generated targets where the viewers did not receive any feedback.[13]

• Finally, the data show that the sooner the participants get their feedback, the greater the hit rate. That is, it appears that for forced-choice targets, it is easier to foretell the immediate future than the distant future. In laboratory experiments, people did very well in predicting events seconds or minutes in advance, but did less well looking hours or days in advance. This seems to be the case for naturally occurring precognition as well. On the other hand, it is also possible that people tend to forget dreams about the distant future before the events can be corroborated.

Thus, the four factors that are important in these studies are: (1) Practiced vs. inexperienced subjects, (2) Individual vs. group testing, (3) Feedback vs. no feedback, and (4) Short time interval between subject response and target generation. In the whole database of the Honorton-Ferrari analysis, there were some experiments that had all four favorable factors, and some that had all four unfavorable factors. After all is said and done, 87.5 percent of the psi-conducive studies were successful and significant, while *none* of the unfavorable studies were statistically significant. Since we now routinely carry out experiments under the favorable conditions, I think that we can say that we have learned quite a lot about psi in the past fifty years — if you do everything wrong, you'll definitely find no psi — which is, unfortunately, what many hope to find.

We also know that forced-choice ESP tests are a very inefficient way to elicit psi functioning. For example, in the above studies, the experimenters, on the average, had to carry out 3,600 trials to achieve a statistically significant result. With the free-response type of experiment, such as remote viewing, we typically have to do only six to nine trials.

In an imaginative series of experiments in the 1970s involving precognitive dreams, Stanley Krippner, Montague Ullman, and Charles Honorton found that only eight trials were needed to show the effects of precognition. These researchers at the Maimonides Dream Laboratory worked with Malcolm Besant, a very successful English psychic and the grandson of Annie Besant, one of the founders of The Theosophical Society. In two formal series of eight trials each, Malcolm was asked to dream in the laboratory about the events that he would experience the next morning. Several dozen of these possible feedback experiences had been previously made up by the creative laboratory staff, and written down on file cards. Malcolm was awakened from time to time during the night, when his EEG showed by the appearance of rapid eye movements (REM sleep) that he was dreaming. His dream reports were all tape-recorded. The next morning other lab staff used a random number generator to choose one of the experience cards. Malcolm would then be given that experience. In one typical case Malcolm dreamed of being in a cold, white room with small, blue objects, while experiencing the feeling of being very chilled. When he awakened, the experimenters randomly chose an experience card that instructed them to take him into another room and drop ice cubes down his shirt, while two blue electric fans blew cold air on him.[14] We would say that the morning's ice cubes were the cause of his chilly dream the previous night.

In our experiments at SRI, the first case of precognition appeared spontaneously. I was sitting with Pat Price in our little shielded room, about to start one of the trials in the formal series described in Chapter 2. I had described who we were and what we were doing for the tape recorder, and Pat and I were chatting about the experiment in progress. Our lab director, Bart Cox, was the target selector for this trial, because he wanted to have the experiment under his complete personal control. He decided to drive out of SRI and turn his car randomly at intersections until he decided that he liked the target location. My colleague Hal Puthoff was with him on this random drive. Meanwhile, Price was explaining to me that we don't have to wait for Bart to actually choose a target. He, Price, could just look "down the time line" and see where they would wind up half an hour in the future! Price's first words on the tape are as follows:

> What I am looking at is a little boat jetty, or a little boat dock along the Bay. In a direction like that from here [he pointed in the correct direction]. Yeah, I see little boats, some motor launches, some little sailing ships, sails all furled, some with their masts stepped, others are up. Little jetty, or a dock there. Funny thing — this just flashed in — kinda looks like a Chinese or Japanese pagoda effect. It's a definite feeling of oriental architecture that seems to be fairly adjacent to where they are.[15]

Pat completed his description fifteen minutes before the travelers arrived at their site. Half an hour later Puthoff and Cox returned to SRI to see what Pat had to say. It turned out that we all had plenty to say, because Hal and Bart had found their way to the Redwood City Marina. The marina is a harbor and boat dock, about four miles north of SRI. It is full of small- and medium-sized sailboats, and it is right next to a restaurant with a curved, sloping roof that looks very Asian indeed. Price had a full precognitive experience of the marina, including a discussion of how much he liked the smell of the sea air, all before the target was even chosen!

The following year (1975) we conducted a series of four deliberately precognitive trials with Hella Hammid. All four of her remote-viewing descriptions were matched correctly to the targets.[16] One of these was especially striking for me. I still remember sitting with her as she described a location with "manicured trees and shrubs … a formal garden." She then went on to describe a path leading to a balcony and steps. After the travelers returned from their target location, Hella and I joined them for feedback on a return visit to their site. It was an extraordinary science fiction-like déjà vu experience to listen to Hella's tape-recorded description of the Stanford University Hospital gardens, just as we were walking through them.

One of the recurring questions in precognition research concerns the source of the mental images that the viewer experiences. Are they from the target, or are they from the feedback? A very clear example of this kind of phenomenon is described in the wonderful book, *An Experiment in Time*, by English engineer J.W. Dunne. Dunne's book, published in 1927, is a treasure trove of precognition data. In one of many examples of his precognitive dreams, he reports that he had a clear impression of a volcanic eruption in which 4,000 people were killed. The next morning he read of that very event in the newspaper, including a report of the fatalities. It wasn't until he prepared his book for publication, and looked again at the article, that he discovered it actually referred to 40,000 people, and not the 4,000 that he originally misread. As it turned out, the number of lives lost in the eruption was different from both these numbers. Dunne writes of this incident:

> Now when the next batch of papers arrived, these gave the exact estimates of what the actual loss of life had been, and I discovered that the true figure had nothing in common with the arrangement of fours and naughts I had both dreamed of, and gathered from the first report. So, my wonderful "clairvoyant" vision had been wrong in its most insistent particular! But, it was clear that its wrongness was likely to prove a matter just as important as its rightness. For whence in the dream did I get the idea of 4000? Clearly it must have come into my mind because of the newspaper paragraph.[17]

The most comprehensive laboratory examination of precognition was done by Robert Jahn, Brenda Dunne, and Roger Nelson at Princeton University.[18] They conducted 227 formal experiments in which a viewer was asked to describe where one of the researchers would be hiding at some preselected later time. They discovered, much to their surprise, that the accuracy of the description was the same whether the viewer had to look hours, days, or weeks into the future. The overall statistical significance of the combined experiments departed from what you would expect from chance by a probability of 1 in 100 billion! Their findings are so strong, that it is hard to read about their work and not be convinced of the reality of precognition, even though we don't understand how it works.

One of our great passions over the years concerns the issues of precognition and probable futures. An outstanding question that arose was our uncertainty as to whether a remote viewer sees the actual future, or the probable future. That is, does he or she view what is *likely* to happen, or what *actually* occurs? My daughter, Elisabeth Targ, and I (Russell) carried out an experiment to investigate this question.[19]

She designed an ingenious experiment with twelve precognitive trials. For each trial there was a target pool of six possible target objects to be chosen by a 0 to 9 random number generator. One particular object would be the target if the generator came up with any number from 0 to 4. So that object had a 50 percent chance of being chosen. Each of the other five objects would be chosen if its corresponding number of 5, 6, 7, 8, or 9, came up. Thus, each of these objects had a one in ten probability of being chosen. The viewer's task, as always, was to describe the object that she would be shown at the end of each trial. The question asked by the experiment was whether the presence of a 50 percent likely target would interfere with the viewer's ability to correctly describe a 10 percent object when it was chosen by the random number generator. What we found was that there is no such interference. A viewer sees the actualized and chosen future, not the probable future. Thus, from a psychic point of view, what you see is what you get.

This suggested to us that we could design an experiment that could be tested in the marketplace, and use remote viewing to forecast the future.

ASSOCIATIVE REMOTE VIEWING

As we have described earlier, remote viewing is not generally suited to acquiring analytical information, such as words or numbers. So, in order to apply this capability to number-guessing tasks such as stock market or horse race forecasting, one would have to use another strategy. It would be nice if we could say to the viewer, "Close your eyes and tell me the number of the horse that is going to win the next race at Bay Meadows." But that definitely does not work. Instead, we can encode the numbers or information we would like to receive psychically, into associated target objects matched to each possible outcome. A viewer can then precognitively see the associated target objects on his or her mental screen, and describe or draw them.

In a horse race example, there might be six horses running in the race you have selected to forecast. For this task, we would assign an interesting household object to each of the six horses. We then ask the viewer, who has no knowledge about any of the objects, to describe the object that we will show her after the race — the object that has been assigned to the winning horse. The viewer's task, therefore, has nothing to do with selecting the winning racehorse. Her only desire is to describe the object that will be placed in her hands later in the afternoon.

Elisabeth Targ was a viewer in such an experiment. She said that she saw some kind of glass sphere as the target. Since one of the targets was a spherical apple juice bottle, the experimenter decided that Elisabeth's description was a good correspondence. The bottle had been previously assigned as the target object associated with a horse named Shamgo. An hour later, we learned that Shamgo, against great odds, had won the race. Elisabeth was then shown the round apple juice bottle.

For another example, you might want to know in advance whether a particular silver contract will go up or down in a particular period of time. You would need three participants for this experiment: an experimenter, an interviewer, and a viewer. The experimenter makes his or her private assignment of objects for this test. He could decide, for example, to show the viewer a champagne bottle if the silver went up in four days, or a pancake if it went down. The interviewer, on the other hand, knows nothing about the target objects or their associations with market changes. His sole job is to interview the viewer.

A skillful viewer might say that he or she sees something flat and round, damp and floppy, with a funny smell. The interviewer would then call the experimenter and tell him what he had recorded. At that point, the experimenter would tell the interviewer what the targets were, and together they would make a decision as to which, if any, of the targets had been described. In this case, it would be easy to determine that the viewer had described the pancake. If that were the "down" object, the interviewer would call the broker and have him sell the silver. At the end of four days, if you learned that silver had indeed gone down, you would show the viewer his pancake for feedback. If the price of silver had gone up, you would show him the "up" object instead, to fulfill the promise to show the corresponding object.

We believe that the feeling of consensus of purpose and mutual trust among participants are essential prerequisites for enduring reliable psi-functioning, so we carried out an experiment of this kind with our friends. We wanted to investigate the reliability of precognitive remote viewing, without actually betting any money.

In this 1994 experiment, the authors took part as viewers, and worked with two independent judges to design and implement a demonstration of associative remote viewing.[20] We used what is known as a "redundant protocol," which is described below, to eliminate some of the problems experienced by many of us who have tried to harness psi for real-world applications. We carried out nine weeks of remote-viewing trials, in which each viewer was to describe the target that he or she would be shown two days in the future. For each trial, the two viewers had their own separate target pools consisting of two targets, about which they knew nothing. A total of eighteen viewings were carried out at the rate of one per person per week. Targets were randomly assigned "up" or "down" status by judges previous to the viewing. If the viewers both accurately described the targets of different directions, then the trial was considered a pass. Additionally, if a viewer's target description failed to be awarded a rating of 4 or more on a 0-7 point scale rating, his or her call was declared a pass.

Of the twelve viewings that were not rated pass by the blind judges, eleven correctly described the object that the viewer was shown at a later time — that is against odds of more than 3 in 1,000. The objects shown to each viewer corresponded to the direction of the one-day change in the price of silver futures. Of the nine two-person trials carried out, two were passed for various reasons, and seven were recorded as traded in the market, although no purchases were actually made. Six of the seven trade forecasts were correct.

Several groups of people have used associative remote-viewing techniques successfully to forecast changes in various markets. Unfortunately, this approach is not 100 percent reliable, even with the best of viewers. Sometimes they give excellent descriptions of the wrong target, causing the investors to go into the market with a high degree of confidence, only to lose their entire investment.

We believe that it is incorrect to say that the Universe will not let you use your psychic abilities for personal gain. Rather, it is our observation that many people who have made significant progress in the development of psychic abilities seem to mysteriously lose interest in applying these talents to mundane activities such as silver futures forecasting. Human potential innovator Michael Murphy sums up this situation very nicely in his book, *The Future of the Body*:

> We live in an evolving universe. I think in the most fundamental sense, the universe is in the business of manifesting the divine nature. So I say that all metanormal attributes [psychic abilities] are the budding limbs and organs of our latent super-nature, and that this latent super-nature is closer to the divine than our present way of being in the world....[21]

chapter six

Are Psychic
Abilities Sacred?

There is no such thing as a unique scientific vision, any more than there is a unique poetic vision. Science is a mosaic of partial and conflicting visions. But there is one common element in these visions. The common element is rebellion against the restrictions imposed by the locally prevailing culture, Western or Eastern, as the case may be.

— Freeman Dyson
"The Scientist as Rebel"
The New York Review of Books

And though I have the gift of prophecy, and understand all mysteries, and all knowledge; and though I have all faith, so that I could move mountains, and have not charity, I am nothing.

— I Corinthians 13:2
Holy Bible

As we learn to exercise our psychic abilities, ethical issues arise that are outside the understanding of modern science. Are psychic abilities sacred? Is it appropriate to think about using them for mundane purposes, such as making money in the stock market? Is healing sacred, and what does it have to do with our psychic capabilities?

Our psychic abilities allow us to experience mind-to-mind connections with each other, and many people regard these experiences as profoundly spiritual. There is no doubt that psi gives us a unique window on our non-local reality. It allows us to have contact with a kind of omniscience that none of our other senses makes available to us. Buddhist teachings would have us believe that psychic powers do, indeed, exist, and can be used for beneficial purposes. However, if a person shows an interest in developing these powers, then he or she is not yet ready to use them. In this tradition, ESP in all its forms is widely regarded as a stumbling block to be overcome on the path to enlightenment. One might well consider that using these abilities to spy on the Russians or to make money in the commodities market is a trivialization of a sacred gift.

We have chosen to discuss the psychic spying described in Chapter 2 as an example of psi functioning, because it illustrates that ESP abilities are available, useful, and abundant. We look forward to the time when different applications of our psychic abilities are studied and developed to a reliable and useful stage.

We often hear that psi is a weak and unreliable faculty. Arthur Koestler, in his pioneering book of 1956, *Roots of Coincidence*, spoke of the "ink fish phenomenon," wherein psi disappears in a murky cloud whenever you try to get too close to it.[1] This may have been true of available evidence in the 1950s and '60s, but current laboratory data, especially for remote viewing, show that psychic perception is about to take its place alongside other perceptual modalities we know and trust. Now that the U.S. government has declassified some of its highest-quality ESP data, these results should begin to find their way into mainstream scientific inquiry, rather than hovering at the edges of credibility in the tabloid newspapers.

The new perceptual data of remote viewing has aspects in common with recent double-blind clinical studies of remote healing. We now know that although some individuals have a special talent for remote viewing, anyone can learn to do it. Similarly, although shamans and medicine men are given special training to develop their gifts for healing, it appears that all people have the capacity to be healers, to a greater or lesser degree. For example, a mother's cuddling of her sick child lets loose a rush of endorphins and endocrines that can ease the infant's suffering and promote its healing. While we don't consider this to be "paranormal," we believe it is on a continuum of what a healer is able to do remotely. The remote-viewing data shows unequivocally that information can be accessed across distances of space and time. We believe that a healer makes healing information available from a distance. The information becomes available through a channel created by the healer's focused attention, healing intent, and surrender of separateness. Thus, a healer sends a healing message, rather than healing rays, to the patient.

Most healers believe that there is a spiritual aspect to what they do. This raises the important question as to whether all psi functioning should be considered sacred. Dr. Rachel Naomi Remen, medical director of the Commonweal Cancer Help Program in California, has written about the discrepancy between our "level of technology and the level of moral and ethical wisdom appropriate to the use of that technology."[2] She recently wrote about the issue of this discrepancy as it relates to the sacredness of psychic abilities, as compared with our other senses. She says:

> Our intuition informs us of the intangible, and may offer a glimpse of the great laws that govern the workings of the world. Yet, is the particular capacity by which we may experience an aspect of sacred reality necessarily sacred in and of itself? Is the eye which perceives holiness necessarily holy? In fact, can't any of our senses become a doorway to sacred experience?
>
> Anyone who has seen the light pour through the great stained glass window at Chartres knows that vision can lead to sacred experience. Anyone who has heard the *Messiah* or the *Allegri Miserere* knows that hearing can evoke a powerful experience of the sacred, and anyone who has had really good sex knows the power of touch as a bridge to sacred experience. Yet seeing, hearing, and touch are simple human functions. Is psi a simple human function as well?[3]

Remen suggests that we consider psi as an expanded, rather than an exalted, human function. As such, it is subject to individual discretion, as well as to human frailty. A sacrament can be any procedure or ritual that we use to contact our spiritual aspect. We believe that all of our senses can be

thought of as sacred in this regard, and psi does not necessarily have a priv-
ileged position. It is how, and in what context, we choose to use any human
capacity that seems important. For what purpose? Serving which values?

> Why does this applied science, which saves work and makes life easier,
> bring us so little happiness? The simple answer runs: Because we have
> not yet learned to make sensible use of it.
> — Albert Einstein

The scientific study of psychic abilities is relatively new, but the knowledge of their existence has been described in the historic spiritual teachings
of Hinduism, Buddhism, Islam, and in the Bible. According to all these
paths of wisdom, we are "spiritual beings" temporarily residing in bodies
and learning how to be human. We believe that the study of psi offers us
insight into our spiritual nature as well as the nonlocal dimension of consciousness uniting us all. It also offers us the opportunity to evaluate the
same issues of integrity and responsibility that we confront in other aspects
of our lives.

> I maintain that cosmic religiousness is the strongest and most noble
> driving force of scientific research.
> — Albert Einstein

The emergence and exercise of our psychic capacities offer us opportunities to consciously join minds with others for purposes of learning, helping, healing, or even having fun. However, our capacity for psychic activity
also presents us with additional temptations of power and greed, which
serve to enhance our illusion of separateness. Kenneth Wapnick has written
extensively on this subject in his commentary on *A Course in Miracles*:

> What renders a thought spiritual is its purpose.... Abilities of the
> mind can be powerfully used on behalf of truth. This is especially so
> when these abilities demonstrate to others and oneself that the mate-
> rial universe is not what it seems.[4]

According to Rabbi David Cooper, in the Jewish tradition, "prophecy is considered to be one of the highest levels of attainment in Jewish contemplative teaching."[5] The Christian apostle Paul wrote that prophecy was a gift "given by the Spirit," and available to all for the benefit of all, whether or not a person was Christian.[6] There are frequent references to psychic abilities throughout yoga literature, but they are not treated as something to be sought after or prized.[7] Nor are they seen as miraculous, but rather, they are considered as being governed by natural laws as yet unknown to modern science.

> "The word *Siddhis* is used generally for the extraordinary powers acquired through the practice of Yoga, but its real meaning is best expressed by the words 'attainments' or 'accomplishments'...concerned with the attainment of the highest states of consciousness."[8]

SOME SERIOUS CONSIDERATIONS

The Indian sage Patanjali in the fourth century B.C. instructed that "These [psychic] powers of the spreading or outgoing mind are injurious *to contemplation*" for an aspirant seeking enlightenment. [Emphasis added.][9] This is not because they are evil or even bad — it is because they are distracting for a person seeking unitive consciousness and "the experience of inward illumination beyond all sensation." He believed that our psychic abilities could potentially intensify a person's fascination with sensations, objects, or the illusion of the separate self in daily life.[10]

Patanjali mentioned that psychic abilities may arise from causes other than the practice of yoga meditation. They are sometimes present at the time of birth, and they may also be produced by taking certain drugs, chanting mantras, or practicing austerities. Among the examples of siddhis or psychic powers that Patanjali said could be produced by diligent meditation practices are:

> ...knowledge of past and future; understanding of the sounds made by all creatures; knowledge of past lives; knowing what others are thinking; prior knowledge of one's death; the attainment of various

kinds of strength; perception of the small, the concealed, and the distant; knowledge of other inhabited regions; knowledge about the stars and their motions; knowledge of the interior of the body; control of hunger and thirst; steadiness; seeing the adepts in one's own interior light; general intuition; understanding of the mind; entering the bodies of others; lightness and levitation; brightness; control of material elements; control of the senses; perfection of the body; quickness of the body....[11]

Most ancient sacred teachings emphasize the seductive distraction of psychic abilities; they entice us to stray off the spiritual path with thoughts of using them to enhance our individual power or prestige. However, one of Patanjali's goals of meditation was to bring a person out of normal, everyday sensory awareness, and into a nonlocal awareness of unity consciousness. We believe that for those of us who are actively involved with working, thinking, playing, and moving in the physical world, our psychic abilities have much to teach us about the illusion of our separate selves. The acceptance of the reality of our mind-to-mind connections can inspire others, as it has done for the authors, to seek our highest potentials as human beings.

Our psychic abilities become accessible when we are open-minded, and share commonality of purpose and mutual trust with one another. Indeed, the revered seventh-century Hindu teacher Shankara referred to psychic abilities as "powers of the unobstructed life."[12] We find the processes of achieving the consensus and rapport with others to be worthwhile activities in themselves, in line with what Shankara called "the joy of harmony with the intent of our being."[13]

What else might we discover as we remove the psychic barriers to our awareness of our connected natures? Exploring these states of nonlocal consciousness together with friends has given us many richly rewarding experiences. The emergence of our psychic capabilities is a natural occurrence as we learn to focus our attention with mindfulness. As we discover more and more ways to apply our psychic abilities to real-world tasks, we will all have many opportunities to choose which applications of psi are ethical and appropriate for us.

USING PSYCHIC ABILITIES IN OUR LIVES

No discussion about applying psychic abilities in daily life would be complete without mentioning the term "intuition." For us, intuition is a nonanalytic awareness that can come from either internal subconscious processes, or psychic sources such as mind-to-mind connections, or direct clairvoyant perception of the outside world. Medical intuitive Caroline Myss believes that "intuition is a natural by-product of the flowering of a mature self-esteem and sense of empowerment — not power over, but power to be."[14] Myss also believes, as we do, that intuition and psychic abilities are our birthright, and are trainable, rather than being capabilities possessed only by a few special people. We discuss Myss' highly developed intuitive faculties in the field of illness diagnosis later in this chapter, as well as in Chapter 10.

Four different types of applications of intuition in the real world have been suggested to us by Dr. Jeffrey Mishlove, author of the informative and engaging book *The Roots of Consciousness*.[15] Mishlove is also the director of the Intuition Network, an organization devoted to developing and incorporating greater use of intuitive processes in the workplace as well as in other venues of daily life.[16]

From Mishlove's business perspective, *evaluation* is one of the key psi application opportunities. Evaluating design and construction alternatives, investment choices, research strategies, and technology alternatives are all applications with significant business potential. For these applications, the distinction between intuition and psi is somewhat murky. Some would say that intuition involves access to and associations with subconscious material buried in one's memory. Others use intuition interchangeably with a psychic sense that accesses material coming in from beyond one's actual life experience. We are aware that once we are dealing with a world that includes psi data, there is no firm boundary between internal and external information. But we can be quite clear about what has actually been experienced during the course of our life's activities.

Mishlove's second category of workplace applications for psi is that of *location*. Locating oil, mineral deposits, and buried or hidden treasure has held a fascination for people as long as they have tried to span space with their thoughts. The ancient Chinese, for example, at least as far back as the time of Christ, used a meditative process called *feng shui* to determine everything from the best location for a new village to the most propitious site for a new house, and even the placement of objects within the home. These decisions would be made by a village shaman sitting by himself in the dark, and visualizing the answer. In their cosmology, all power came from the north, and they oriented their maps by the North Star. However, they had also found that if they carved a Chinese soup spoon to look like the Big Dipper in the sky, this magic spoon would swing around and point to the north all by itself. (This was, of course, because they had learned to carve the so-called magic spoons out of lodestone — later used to make the first compasses.)

Another application of this approach to location has been pioneered by Stephan Schwartz, former president of the Mobius Group, an international association of archeological scientists and psychics based in Los Angeles, which has now disbanded. Schwartz has had a lifelong interest in pursuing psychic archeology, and he has written two books about his spectacular discoveries, *The Secret Vaults of Time* and *The Alexandria Project*.[17] In one of his many adventures, Schwartz was looking for a buried Egyptian temple in a desert region called Marea, outside Cairo. Our indefatigable friend Hella Hammid was with him in the desert, along with psychic archeologist George McMullen, to do the actual psi locating.

Schwartz's research had led him to believe that the temple was somewhere near their encampment in the trackless sand. Although the Egyptian authorities kept assuring him that there was nothing to be found, Hella sensed otherwise. She made a promenade back and forth in the 105 degree temperature, over a quarter-mile area. She dropped the tent pegs onto the sand to mark the locations where she sensed that the temple walls would be found. By the time Hella was finished, she had marked out a long rectangle, and had described a specific location inside the building where she predicted they would find green tiles. After the tent pegs had been driven into the ground to mark the perimeter, and the backhoes had cleared away the sand, the building shell was found to be just where she had marked it. So, too, were the green tiles set in what is thought to have been a ceremonial bath in the temple.

A third application of intuition or psychic abilities in the business world is in the area of *diagnosis*. Diagnosis of medical problems, mechanical problems, safety hazards, sources of human error, and health and environmental hazards are all possible applications for psychic and intuitive practitioners.

One example of such a mechanical diagnosis occurred on a recent sea voyage in search of underwater treasure in the Indian Ocean. When the ship's engine would not start in the Port of Mauritius, psychic Alan Vaughan offered a diagnosis of the problem. He said that he saw some kind of "gunk" clogging the filters in the fuel pump. The ship's owner said that was an interesting suggestion, but the filters had already been cleaned. Alan said, "That's all right. You're just going to have to clean them again." And, in fact, they were not able to get under way until the filters had been taken ashore and cleaned ultrasonically. Alan's diagnosis was exactly correct.

The diagnosis of disease by psychic means has been described in many cultures throughout history. Psychic diagnosis is an application of our extended abilities that is attracting more attention as people seek to become more involved in healing. One of the best contemporary examples of controlled research in this area is described in the book *The Creation of Health* by C. Norman Shealy, M.D., and Caroline M. Myss, which is about merging medicine with intuitive diagnosis.[18]

The process of psychically diagnosing illness is similar to remote viewing in that the distance separating the patient and the person doing the psychic diagnosis does not affect the accuracy of the diagnosis. Such distance may even be beneficial, because it prevents the intuitive practitioner from being bombarded with the analytical noise that accompanies sensory input. Myss believes that a physical separation between her and the person she is diagnosing is desirable, because it permits her to "receive information that a more personal connection would otherwise tend to block."[19]

An earlier lengthy study of psychic diagnosis was carried out by Dr.

Shafica Karagulla, who investigated and reported many cases of this remarkable ability in her book *Breakthrough to Creativity*.[20] In addition, Jane, with her many years of experience as a healer, has found that it is common for her and other healers to feel the same physical symptoms as their patients are experiencing, before the patients have described or given any other evident clues about their condition. We have written more extensively about the ability to do psychic diagnosis in Chapter 10.

Forecasting is the fourth area of application of psychic faculties that Mishlove describes. Forecasting earthquakes and volcanic activity, political conditions, technological developments, weather conditions, and interest rates and investment opportunities, as well as prices of commodities and currencies, have all been approached psychically. It is the latter applications that have always attracted the greatest attention. One reason for its appeal to researchers is that it lends itself so easily to the study of precognitive remote viewing. Whether or not any money is actually traded, the process of conducting the research is always stimulating and entertaining.

PSYCHIC AND SPIRITUAL HEALING

In healing, as well as remote viewing, the willful participant invokes information and acts as a messenger. In remote viewing, the viewer translates impressions of the information into drawings and language. In psychic healing, the healer transposes intuitive impressions into thoughts and specific healing actions to remedy a perceived problem in a patient's body. In spiritual healing, no translation of the accessed information is done by the healer at all. The spiritual healer maintains his or her awareness in a nonlocal state of unity-consciousness throughout the healing session. All judgments are absent during the practice of spiritual healing, as spiritual harmony is not necessarily in accordance with a healer's, any other person's, opinions. A spiritual healer's job is to maintain his or her state of awareness in a timeless everpresent now, allowing an infinite consciousness, intelligence, and love (known as God, or nonlocal mind) to express Itself through the healer's awareness.

When minds are merged, and one has the focused intention of surrendering individuality and being used as an instrument of help or healing, that condition allows nonlocal healings to occur. The joining of minds between healer and patient is made possible by trust, and by the absence of fear or guilt. A spiritual healer's focused intent is that his or her consciousness be used as an expression of nonlocal Infinite Mind, which some know as God. No thoughts of personal profit or failure on the part of the healer, and caring intent with nonattachment to the outcome, are the essential components in spiritual healing. It is as though the healer's receptivity acts as a *conduit of information, or makes available a template of healing information, that enables and activates the patient's own self-healing ability.* A spiritual healer's intention is to be helpful, and this impersonal mind state of merged consciousnesses, wherein nonlocal mind is acknowledged and shared, could be called "loving one's neighbor as oneself." In the following chapter, Jane tells about how she came to understand and use this capacity for enabling healing in others.

chapter seven

The Making
of a Healer

Life is not so much a journey as an awakening.
— Anonymous

All suffering prepares the soul for vision.
— Martin Buber

I *(Jane) was weeping silently as I lay on my bunk in the dark, all by myself, at night* in a dusty youth hostel in the Philippines. I couldn't bear the pain from my throbbing headache any longer. I was 26 years old, and feeling miserable, exhausted, and confused.

The year was 1974, and the troops enforcing the curfew under Marcos' martial law were pacing the streets of downtown Manila. It was quiet outside, but tension pervaded the stillness, and the air was hot and muggy. From my second-floor room I could hear every creak in the old building, and the dripping faucet of the bathtub down the hall was exacerbating the pounding in my head. There were so many spiders and crisscrossing webs in the tub that I hadn't had the energy to deal with bathing. So I lay sweating in the humid heat. The widow who owned the old mansion lived in a separate building, and it was too late for any other travelers to be arriving for the night. I was very much alone in the dilapidated building, and I had been tolerating more continuous pain than I had ever experienced before in my life.

I had never had a headache anywhere near as painful or as long-lasting as this one. It was now in its third day, and massive doses of aspirin hadn't touched it. Lying down, practicing deep, rhythmic breathing, and massaging my temples hadn't helped either. The pain was awful, and it never let up. I felt dizzy, nauseous, and very disoriented.

I remembered the Zen teacher Alan Watts said, "Go into the pain." Whatever that meant. I tried it. I was inside the pain, and it really hurt. I became the pain. I was pain. It still hurt. After awhile, I couldn't maintain my focus anymore, and I went back outside the pain. I couldn't handle the headache. I started to cry. It didn't matter if I cried or not; the pain still kept coming. I sobbed, "Somebody, help me. Please, help me!" No one came.

> There is a dark night through which the soul passes in order to attain the Divine light.
>
> — St. John of the Cross

I hoped I would lapse into sleep. Sleep...sleep.... I was wide awake, and the pain continued. I began to wonder if I might die from the pain. I began to wish that I would die. I was crazy from the pain.

So crazy, I was driven to prayer. I had never really prayed before. As I lay there, I contemplated my experience with prayer, and I remembered saying, "Now I lay me down to sleep..." with my babysitter after she tucked me into bed, when I was about five. I remembered going to church and bowing my head when the minister said to, and opening my eyes and peeking at all the women in silent concentration, and wondering what they were really *doing*. Now, for the first time in my life, I prayed. I had no idea how. I hadn't been to church since the seventh grade, and I certainly didn't pray then. I had gone to meet boys. When that didn't work, I quit going.

But my hopelessness that night in the Philippines was much worse than my adolescent angst had ever been. I felt deranged, and unable to lift my head from the bed. I would do anything to escape the pain. Unable to help myself, and with no one else there to help me, I felt completely hopeless.

A Course in Miracles says prayer is a testable hypothesis, but I knew nothing of that then.[1] I figured I had nothing to lose. So I prayed. I asked silently, "If there is anyone out there hearing me, please take the pain away. If there is a God, please help me. Or just please kill me, I don't care. I'll die, if that's what it takes. Please take me out of this misery. Please help me die."

Then, a most unusual thing happened. What I experienced next changed my life profoundly....

The reason I had gone to the Philippines in the first place was to investigate firsthand what was going on with the Philippine healers, or the so-called psychic surgeons. I was on the last leg of a yearlong trek around Southeast Asia, and I was ready to return home. But I had promised myself that I would see "the healers" before going back to Seattle. A friend who had multiple sclerosis had gone to see the healers in the Philippines the year before. She had not been cured, but she was not at all sorry that she had spent so much money to go there and visit them. She felt her symptoms had gone into remission after her trip. She also told me that everyone in her travel group felt improved, too. She said that she knew that some healers used sleight of hand to make it look like they were pulling tumors out of people's insides, but that one woman in her group had apparently been completely healed of cancer. My friend said that something remarkable and unusual was going on in the Philippines. She suggested I check it out for myself, and see what I could make of it.

Before I left town, I visited the woman whose cancerous tumors had disappeared during her trip to the Philippine healers. She told me that her story had been filmed by KOMO-TV in Seattle, and that they had planned to air it on television, but at the last minute her doctor would not allow his name to be used in the documentary. He felt it would ruin his reputation, because everyone would think he had misdiagnosed her malignancy. So the story never went public.

I had been following the newspaper stories about different travel agencies in Portland and Seattle that were advertising low-priced tour group trips to visit the "psychic surgeons." The Federal Trade Commission was planning to prosecute the agencies for fraudulent advertising, but they were unable to find any disgruntled patient who would bring suit against the travel agents. Of all the hundreds of Americans who went there, not one person wanted to complain about their treatment. Apparently, almost all of the ill people who saw the Philippine healers were positively affected in one way or another.

I told my longtime friend Henry MacLeod, who was the managing editor of *The Seattle Times*, about my plans to observe the healers. He said that the healers were of great interest to many *Times* readers, and that he would like to print my reports and comments about the trip. So, in my role as cub reporter, I wanted to report accurately what I observed.

In retrospect, I didn't consider the healers as contenders to help me with my headache, because I doubted their ability to do anything helpful. I believed it was "faith healing," and I didn't have the faith. After all, I was a straight-A student in high school, and my family was known for its brains. My father and brothers were distinguished in their science-oriented fields. We didn't do religion....

The Philippine healers were Catholic Spiritualists. At that time in my life, I was entirely ignorant about the power of faith. For me, the fact that someone actually believed in something like an active, intelligent, organizing Principle in the universe outside their own ego made them suspect. And the idea that prayer might be efficacious beyond the placebo factor was one I could not understand. I had never heard an adult discuss why Catholicism was meaningful to her. I certainly had never known a Spiritualist before. Years later I learned that some of the world's most gifted healers were and are highly intelligent, ethical Spiritualists, who believe that they are used as channels by God for healing.

I thought my headache would go away by itself eventually, just like they always had before. The most important reason why I never considered going to the healers for help, even out of skeptical curiosity, was that I knew from what I'd already seen that long lines of people would be patiently waiting their turn to have a private session with one of them. As they congregated in the lobbies and elevators of the hotels in which the Manila healers operated, I had overheard hopeful pilgrims discussing their catastrophic ailments. Most suffered from debilitating, life-threatening, or highly painful illnesses. They had anxiously anticipated their trip to see the healers for many months. I was not about to mention my headache to anyone. I was grateful for my healthful mobility, until that night when the pain got so bad that I lost all desire to live.

The healers weren't interested in convincing anyone of their effectiveness. They charged nothing. They didn't have to. People gave to them generously. Each day, multitudes of people came to the healers, and seemed to get better, or at least feel better, no matter what I or any other skeptic might have thought.

After I had learned where the healers worked in Manila, I tried to figure out how to watch them do whatever it was that they did. I contemplated the problem, as I wandered around the crowded second floor of the Manila Hotel, where several Americans had come to be healed. Before I had time to meet anyone, a bright-eyed, salt and pepper-haired man came right up to me and introduced himself. With a sense of urgency, he explained that he was next in line to see the healer Thelma Zuniga. Then he anxiously asked if I would be willing to video his hemorrhoid operation.

I was taken off guard, and before I had time to answer, he handed me his camera, and showed me where to look and what to push. "Now, don't be bashful!" he urged. "Get right up close to her hands, and get it all on film! This is amazing stuff! I brought my seventy-two-year-old mother here last year, and they took out her tumors and healed her cancer. So this year, I came to have my hemorrhoids out, and I want to show my friends and family what they did when I go home!" So I said, "Okay." I had only the vaguest notion of what a hemorrhoid was, but the situation provided me with a perfect vantage point from which to carry out my mission.

I got right up close and filmed the healer, Thelma, pressing on his bare buttocks with her fingers. Watery, bloodlike fluid oozed down his thighs, and in a minute or so some purplish tissue appeared in Thelma's fingers. It looked like clusters of tiny grapes. She wiped his bottom with a wad of cotton and said, "Okay. Finished." As he pulled up his boxers, I looked askance and mumbled something, handed him his camera, and made a hasty getaway.

The next morning when I returned to the second-floor lobby of the hotel, I reluctantly encountered the man again. I asked him, sheepishly, "So, how are your hemorrhoids today?" and he said, "Honey, they're gone! It's great!" I questioned him skeptically, "Are you sure?" He exclaimed, "You bet

I'm sure! I've been tucking those darn things in every morning for the past fifteen years, and when I tell you they're gone, believe me, I know what I'm talking about! They're gone!"

That day, another unexpected event took place. Thelma invited me into the hotel room where she was doing her operations. Her assistant told her that I was a reporter, and that I shouldn't be allowed to observe, but Thelma shushed her away, and turned toward the buxom Swiss woman who was disrobing for a varicose vein operation. The woman lay facedown on the bed, clad only in her underwear, and Thelma began to massage her thighs laboriously, as red fluid squished and splattered all around us.

Thelma told the woman and her concerned husband to pray. The husband stood at his wife's side with his head bowed, and he held her hand as they murmured hushed words together in German. I was moved by their devotion to each other and to their God, by the man's gentle sensitivity to his wife, and by his relinquishing of control to Thelma. They had something I had rarely seen before, something that was entirely foreign to me. These seemingly intelligent people believed in a Higher Power that was real and had meaning for them, and they believed that their prayers might be beneficial for healing. For me, it was like watching a play. I could not understand why they would spend their money to come here and pray in a hotel room, while this Philippine woman put on a spectacular performance of trickery with animal entrails and blood. It was as if we were all agreeing to participate in some cathartic ritual.

All of a sudden, I realized that I was *in* the play, but no one had ever given me a script. I was enveloped in the loving, prayerful ambiance in that hotel room. All was quiet for a few moments as I felt my mind joined with theirs, hoping for healing.

Right in the middle of the operation and prayers, a dark-suited man followed by two others barged into our room, and announced that he was an agent of the U.S. government. He acted like a character in a James Bond movie as he ponderously declared that he would be staying all day to observe the proceedings. I was outraged at his rudeness, and felt embarrassed to be of the same nationality. He was oblivious to the naked Swiss woman's shock and embarrassment, as she groped for her clothing and asked in flustered German, "What is going on?"

Whatever else I had thought about Thelma up to that point expanded to include respect at that moment. She never missed a beat. She was calm and soothing, as she gently assured the woman that the agent's presence was no deterrent to either her concentration, or to the efficacy of her healing treatment. She conveyed genuine concern for the woman's emotional well-being. I liked her, even if she was a charlatan. I thought it was ironic that our government sent people like him to save us from people like her. It was my first insight that what was occurring here under the heading of "healing" was far more complex than what could be conveyed in an answer to the question, "Is it sleight of hand, or is it not?" — or even, "Are the healers fraudulent, or are they not?"

I never got to see if the Swiss woman left with varicose veins in her legs or not. It didn't matter, because I hadn't gotten a good look at her legs before Thelma did her treatment on them, anyway. What was most interesting to me was what happened when Thelma directed her attention to the U.S. agent, who had removed his jacket during the heat of the fuss.

She introduced herself to the officer, and welcomed him to observe her healing, with far more courtesy than he deserved. Then she pointed to a ridged bump on his forearm, which was about an inch long, and purplish in color. "What's this?" she asked. "Oh, it's nothing," he stammered. "May I look at it?" she asked. He held out his arm reluctantly, uncomfortable with everyone's attention on him. "It's really of no consequence," he protested. "It's been there for so many years, that I'd forgotten it was even there."

"Would you like me to get rid of it for you?" asked Thelma.

Why do anything at all for him, I thought. Why voluntarily put yourself under this boor's scrutiny, and lay yourself wide open to be caught doing fakery?

The man was in a tight spot. What would he do now, I wondered? He mumbled something in embarrassment, as Thelma led him towards the bed, and motioned for him to lie down. I stood at the man's head, and watched intently. I observed him as the healer moved her hand back and forth about an inch above the bluish protrusion. She gently swept the air over the lump with the palm of her right hand. Then she held her right palm open above the bump, and kept it there for awhile. I was surprised that she didn't look at the man's arm. She gazed downward, and appeared to be intent on something she was feeling or sensing within herself. I wondered if she were praying, or listening for an answer.

Then I looked at the man, and noticed that he was sweating profusely, despite the air-conditioning in the room. Beads of perspiration rolled down his red face. I whispered to him, "Does it hurt?" "No," he said.

"Do you feel a lot of heat?" I asked.

"No," he said again.

"Then why are you sweating so much?"

"I don't know. It's very strange. I don't feel anything. I feel very light."

Thelma began to scratch the lump with her thumbnail. For the first time, I noticed a dark speck, like an enlarged pore, on the surface of the bump. Thelma picked at it a bit with her fingernail, and pulled up, seemingly from out of the pore, a thin, elongated piece of tissue. It looked like an inch-long dendrite, the shape of which I remembered from high school biology. She told the man it was the root of the growth on his arm, and now that it was removed, the lump would recede and be gone within two weeks.

The man was obviously flustered. He left abruptly, without a thank you, or an apology for his obnoxious behavior.

Two days and many healings later, when I arrived at Thelma's hotel room in the morning, the U.S. agent was already there. He stood quietly and courteously over to one side of the room, as he observed the day's "surgeries." His respectful manner was extremely different from that of his first encounter with Thelma. I was surprised at his transformed demeanor. I asked him, "How is that growth on your arm?" He showed me the place where Thelma had scratched a few days before. The ridge was one-third as high as it had been previously, and its color had changed from purple to pink. "Oh," he assured me, in a matter-of-fact tone, "It's almost gone now. I think it will be entirely gone by the end of the week." I wouldn't have believed it was the same man if I hadn't talked to him myself!

After a week, I'd seen many so-called psychic surgeries, most of which my rational mind told me were sleight of hand, and yet which my observations told me were efficacious to varying degrees. I saw things that looked like animal entrails appearing as if they were being pulled out of people, and things that looked like real incisions cut into people, through which globs of who-knows-what appeared. I mostly saw sick people feeling better, speaking a common language of hope and fellowship to each other, in a community of affirmative expectation.

I was looking forward to seeing the renowned healer, Alex Orbito, do his famous eye-check procedure. I decided to team up with an American woman who was writing for a Yakima, Washington, newspaper. With two pairs of eyes to scrutinize, I thought we ought to be able to discern what was going on. We walked over to the chapel courtyard where Orbito was doing his procedures. Long lines of Filipino people of all ages were waiting patiently to be treated.

The reporter stood on one side of the patient's head and watched Orbito's hands, while I stood on the other side with my face down, eye-to-eye with the patient. It looked as if Alex had his finger behind the man's eyeball, and that the eyeball was popped forward in its socket and pushed off to one side. I thought to myself, it might be easy to palm a fake eyeball, but why can't I see the man's real eye in there? And how does he get the glass eye to just hang there? I asked the patient, "Doesn't that hurt?" and he answered, "No, but it feels strange — a bit ticklish. I can feel his finger in the socket."

Later I wished I had asked him if he could see with his dangling eye. I'm not sure what the procedure was meant to accomplish, or whether it was helpful or not, but it certainly was impressive to watch. When I compared notes with the other reporter after Orbito's eye show, we were each disappointed that the other didn't have an intelligent explanation for what we saw.

At that point, I had seen many surgeries. I didn't know what to believe, and I didn't trust what I thought I saw. Some of the operations I observed had been quite bloody, and others not at all. When I asked Thelma why that was, she told me that "Some people do better with lots of blood." I assumed she had meant that they more strongly believed in the power of God to heal them, or that they healed themselves better.

Why did the healers palm chicken guts if they could rearrange eyeballs painlessly, and remove hemorrhoids with their bare fingers? I thought I had seen a tiny razor blade under one healer's fingernail, so, aha! He wasn't cutting people open with his finger! He was simply using a razor blade! (And then reaching inside people's bodies with his bare hands and pulling out tumors, while the people felt no pain?) Or did he cut people and use chicken guts, so they would believe they were being operated on — and actually heal themselves?

I gave up the idea of writing anything about the healers for the newspaper. It wasn't possible for me to figure out what was actually going on. Smarter people than I had been perplexed by this. It didn't seem to be all fraud, all the time. And besides, I wanted people to get better, so why did it matter *how* it happened?

So what if the so-called operations were frauds, as long as people got well? If reporters think it's a problem, but sick people don't, is it meaningful to ask if the psychic surgeries are real or fake? Maybe, as the Buddhist philosopher Nagarjuna postulated, they are both real and not real.[2]

In any case, when I tried to make sense of it, my headache began. It was made worse by the fact that I had barely eaten anything in the past few days, because I was out of money and was waiting for the arrival of funds via Western Union. Also, I had not been sleeping well at all. In retrospect, my stress, my unintended fast and dehydration, physical exhaustion from months on the road, and the assaults by the healers on my view of reality all contributed to a situation that, in many ways, resembles a contemporary shamanic vision quest, or brainwashing.

I once heard it said that "mystical experiences are to religion what basic research is to science."

— Anne Gordon
A Book of Saints

I have no recollection of even one more moment of pain after I prayed.

In fact, I have no recollection of being awake at all after praying that night. What I do remember is the most vivid, startling, phenomenal dream I have ever had in my life. It disturbed me so much that I thought I was going crazy. Now, twenty years later, I see books and workshops advertised for people who have had spiritual crises. Stanislav and Christina Grof refer to these episodes as opportunities for spiritual *emergence* in one's life.[3] For me, it was an extreme spiritual emergency, and for some time afterward I did not feel I could discuss it with anyone.

Twenty years later, in 1994, I met a physician who wrote an inspiring book about extraordinary, "spiritually transforming experiences" that radically change ordinary lives, if anyone's life can be said to be ordinary. The book *A Farther Shore* is written by Dr. Yvonne Kason, and it is about her amazing brush with death.[4] Kason survived a small-plane crash in a blizzard in Manitoba, Canada, only to be faced with the challenge of having to swim to an island in freezing cold water, and then to survive in subzero temperatures until she was dramatically rescued. She wrote about her encounter with light, and a great loving and peaceful Presence, who guided her to safety. Reading about her experience gave me courage to write this account of my life-changing dream, and subsequent healing encounters.

> The most beautiful thing we can experience is the mysterious. It is the source of all true art and science.
>
> — Albert Einstein

The dream I had after praying gave me instructions about how I myself would do healing with my own hands. This information came to me from an extremely bright light that communicated with me in a dream that I did not want, and patiently debated with me when I declined to believe or accept the instructions. The voice in the light conveyed compassion when I began to sob out of fear that I was cracking up. The dream greatly frightened me, because when I tried to escape the instructions and the light by waking up, I was unable to awaken myself.

The details of what seemed to be an interminably long tutorial are not important. I received advance information about people I would meet, and events that would happen to affect my development as a healer. I repeatedly argued with the light in my head: "Stop! Wait! Clearly, there's been a mistake! You have the wrong person! It's not me you mean to be talking to! I don't believe in God! I don't go to church! I swear! And I *covet* — I'm sure you've mistaken me for someone else!"

No one was more surprised than I, when the events came to pass, when I met the people who had been described to me, and when sick people told me they felt relief when I brought my hands near their body.

It doesn't seem to me that I consciously or unconsciously "chose" to give myself instructions about healing in a dream, and then decided to become a healer. I was an artist and a teacher at the time when the "gift of healing" was given to me. I was a most reluctant recipient of the gift. It wasn't what I planned to do with my life. I've had to grow into it. It has often been inconvenient and embarrassing for me. It carried great negative status at the University of Oregon, where I earned my Ph.D., and where I taught a variety of health courses for many years. It draws little financial remuneration. It has often caused my family and friends to treat me awkwardly. One boyfriend told me that he was afraid that I would expect him to become spiritual, or that I might try to use the power to control him.

I've been called stupid, silly, deluded, crazy, a religious fanatic, just plain weird, and inappropriate to be on a university faculty — all for practicing this gift which I don't understand, but which seems to be efficacious. Fundamental Christians have told me that I'm in cahoots with the devil. One friend said she could no longer associate with me after she heard that I offered this gift to help alleviate someone's pain. In retrospect, I felt a bit like the heroine in the film *Resurrection*. In that film, the heroine becomes a healer after nearly perishing in a car accident. Then she is harassed by a Bible-waving preacher, shot at, and run out of town.

So why do I practice healing? Because it helps people in need, and because I have come to care less and less about what others think. Because I've changed — I've adopted a lifestyle that does not require much money, and because the status and profession of being a university professor means less to me now than it did before. Because healing is a wondrous "calling."

It is always interesting — no two healing encounters are ever the same. I never know what will happen. I am continually amazed by what occurs. *A Course in Miracles* teaches that "There is no order of difficulty in miracles." A miracle in this context means a change in a person's thought or perception. Similarly, there is no limit, or order of difficulty, in healing.[5] It is exhilarating work.

In that long-ago dream, I was told that *the very next day*, I would put my hands on a stranger, and she would be healed. I vehemently denied it. "No way! Absolutely not! I wouldn't do that to a friend, much less to a stranger!" The voice told me that it would, indeed, happen, but that I would not remember my dream or these instructions until after the healing had occurred, because I was so distraught.

I argued with the light-being. "I won't do it! Even if you say I will be able to do healing, I won't! You can't make me do it!" The being was amused. "No one will force you. You will do it on your own accord." "Please give me some sign," I asked, "Show me, somehow, that I have not lost my mind. Please!"

The voice in my dream told me that in due time I would meet two men who would help me to understand. I was told that each man would approach me and introduce himself. As I wondered to myself how I would know the difference between a man coming to offer guidance, and one whose motives were not so pure, my concern was addressed. I was told specific words that the mentors would use during the encounters, so that I would be able to identify them as the people who would be trustworthy and helpful.

Then the voice in the light told me to hold out my hand. So I did. "Stretch out your arm," it communicated, so I did that. Then a most amazing thing happened.

I was zapped with blinding light. I felt a sensation much like one I experienced when I was four, when I stuck some wires into an electrical outlet. A powerful surge of electrifying current passed down my arm, and coursed through my entire body, with a *whoosh*. An explosion of light erupted within me. Fireworks went off inside my head. I was stunned, and overcome by the brightness. I felt like I had no body. I was radiating light. I was pure energy. I was elation.

I awoke to find myself standing in the middle of the room. I knew it was no longer night by the light coming through the windows. My right arm was outstretched above me. My nightgown was sopping, and clung to my wet body as tears rolled down my face. I felt absolutely energized. Completely alert. Blissfully radiant. Ecstatic. Not at all like a person who had been tormented by unrelenting pain for days. Not at all like someone who hadn't been sleeping well, or hadn't eaten anything in recent memory. All the pain I'd felt the previous night was gone.

And then, I panicked. I thought I had gone completely mad. I was terrified. I quickly dressed, and went outside. The early morning light made everything look extremely clean. Even the sidewalk, which the day before had appeared a dingy gray, seemed beautiful. Plants and people were luminous. I felt joyous and loving towards strangers. The air smelled inordinately fresh. I noticed colors everywhere, more vivid than they had ever been. But the dream was forgotten.

I hastily made my way to the Western Union office. My body felt nearly weightless. I felt extraordinarily alert and strong. The beauty I saw all around me brought tears to my eyes. I felt such love for being alive. I seemed to be aware of everything all around me, all at the same time. And I knew I had to get home right away.

The money I had been waiting for had arrived. I immediately bought a ticket for the next available flight out of the country. I had not looked at a calendar for quite awhile. I had been traveling in Asia, through hot, humid, exotic places for almost a year, with no particular schedule, so that my normal methods of measuring time no longer applied. I realized that not only had I forgotten what day and week it was, I could not even remember what month, season, or even year it was. I could not even remember my age. In spite of my buoyancy, I feared that what had begun as a quest for consciousness expansion had culminated in mental illness.

"Oh, God, Jane, get yourself home while you can still walk. Don't collapse here, now." While I was downtown, however, I decided I must say a last good-bye to Thelma and Alex. I couldn't leave the Philippines before I had thanked them for being so accepting of me. As I rode the elevator to the second floor of the Manila Hotel, I thought how unusual it was to feel so well-rested and vitalized in my physical body, while my mind was obviously so confused. I felt like a different person from the one who had been suffering with the headache . . . whenever that was. It seemed so long ago.

The elevator doors opened, and I stepped out into a small sitting area. As I headed towards Thelma's room, I noticed a woman lying on a couch, off to one side of the hallway. As I approached her, I saw that she was agitated. As I came closer, I heard her groan, and I sensed that she was not well. I asked, "Are you all right?" And she said, "No," that she had been having a horrible migraine headache for two days, that she was nauseated and dizzy and couldn't walk, and that she was in agony. Her husband had gone to look for a doctor.

I asked her if she would like me to wait with her, and she said, "Yes." As I stood there, watching her suffer, I asked her, "Would you like me to massage your scalp while we wait? Maybe it would help." And she said, "Sure. Try anything."

As I bent over her, with my hands over her hair, I tried to decide what to do. Just as I was about to put my fingers on her head, I got the idea that it might be better if I massaged the back of her neck. But she was lying on her back, and I couldn't get to her neck without asking her to change her position. So I decided to go back to my original plan, and massage her scalp. Just as I was deciding whether to start above her ears, or below them, she heaved a huge sigh of relief, and exclaimed, "Oh! *Thank* you! Oh, what a relief! Thank you so much."

I was totally taken aback. "But I haven't done anything yet! I was just about to start!" She quickly exclaimed, "Oh, yes, you did! I felt it when you brought your hands near. I felt the surge of energy! It felt so wonderful! It took the pain right away! My head felt so light. It was such a relief! It felt like your hands opened a dam, and all the pain just poured out! Thank you so much!"

Then I remembered my dream from the night before. It all came back to me. And I shook my head in disbelief at what I'd done, and thought to myself, "You were right. I did do it!... And she was a total stranger!" I looked at my hands and wondered why I hadn't felt any energy leaving them, if the woman had felt energy flowing into her. If I had done something, wouldn't I know it? How could something like that happen, with my body, without my knowledge? Who was doing this? What was going on? I was more bewildered than ever.

I am now aware that laboratory data offers strong evidence for the existence of a mind-to-mind connection in psychic healing. Among people who actively practice healing today, however, the mind-to-mind hypothesis would be a minority opinion. Millions of Asians, Indians, Egyptians, and Polynesians throughout history have believed in an "exchange of energy" associated with psychic healing. Their experiences are not unlike those of modern day practitioners of Therapeutic Touch, Reiki, Polarity, Joh Rei, Huna, Raimondi, Chi Gong, or Pranic Healing, who also feel that energy is transmitted between healers and their patients.

When involved in healing interactions, my clients and I also experience feelings akin to energy flows and vibrations, accompanied by heat. In addition, I sense a kind of mind-to-mind attunement that accompanies the feelings of energy movement. Neither of the authors of this book pretend to have an explanation for the mechanisms of psychic or spiritual healing, any more than we do for ESP. However, that in no way diminishes our confidence in the efficacy of the former, or in the existence of the latter.

Before I left the Philippines, I met one of the two men I had been told I would meet in my dream. He was a physician and Yoga teacher, who had been investigating and observing the healers for many years. This doctor encouraged me to learn about the science of Yoga, which actually means union with God. It comes from the Sanskrit word meaning "yoke," or connection, or bringing together. He told me that all of the world's great religions contained teachings about this union or enlightenment path of wisdom. The teachings were known as the mystical branches of the faiths, and went by such names as Sufism, Zen Buddhism, Yoga, and Kabbala. The mystical form of Christianity is found in the words ascribed to Jesus in the Bible, and in the writings of St. Teresa of Avila, St. John of the Cross, Meister Eckhart, Teilhard de Chardin, and Thomas Merton, among others. All of the teachers who have been most influential to me have encouraged me to read works by the mystical poets and leaders of the world's great wisdom and religious traditions.

The thread throughout all of these texts is the quest for union with the sacred, or *cosmic consciousness*, a term described in the 1901 book of the same name by Richard Bucke, M.D.[6] Many have written that the ultimate goal of all the world's great faiths is "a transforming communion with the Divine in which the self dissolves to become united with God."[7] Sanskrit scholar Ernest Wood, who has translated sacred Indian texts, has said God is a good word if we remember that it is a word of discovery and not a word of definition:

> In science we have words of definition, but here we have a word with which to give *direction* to the mind, a word which is like a boat, such as Columbus used when he set out to discover something that he did not know.[8]

"The mystical experience of God, the immediate intuitive experience of God…is the very heart and soul of Christianity," according to contemporary Carmelite mystic Mother Tessa Bielecki.[9] An unknown medieval author wrote that "God may well be loved but not thought."[10] This experience is what I think Jesus, St. Paul, and other mystics are trying to convey. Poetry by Blake, Whitman, Tagore, Gibran, Kabir, Rumi, Bashō, Rilke, and Dickinson reflects the timeless, blissful state of love, gratitude, and connectedness that is characteristic of spiritual mystics the world over.

Philosopher Bertrand Russell tried to define the characteristics of a mystic's perception of reality. In an essay on mysticism and logic published in 1925, he reports that mystics gain information from a source other than the known senses. They perceive time as an illusion, they are aware of a fundamental unity to all things, and they perceive evil as an illusion that changes when one shifts one's field of perception.[11] Evelyn Underhill wrote a sort of Bible of mysticism in 1912, in which she says that mystics shift their field of perception from one level of consciousness to another, and actually *unite* with an aspect of reality that is different from ordinary waking consciousness.[12] Because the reality of the mystic is timeless, and all things seem interconnected, it becomes difficult to describe and categorize mystical perceptions into language when a person shifts her field of perception back to the more ordinary sensory awareness. As I gained experience as a spiritual healer in the years that followed, I realized that the state of consciousness typical of a healing interaction was similar to that of the mystics.

The man who introduced himself to me before I left the Philippines in 1974 told me that, in the Hindu tradition, the concept of light was equated with the expansion and intensification of consciousness, the creative impulse, and bliss. He said that I could read about people's experiences of light, expanded awareness, and merging with a unity-consciousness from a more contemporary Westerner's point of view in Richard Bucke's book, *Cosmic Consciousness*. Bucke was the physician to poet Walt Whitman.

Their association influenced Bucke to investigate and write about the illumined state of awareness wherein self-consciousness is transformed, and an enduring sense of oneness with all creation is experienced. Buddha, Jesus, the apostle Paul, Moses, Isaiah, Muhammed, Ramakrishna, St. John of the Cross, Blake, Dante, Socrates, Swedenborg, Spinoza, and Whitman were all among the ranks of those who had, in the opinion of Bucke, encountered varying degrees of cosmic consciousness. The eminent American philosopher William James, author of *The Varieties of Religious Experience*, wrote that Bucke's book was "an addition to psychology of first-rate importance."[13] James himself had written of the experience of "the light," which he called "photism." He told of many people throughout history who had had such an experience, and he declared it to be fully normal.[14]

Dr. Bucke described his own experience of illumination, which he defined as the temporary entry of a percipient into the cosmic consciousness:

The person, suddenly, without warning, has a sense of being immersed in a flame.... At the same instant he is, as it were, bathed in an emotion of joy...ecstasy.... Like a flash, there is presented to his consciousness a clear conception (a vision) in outline of the meaning and drift of the universe....That the foundation principle of the world is what we call love.[15]

He went on to say that people who had the experience of illumination were at first alarmed by the vision, wondering if it were a symptom or form of insanity. He then pointed out that all of the world's great religions and spiritual practices are based on such "insane" visions, which challenge our everyday concept of the nature of reality. How, then, asks Bucke, shall we know that this sense of cosmic consciousness is not insanity, but truth? He answers that the characteristics of illumination are universal to all who have experienced a temporary entry into cosmic consciousness. They include self-restraint of the ego, a sense of love for all of life, an awareness of an all-pervasive connectedness to others, and an acceptance of the teachings of other people throughout history and from other cultures who "have passed through the same experience."[16]

I find Bucke's descriptions of the effects of illuminations to be remarkably similar to the life-changing aftereffects of near-death experiences (NDEs) on people's lives, which are described in many recent bestselling books. Some researchers who study people who have had near-death experiences perceive NDEs to be one of a family of related mystical experiences that serve as catalysts for spiritual awakening and development. NDE researcher and author Dr. Kenneth Ring believes that such experiences are actually evolutionary mechanisms thrusting us forward, toward a higher state of consciousness for all humanity. Melvin Morse, M.D., who wrote about his research with children who had experienced NDEs in the book *Transformed By the Light,* and Kenneth Ring, author of *Heading Toward Omega,* have found the experience of light "to be the keynote event of the near-death experience, the element that always leads to transformation."[17]

Included in the personality-transforming illuminations of NDEs are the illuminations accompanying what Morse has called "fear-death" experiences (FDEs). These are dissociative reactions to intensely stressful or life-threatening situations. I consider myself to be a member of this latter cohort. I do not know whether or not my experience in the Philippines was actually an NDE, as characterized by Raymond Moody in *Life After Life* by such bodily symptoms as cessation of breathing or heartbeat, or drop in blood pressure or temperature.[18] Nonetheless, I experienced radical long-term changes in my worldview, values, and priorities due to a set of interactions "in the world of light." Spiritually transforming awakenings come in many forms, and nearly dying is only one of the circumstances that tends to be conducive to them.[19]

I am deeply grateful to all those who have researched and written of these transcendent experiences of light, as they have helped me to integrate my own experience into my life. An additional aspect discovered by Morse, in his study of people who had had such experiences, is that the illumined NDE group reportedly had more than four times the number of validated psychic experiences as did the well or seriously ill groups of people with whom they were compared. He described many instances wherein people who had experienced light as part of their near- or fear-death experiences were surprised by influxes of precognitive information, clairvoyant vision, and healing ability after their illuminations.

Other researchers who have conducted surveys of the range of after-effects experienced by those with NDEs (NDErs) have also reported that a perceived increase in psychic phenomena is common, but those are not the most significant changes to come about in the lives of the experiencers.[20] Far more important for them were the changes in life direction, and the focus on spiritual growth. These aspects have been true for me, as well. As Raymond Moody wrote in *The Light Beyond*:

> Upon their return, almost all [NDErs] say that love is the most important thing in life. Many say it is why we are here. Most find it the hallmark of happiness and fulfillment, with other values paling beside it.[21]

Elisabeth Kübler-Ross wrote that the near-death experience is often "a spiritual, sacred experience, which leaves the person profoundly transformed."[22] Such was the case for me, as I found I had received a calling to be a healer from my illuminating experience. Although I did not consciously choose this way of life on my own accord, this mission does give purpose and direction to my life. However, it has not been easy to feel compelled to practice something that is not only not understood, but is often ridiculed, or condemned for being offensive to someone else's religious or scientific beliefs.

The most difficult part has been accepting the difference between who I am and the person that others expect someone with a gift for spiritual healing to be. I have come to believe that this is, in fact, the most important part of the calling. It has shown me, at least, that revelations of God as an overwhelming feeling of love occur to ordinary people who ask for help. It demonstrates our enduring connected nature, despite our ignorance, or refusal to believe it. It shows, as does remote viewing, that we are all capable of higher sense perceptions. Further, it invites us to act responsibly, by cultivating an awareness of our inherent connection to each other, and connection to a transcendent, unifying intelligence. It has taken me many years to grow into these beliefs, as well as into the practice of healing.

I left Asia in 1974 in hurried confusion, and returned home to Seattle. On my first day back, I was "coincidentally" drawn to walk by a *Quest* bookstore, which specializes in books published by the Theosophical Society. Since the founding of the Theosophical Society in New York City in 1875, the primary mission of that international organization has been, "To encourage the study of comparative religion, philosophy and science; to investigate the unexplained laws of nature and the powers latent in man; and to form a nucleus of the Universal Brotherhood of Humanity, without distinction of race, creed, sex, caste or color."

Theosophy incorporates the idea that we live in an ordered universe in which consciousness is evolving, and in which humans have an innate purposeful drive to develop and expand their spiritual awareness. This philosophical system teaches that knowledge and experience of a transcendent reality can come through meditation, revelation, and other avenues. Helena Blavatsky, the founder of Theosophy, said that the essence of the philosophy is in the harmonizing of the divine with the human in man. She said, in 1888, that kindness, the absence of every ill-feeling or selfishness, and the presence of charity, goodwill to all beings, and justice to others and oneself are Theosophy's chief features. This sounds similar to the revelations of near-death experiencers, as well as the teachings of "loving thy neighbor as thyself" by Jesus, and Buddhist teachings of compassion and noninjury to other beings.

Through Theosophy, I "coincidentally" met Mr. Bing Escudero, who was the Director of Education for the American Theosophical Society at that time. He was of Philippine nationality, and again coincidentally, had been close boyhood friends with the man in the Philippines that I was told in my dream I would meet. I realized that Mr. Escudero was the second man foretold in my dream. Under his guidance, I studied Raja Yoga, which includes methods of concentration, contemplation, and meditation. Such study was for the purpose of nurturing the inner impulse for illumination and union with God, which is said to be an inherent instinct in all of us, according to both Yogic and Theosophical philosophy.

Through my association with Mr. Escudero, I had an opportunity to study healing with Dora Kunz, a renowned clairvoyant and healer. She was also the president of the American Theosophical Society, and the teacher of healing to Dolores Krieger, who together with Kunz originated the Therapeutic Touch healing method. Kunz's remarkable higher sense perceptions are described in the book *Breakthrough to Creativity* by physician Shafica Karagulla, who studied Kunz's ability to do clairvoyant diagnosis.[23] Kunz's own book, *Spiritual Aspects of the Healing Arts*, is also inspiring.[24]

Through the Theosophical Society, I found the companionship and support of many heartful people who had experienced spiritual awakenings, and unusual psychic and artistic capabilities. Most of the people I met in the organization understood my confusion, and the experience of alienation from friends, family, and my previous way of relating to the world, after my illumination and dream. We shared a bond of the transforming and ineffable life experiences which affected us profoundly, but about which we could not speak to the majority of our acquaintances without driving them away.

Today, twenty-six years later, there are a variety of groups for a spiritually inclined, mystically minded or "illuminated" person to join for social support and education. I used to think the word "mystic" referred to a permanently spaced-out and irrational person who was strangely cut off from reality, until someone called *me* one. Since then I've learned that I am a generic mystic, and, as Gordon puts it, "In fact, all of us are born mystics . . . [because of] our capacity to experience wonder and a primal sense of connectedness . . . to one degree or another."[25]

> The men and women we call mystics differ from the rest of us merely by giving these experiences the place they deserve in everyone's life. What counts is not the frequency or intensity of mystic experiences, but the influence we allow them to have on our life.
>
> By accepting our mystic moments with all they offer and demand, we become the mystics we are meant to be. After all, a mystic is not a special kind of human being, but every human being is a special kind of mystic.[26]
>
> — Brother David Steindl-Rast

The great teacher and writer Joel Goldsmith, whom I refer to in later chapters, taught that the mystical life was a life lived by a person who recognized that the presence of infinite consciousness, knowledge, and love within him or her was the true reality. An important conclusion from this is that a mystic finds the source and substance of joy, peace, wisdom, and love within herself — realizing that those inner qualities or the absence of them are the source of one's outer experiences.

I've heard the aphorism "A razor must be sharpened before it is useful." My writings here are an attempt to record my quest on the path of sharpening, of learning to accept my mystic moments with all they offer and demand. My experience has been that I was offered a calling by grace, and that the gift or talent of healing has been accompanied by a responsibility to discuss it, practice it, and to earn a Ph.D. in the field of health research so as to be able to teach, study, and write about it.

An important part of my education has been the study of *A Course in Miracles*. It is a nonsectarian course in mind-training, which teaches about becoming aware of our connected nature. It gave me a perspective for my "mystical" experiences and my newfound healing abilities. The main focus of the course is to show people how their present experiences are profoundly affected by their past perceptions and fears. It teaches that we can have more peace in our lives, and more satisfying relationships with others, by changing our mind. The teachings deal with universal spiritual themes, but clearly state that they comprise only one form of the many spiritual pathways to inner peace that are taught throughout the world.[27]

A Course in Miracles states that the teachings of different religions will always engender controversy, because all terms of language vary in their interpretation, and beliefs are subject to doubt. Therefore, it says, "A universal theology is impossible, but a universal experience is not only possible but necessary."[28] In his book *An Introduction to the Course in Miracles*, Robert Perry says that the teachings undoubtedly have something to offend almost everyone:

> For a secular age, it is too spiritual. For those into alternative spirituality, it is too Christian. For Christians, it is too Eastern. For those into self-help, it is too emphatic about helping others and being helped by God. And for all of us, it presents deep, seemingly insurmountable challenges to our ego.[29]

The late psychiatrist Dr. Viktor Frankl, a survivor of Auschwitz and Dachau, explains in his powerful classic, *Man's Search for Meaning*, how he discovered his power to choose the attitude he wanted to have as he went through his life, after losing his father, mother, brother, and wife in the Nazi death camps.[30] His summary of how to find meaning rather than resentment from suffering is similar to the lessons of *ACIM* that have been so meaningful to me:

Everything can be taken from a man but one thing: the last of the human freedoms — to choose one's attitudes in any given set of circumstances, to choose one's own way."[31]

A Course in Miracles says that we are both teachers and students to each other, and it is in that spirit that we share our learning process here. It is the authors' hope that others will benefit from our efforts to explore the inner and outer spaces of that which we share together — our unique individuality and experiences, as well as our mutual interconnectedness.

In the following chapter, I describe some of the experiences I've had as a practicing spiritual healer during the past twenty years. These healing interactions have convinced me that my focused attention, infused with an attitude of willingness to be used as an instrument of healing, is actually effective in assisting the self-healing of others. I have learned that healing, like remote viewing, occurs in a stress-free environment of trust, where both healer and client maintain an attitude of openness and expectancy. I have come to approach each healing interaction as an experiment, and I ask my clients to regard healing sessions as experiments among friends. This allows for what feels like a merging of our consciousnesses, which can only set the stage for the "unreasonable" nonlocal healing to occur.

When I participate in a healing interaction, I offer my imperfect faith, my ignorance, my willingness to help, and a talent for merging minds with others. My perceptions of illness and disease are from the point of view of a spiritual healer, and remind me of the poem *Anthem*, by Leonard Cohen:

> Ring the bells that still can ring!
> Forget your perfect offering.
> There is a crack in everything:
> That's how the light gets in.

Our pain and suffering can push us to the brink of our sensory and analytical awareness, and force us to open ourselves to the possibility of help from a greater nonlocal spiritual realm. That was the gift my suffering gave to me.

chapter eight

The Healing
Experience

If we do not expect the unexpected, we will never find it.

— Heraclitus

Ever since *my first experience with the so-called "healing touch" in the lobby of the* Manila Hotel, I (Jane) have read everything I could find written by heal-ers, and about healing. One of my favorite books is the autobiography of an American spiritual healer who moved to England before World War I to practice his healing gift, because spiritual healing is accepted and legal there. William MacMillan titled his book *The Reluctant Healer,* because he, like I, was often troubled or puzzled about this "calling" or talent for healing.[1]

We shared much in common. Both of us had the gift revealed to us in a strange and unsettling way: MacMillan, who did not believe in psychic phenomena, had been seated next to a psychic at a dinner party. He had never before encountered a psychic, and was taken aback when the woman casually announced to him that he had the gift of healing. Later, his reac-tion was much the same as mine, wondering how an unexpected declaration from another person could come to influence our lives so strongly. Neither of us understood much about how the phenomenon worked, or why it hap-pened to us.

We both continuously wondered if the "gift" would stay with us if we didn't use it for a long time, or if we committed some act that made us feel guilty or unworthy of the talent. We both wondered if we might inadvertently harm a person while healing, or if the ability would vanish sometime, just as mysteriously as it appeared.

Joel Goldsmith was a world-renowned twentieth-century mystic and spiritual healer. He wrote that no one should practice spiritual healing "unless God takes him by the nape of the neck and pushes him into it," and he is unable to resist the call.[2] This was because he knew that nontraditional healers in the United States would encounter vigorous antagonism to the idea of spiritual healing. I've certainly found this to be true, and to tell the truth, much of the skepticism that I have encountered has come from my own mind.

This chapter deals with how I learned about spiritual healing by direct experience. It is only after years of healing encounters that I have come to accept the reality of nonlocal healing, though I still don't understand how the healing takes place.

After I returned from Asia, a few months passed before an opportunity arose for me to offer healing to another. This time someone I knew and cared about was injured, so I was highly motivated to help, and did not fear failure or ridicule.

EXPERIMENTING WITH A SKEPTIC

The first opportunity for me to experiment with my newfound "healing energy" came when my boyfriend smashed his thumb with a hammer while pounding nails into drywall. I cupped my hands together, and told him to stick his thumb in the space between my palms. He was skeptical, and I was curious what would happen with a "nonbeliever." As I have discovered over the years since then, the more pain someone is in, the more likely they are to try nontraditional healing. In a moment of immediate crisis, they are open to receiving help from wherever it may come. This state of openness is so important for the influx of spiritual healing information to occur. No matter how clear the channel provided by the healer may be, the message cannot flow through the recipient's psychic defenses, if they maintain separateness and prevent the joining of mind-to-mind connections.

In fact, I have come to believe that the pain and isolation I had experienced in the Philippines were, for me, essential precursors to the illumined vision of life, which has brought healing and meaning to me. I would not have asked for help if I had felt able to manage on my own. The availability of pain-altering drugs, helpful friends, or medical personnel would also have prevented me from asking for help. Pain and crisis brought me face-to-face with my pride, and forced me to let down my barriers of defensiveness that separated me from any concept of God.

I believe that the removal of barriers, which opens the way for mind-to-mind connections, or what we call intimacy, is incorporated in the concept of "forgiveness" extolled in many religions. This state of trust, vulnerability, or defenselessness, makes healing possible. Remembering painful past experiences engenders fear, and unresolved fear leads to anger, which becomes resentment. By forgiving, we let go of resentment, which keeps us focused on the past, and impedes our own healing. I have also learned that one need not be sick, as I was, to "get better." In this context, getting better means developing a spiritual practice of quieting one's individual mind activity to allow merging with a greater transpersonal Mind.

When my friend inserted his smashed and throbbing finger into the little haven between my hands, his pain disappeared, despite his skepticism. In the ensuing weeks, his thumb turned purple, and his nail turned black and dropped off, but he never felt another moment of pain from the injury.

Healing experiences like this one, where pain ceases for a period of time or never returns, are common for me. It feels to both healer and patient as if a forcefield is created between my hands, but I also perceive the merging of our minds with a common focus on healing that activates a healing potential. The "healee" need not have any faith, but he does need to be open and receptive to the possibility of healing. He has to be willing to suspend judgment, which I interpret to be the same as removing barriers to the possibility.

GAINING HEALING EXPERIENCE

Over the course of that summer, I had many occasions to enter into healing interactions with ailing children at the Theosophical camp where I was teaching crafts. There I was able to offer help to open-minded, trusting youngsters, and practice my "gift" without fear of scorn or ostracism. This opportunity was of primary importance for me. I gained confidence in the healing process in a relatively short period of time, because I came in contact with a constant flow of minor ailments in children who were receptive to healing. The children were much more scientific than adults: They were curious, and willing to experiment.

I learned that the healing "energy" did not come from me. It seemed to be available when I allowed myself to be used as a sort of channel or "soda straw" for it. I discovered that I did not do something to someone else in the process, but rather, it was something we did together, in collaboration with an ostensibly transpersonal mind. It felt like I was instrumental in creating the condition that permitted the information-energy to flow, but I was not in control of it — I gave myself over to it. It is a process of not-doing, and therefore, not being responsible for what does or does not occur. It is a peaceful state of surrender to a source of active, organizing intelligence. What feels like energy flowing may actually be an expression of a limitless, omnipresent potential, which is activated when people join minds for the purpose of healing.

SPIRITUAL HEALING IS NOT A LOGICAL PROCESS

After that summer, I decided that I should study anatomy and physiology, and learn some established method of healing. I thought that I would be a more responsible healer if I understood more about the workings of the body's systems and organs, and could explain to the patient a bit about what was going on. I also thought I should know what kind of healer I was, and to do that, I would have to become knowledgeable in some system of healing that people had heard about, one that was acceptable to those who were open to alternative healing techniques.

I started to take classes in Polarity Therapy and later, Reiki Healing, which are methods of energy healing; but whenever I tried to follow a specific system of procedures and techniques, I found that my analytical mind and self-consciousness interfered with the healing process. I began to be concerned with whether or not I was doing it right, rather than focusing on being helpful. "Let's see... does this hand go here now? Where is my other hand supposed to be if I'm standing on this side?... Oh, dear, let me look at the book again."

It occurred to me that I'd never studied healing before the "gift," or compulsion, originally appeared. I realized that whatever I had been doing previously — without any study or teaching — was more effective for me than anything I had learned since I began studying. Once again, it was difficult for me to part ways with logical systems and techniques, because I very much wanted someone else to be able to tell me the right way to do healing. However, I returned to relying on my own sensations and intuition to guide me. Once again I was free from books and memorizing, but now I began to encounter my own fears and limiting beliefs about the extent to which this healing "energy" — with me as a channel — could be effective.

NONCONTACT HEALING TURNS OUT TO BE MORE EFFECTIVE THAN LAYING ON OF HANDS

By this time, I had experienced a significant amount of distancing by friends and family from this "different Jane" who had returned from her year in Asia. It was painful for me. I quit talking to others about my experiences with healing. I decided it was important for me to move away from the people with whom I had formerly sought social support and approval. I wanted anonymity to explore my spirituality and the healing potential.

I moved to Eugene, Oregon, and taught healing through the Theosophical Society, as well as through a private organization. I took no payment for the healing interactions I participated in, since I never understood what was occurring, nor knew what was going to happen. Therefore, I have supported myself financially with other jobs. I am always curious as to the outcome of each healing encounter, and I approach each of them as experiments. Otherwise, I would never have the confidence to practice healing.

During that time in Oregon, I offered healing spontaneously to friends when I was aware that I might be able to help them. I soon learned to assess the quality of my friendships before offering the experiment. Initiating the subject made many people uncomfortable in such a way that it affected the nature of our relationship. However, I never met a child who was not responsive, although their open-mindedness often changed after they told their parents.

Around this time I learned about Therapeutic Touch, a version of "laying on of hands" healing that was being taught to nurses at New York University and other nursing schools. It was being practiced in hospitals to reduce pain, swelling, and trauma of patients; and its effectiveness was being actively researched in a variety of clinical settings. (Therapeutic Touch is more fully discussed in Chapter 10, in the section on energy healing.)

I knew I could be an effective teacher of Therapeutic Touch (TT), because I had been using a similar technique of healing for years. I worked briefly with Dora Kunz, a co-founder of TT, and I studied Dolores Krieger's and Patricia Heidt's books on the method.[3] I began to offer opportunities for other health professionals to learn and practice this noninvasive and surprisingly effective version of what the ancient Hindus called "pranic healing."

Until this time, I had done laying on of hands healing only, because that was all I knew. From teaching TT I learned that noncontact healing was just as effective. When I would bring my hands near to a person's body, he or she could feel the same pleasant sensations of heat, energy, and tingling that they felt when I did laying on of hands. I learned that my students could sometimes feel what I felt if I put my hands on theirs when they practiced Therapeutic Touch.

Today, noncontact healing is the norm for me, and I only apply touch if I sense that it will add a helpful element to the healing interaction. Touch is definitely not helpful when a patient is in a lot of pain; where there are bruises, incisions, open sores, or bleeding; where sterile conditions are a concern; or whenever it is perceived to be intrusive to the patient. Touch is also undesirable when it would attract unnecessary attention that would impede the patient's ability to relax, or when a patient might interpret it as sexually stimulating.

HEALING IN HOSPITALS

I learned that Therapeutic Touch was highly controversial among nurses, doctors, and hospital administrators. The director of the nursing program at the community college in Eugene told me that she was very skeptical of TT, but since many nurses were requesting it and speaking highly of my class, and since the course brought money into the department, she would continue to list it on the class schedule. (A workshop on TT for hospital nurses had filled two sessions, each with over three hundred registrants.) The nurses who attended the workshops were excited, but their supervisors and scornful co-workers were not. The phenomenon of Therapeutic Touch was apparently polarizing the local nursing community. TT students told stories of supervisors forbidding them to use the method, and of signs posted in the nurses' entry declaring "There will be NO HEALING done in this hospital."

Nonetheless, many nurses became aware that I did healing, and throughout my twenty years of residence in Oregon, they referred patients to me both inside and outside of hospitals. Furthermore, patients who knew about Therapeutic Touch requested it from the night nurses, who were less likely to be discovered and criticized. Also, much of night nurses' work involves ministering to patients experiencing pain or stress, and many members of the late shift knew that TT was often effective under those conditions.

In order to have Therapeutic Touch administered in some hospitals, the regulations were that a patient had to have a prescription for it. I was told that the hospital was legally liable for all therapy administered therein, and they didn't want to be responsible for something as controversial as laying on of hands healing. However, it wasn't possible for me to treat only those with a prescription. I was usually asked to treat someone who was in severe pain, critically injured, or near death, as soon as possible; and I would act immediately at the request of the responsible family member. Usually, nurses referred family members of critically ill or injured patients to me after all available medical treatments had been applied, but had proved insufficient for healing or pain management.

I learned from treating patients whose bodies were inaccessible to me due to medical machinery, wheelchairs, or radiation devices, that whatever occurs during healing treatment isn't affected or obstructed by thick metal, bedding, or distance between me and the patient. I became confident that something involving my mind was really helping sick people, but I wasn't sure if I could depend upon that something's reliability.

I wanted to get more experience with people who were ill or in pain, so I signed up for training to be a hospice volunteer. And later, I volunteered to work with people coming to the local hospital for radiation treatments. My job was to be friendly and supportive, and to help the patients feel comfortable, especially while they were lying down on the metal table and waiting to be irradiated.

Over time, I got to know some of the patients whom I saw regularly. People were so fearful about their cancer diagnoses, upcoming chemotherapy treatments, potential loss of body parts, and possible death, that it was easy to feel helpful, just by being with them. Some of the people with whom I became friends spent most of their waking hours in wheelchairs, because one or both of their legs were either paralyzed or had been amputated.

One man told me that although he had been paralyzed from the waist down for over ten years, his feet were always cold, even though he wore wool socks and down booties. I told him about my so-called "healing hands," and offered to treat him as an experiment. He was willing, so we found a private corner, and I brought my hands close to his feet. He immediately felt vibrations inside his toes, and deep heat welling up from inside his feet. He said his feet and toes felt "toasty-warm," and it was the first time they had been comfortable in years. I was curious how he could feel the sensations he described, when his legs could not feel any pain or touch.

The man became tremendously enthusiastic, and declared that he could hardly wait to tell his buddies about me. I told him that really wouldn't be a good idea, because if word got around the hospital unit I would probably be asked to leave my volunteer job. He protested, and exclaimed that all sorts of the patients would love to try the healing.

So when the man with the toasty toes asked me if I would please try to relieve his best friend's leg pain, I acquiesced. "Okay," I said, "If we keep it quiet and don't attract any attention." Then I learned that his buddy's painful leg didn't exist, because it had been amputated. I hadn't yet heard of "phantom limb pain," and I felt ignorant. But I realized I had to learn to be comfortable with all kinds of injuries and afflictions. Also, I was curious to see if the healing energy that worked through my body would be of help in easing the man's phantom limb pain. So the following week, I tried it. (Looking back on this experience, I can see that I was learning to relate to people's spiritual essence, and not be psychologically blocked by their physical form or appearance.)

LEARNING TO GET BEYOND BODIES

At that time, I believed that some sort of energy was coming out of my hands and going into the patient when I did a treatment. I had no idea where to insert energy for leg pain from a leg I could neither see nor touch. It was definitely a strange experience: I held my hands near to the place where the man's thigh would have been, and felt the characteristic tingles and flowing sensations that I feel when a healing connection is made. Whatever was happening, I began to realize, was far beyond my understanding, and seemed to work in the air.

The man said he felt tingling where he often felt the pain. He did not have active pain at the time I was treating him, he said, so I told him to let me know the following week if he had anything to report. The next time I saw him he said that he had experienced no phantom limb pain since the time of his treatment, which was highly unusual for him. He did not ask for another healing session, and I never saw him again. I felt relieved, because the whole concept of spiritual healing was strange enough to me, without having to deal with the idea of how it could be efficacious for symptoms in a person's extremity that had no ordinary sensations, or for symptoms in a body part that didn't even exist.

LEARNING THAT HEALING HAS NO LIMITS

Since I started doing healing twenty years ago, I have treated hundreds of people for a wide variety of ailments. Most of my healing experiences have taken place outside of clinical settings, either after a person has come home from the hospital, or as an adjunctive treatment complementing their medical care. The treatment seems to be especially effective in promoting pain relief. People also like its effects for the relief of itching, swelling, fever, sleeplessness, fatigue, rashes, ringing in the ears, constipation, nausea, rapid heartbeat, breathing difficulties, stuffy sinuses, stiffness of joints, infections, and inability to feel warm.

After I received my master's degree in health education with a specialty in nutrition, my private practice with women with cancer began to expand. One woman I treated was in great pain after surgery for the removal of one of her breasts and the lymph nodes under her arm. After I brought my hands near to the area of the surgical incision, she felt relief from the pain and swelling for the duration of the time her scar was mending. She exclaimed to me the following day, that for the first time in five years, the pain from a chronic bursitis condition in her shoulder on the side of her body opposite the mastectomy had disappeared, too.

A short while later I treated her for itching at the incision site, and the healing process was effective for that as well. Repeat treatments were needed, however, as the itching sensation returned after time elapsed following treatment.

HEALING AND TIME

When I first began to practice healing, I had no idea what to expect. It is fortunate that I had so many open-minded women friends who were willing to try healing with me, and who I knew would not ridicule me if nothing happened. Another psychic friend told me that the opportunity for her to practice her intuitive skills on adults who cared about her unconditionally was crucial for her development, also.

The first time I treated a relatively new friend who was suffering from postpartum pain resulting from a spinal block, I had an interesting experience that was to be the first of many similar healing encounters. We discovered that each time I tried to help relieve her ferocious headache, the anesthetic effect of the healing only lasted about an hour and twenty minutes, despite the fact that neither of us expected her pain to return after any time frame. Both of us napped in between the healing treatments, which took only about ten seconds, before she would again experience pain relief. She awakened each time her pain returned, and it seemed to recur on a regular schedule.

At that point in my healing experience, I realized that some universal life energy was involved, and I also thought some sort of local forcefield was created during healing that dissipated with time. Sometimes, however, only one treatment was needed for pain to disappear completely without returning. Another outcome was that a person experienced complete pain relief for the duration of his or her life, but they died from the ailment we both hoped would be cured.

While I was a graduate student, I had occasion to participate in healing with an open-minded professor with a sinus infection. This person was a trusted friend, and it took only about a minute to establish the healing connection. I was holding my hands on either side of his head, and we both felt the feeling of energy flowing. The treatment eliminated his symptoms of pain and swelling, and I was feeling the characteristic "high" that I experience from healing interactions. When I am in that connected state, I see concentric spheres of vibrating light behind my closed eyelids. The colors and movements of the circles change as the patient's pain and other symptoms change. I am often able to feel in my body the same symptoms and changes that the patient experiences.

I characteristically keep my hands in the same position as long as I feel the engine-like vibrations moving through my body. Suddenly, the vibrations and "whirring" feeling inside me stopped. For the first time, I realized that it was the client, and not me, who had the most to do with the cessation of the connection. I "felt" his abrupt disconnection from the merging of our psyches. I sensed that the professor had begun to worry about the time, because he was concerned with the amount of work he had to finish in the next hour before he taught class.

I realized at that moment how important it is for me to negotiate time with my clients before we begin our healing interactions. Healing requires letting go of defenses and relinquishing worries during the session, so I must take responsibility for how much time passes. I saw that I must not let our session go beyond the time frame we agreed upon, so the patients can relax. This was a major discovery for me, because I lose all sense of time during healing interactions. Because of this, a pleasant-sounding alarm clock is useful for me.

I asked the professor if he had just, at that moment, begun to worry about the time. He was surprised, and admitted it was true. I convinced him to give the healing process just two more minutes, and trust that I would keep him no longer. I could feel the accompanying feelings of what I call "a clear connection" resume in my body, and the professor continued to feel energized.

At the end of the two minutes, I could feel that his body was "still taking energy," but I disconnected the flow myself, in order to keep my agreement. The professor's sinuses were no longer swollen and painful. Instead, they were secreting mucus, and he reported that his body and mind felt revitalized enough for him to concentrate on analytical processes once again.

A HEALER'S HARDEST JOB

After this experience with the professor, I began to realize that my greatest responsibility as a healer was to help the patient relax enough to allow the healing process to occur. Helping someone to loosen their psychic defenses and let go of self-consciousness is a challenging enterprise. It's not up to me to understand or interpret spiritual healing, but I do know that mind, both local and nonlocal, affects the body. Each person metabolizes his or her perceptions differently, and we each produce and store some amount of toxic emotions in our bodies, disrupting our health. To a certain extent, I view illness as resulting from a block in the flow of a person's vitalizing life forces, which a spiritual healer may be able to restimulate.

I have learned to be patient if more than ten minutes goes by and I am unable to attune to the patient. I just make myself comfortable, listen to the beautiful music which I turn on when possible, and maintain my expectancy. Inability to connect formerly caused me great doubt and self-chastisement about thinking there was anything to this "spiritual healing thing." It has taken me many years to become secure enough to stay with the process, even if I am not able to get the characteristic feelings that indicate to me that a connection is made. I usually allow forty-five minutes per client, and for some people on their first visit, a good deal of that time is spent simply helping the client become comfortable with me. They must open up to the possibility that some healing mechanism we don't understand might occur and actually be efficacious.

Once the "flow" is initiated, it usually feels good to the patient, and the connection seems to maintain itself as he or she becomes progressively more relaxed. It is interesting to me that often a person's disease symptoms change radically in the course of a few minutes of treatment. Changes in skin color, breathing rate, body temperature, mood, and energy level are outcomes that I have observed. On many occasions, a patient's fever abates during the healing interaction. Often, those in great discomfort from pain, chills, or uncomfortable body position due to slings, casts, IVs or the like fall asleep during a healing treatment.

Sometimes patients are not aware of changes in their condition immediately after a healing treatment, but they feel very sleepy. After they have slept and reawakened, their healing process will seem to have greatly accelerated. This has been the case with children with the chicken pox and measles, and young adults that I have treated who had scabies or staph infections. In all of these cases, the discomfort and surface area of skin affected by the rashes greatly diminished during post-treatment slumber. Sometimes chronic conditions decrease in severity or go into remission during the week after one or more treatments. I used to be troubled that

184 • MIRACLES OF MIND

these positive changes were all placebo effects, or the result of some sort of inadvertent hypnosis on my part. It no longer matters to me as long as the effect is positive. In addition, my belief has become stronger that something we call spiritual healing really is occurring.

DISTANT HEALING AND COINCIDENCE

I became interested in distant healing after reading Yogananda's *Autobiography of a Yogi* and the healer Olga Worrall's biography.[4] My first opportunity to experiment with it came when I was asked to do healing from my home on a patient who had been hospitalized for two weeks with a serious condition that remained undiagnosed. The man suffered excruciating pain in all his muscles, and he was unable to move or function, due to his pain and low level of energy. Physicians had done exploratory surgery, suspecting appendicitis. They had not discovered the cause of the man's disease, but they removed his appendix anyway. The man failed to recover from the surgery, and his condition was declining.

At the time of my healing meditation at home, the man's wife and a friend noticed striking improvements in his condition. The man's pain subsided, and he began to rearrange his body position in bed, to converse, and ask for food and water.

When his wife telephoned me from the hospital to tell me that her husband was feeling much better, I asked what food he had requested. She began to discuss his diet with me. I learned that the man had been a vegetarian for over two years. After questioning her about his eating habits in the past years, based on my training in nutrition, I discovered that his diet had probably been seriously deficient in vitamin B12, iron, calcium, and zinc. At my suggestion, the man's wife gave him some vitamin-mineral supplements, and his recovery continued to progress rapidly. He had been experiencing great pain and lethargy for months before the exploratory surgery, but no health professional had ever asked him about his diet. I learned that spiritual healing can take surprising twists and turns.

AN UNCONSCIOUS WOMAN NEAR DEATH

A Hispanic woman who spoke little English had been given the last rites by a Catholic priest in the hospital, because she was unconscious and had failed to recover after intestinal surgery. She had not had a bowel movement for many days since surgery, and she had not regained any desire to eat or drink. She was very pale, and her breathing was weak. She was not expected to live through the day, though doctors did not know why her condition continued to deteriorate.

Although she was unconscious when I initiated the healing, she responded rapidly to my treatment. I could sense and hear things begin to move through her system, which felt stopped-up and congested when I began. Within minutes, she began to groan and move. She opened her eyes and began to react consciously. Color returned to her face. Soon she sat up in bed and talked. She asked if I would hold my hands over her surgical incisions, because she felt something pleasant when I brought my hands near to her body. Then she requested that I hold my hands over other places to anesthetize the areas where tubes had been inserted into her body. It was apparently successful. She asked for food, and shortly thereafter, asked if the tubes into her chest could be removed. Then she asked if I could do something to help her relieve her bowels. I directed my hands and healing intentions to her large intestine, and within minutes she got out of bed, walked with assistance across the room, and had a pain-free bowel movement.

The doctors and nurses were quite surprised, and asked me many questions about what I had done. This dramatic healing experience further convinced me to have confidence as a healer, trust the Source, and refrain from limiting the healing potential with my doubting thoughts.

I DISCOVER HEALING IS A MIND-TO-MIND PHENOMENON

One day I received a phone call from a distraught father whose daughter had been hospitalized and was suffering from unremitting pain. The teenaged girl had multiple injuries resulting from a car accident, including a broken pelvis and back. Her doctor refused to prescribe more pain medication, even though she had been crying out with pain for hours. Her parents were frantic; the girl continuously pleaded with them and the nurses to help her.

I began administering nonstop treatment to the girl. She was apparently unaware of my presence in the hospital room, but her expressions of pain responded to my state of mind nonetheless, and she never cried out as long as I did my healing treatment with her. Finally she seemed to drift off to sleep, so I encouraged her parents to take a break. They had been up all night, so I encouraged them to try to take a nap as well.

I believed I needed to hold my hands near to the girl's body for the anesthetic effect to occur. My back was very uncomfortable, however, because I had been bending over the patient at an awkward angle for many hours. I gradually began to straighten my back and let my arms relax and fall to my sides. As I inched away from the patient, and slowly backed up in order to flex my muscles, I discovered that the effectiveness of my interaction was not at all diminished. To my amazement, I found that I didn't need to use my hands, or even stand near the patient, for her comfort to be maintained. I could back away as far as the wall, and lean against it and still maintain the healing state of consciousness.

I think of this state as being one in which my brain waves are in some way synchronized with those of the patient. The healing interaction in which the patient and I participate feels like some sort of merged consciousness. That day I slowly began to relax my legs, bend my knees, and slide my back down the wall. I soon discovered that I could sit on the cool hospital floor, and support my back against the wall at least twelve feet from the patient's bed, and still not interrupt the healing connection. I entered a state of reverie, lost all track of time, and mentally "floated" away.

My mind began to wander from the healing state after awhile. I began to worry about the time, what I would cook for my daughter's dinner, and if I had enough gas in the car to go grocery shopping on the way home without refueling. Just then, the injured girl on the other side of the hospital room began to moan! Her plaintive groans startled me, and brought my awareness back to the present. Her moaning bothered me greatly. I wondered if the return of her pain was related to my fretting.

I didn't open my eyes or otherwise move. Instead, I put myself back into a meditative healing consciousness and psychically reconnected with the patient. It was difficult to disassociate from her cries of pain, and go within myself to the peaceful mental state of healing. But I tuned her out, and felt my facial muscles relax. I saw the familiar light in my mind's eye. It felt good. The young woman stopped moaning.

I wasn't sure if her silence was related to my changed mental state or not. Maybe it was a coincidence, or maybe she had fallen asleep. I decided to experiment. I stayed perfectly still, and began to think about how late it was getting. I noticed how hungry I felt. Thirsty, too. And tired. Gee, it's really stuffy in here, I thought. Some hot tea would taste good right now. What else would I like to eat?

My dialogue with myself was interrupted by the young woman's moaning. Was I imagining this? Could her pain really respond to my mental state? I immediately readjusted my mental state, back to where I was unaware of any bodily sensations or concerns about time. The groans stopped. I was convinced. And amazed.

Sometime later, the girl began moaning again, and I realized that I was very hungry and had been thinking again about dinner. I opened my eyes, and noticed it was getting dark. It was time for me to go home and resume my role as a mom. I stood up, and made eye contact with the girl's father, who had begun to attempt to comfort his daughter with verbal assurances that he was with her.

I was able very quickly to train the young woman's father to do healing on his daughter. He was so motivated to help her that he was willing to suspend his normal belief system, which recognized neither the efficacy of spiritual healing, nor the possibility that he might be able to do it. His willingness to try something under duress, that he ordinarily would never have considered, reminded me of my introduction to spiritual healing many years earlier in the Philippines.

The girl's father held the palms of his hands close to the bedclothes covering his daughter's broken pelvis. I guided him to close his eyes, and asked him to breathe deeply and rhythmically as I whispered instructions to him. First we inhaled and exhaled repeatedly to the count of four, to focus his attention inward. Then we gradually increased the time between breaths by breathing slowly and deeply to the count of six, and then to eight. I suggested he ask his concept of God to use him as an instrument of healing. To maintain his focus of attention, I suggested he imagine himself gently cradling his daughter in a peaceful cocoon of pink love-light that expanded and contracted along with his breathing, just as if it were an extension of his own body.

We were both relieved to see that his daughter's breathing had slowed down. Her face relaxed, and she ceased moaning.

SOME BARRIERS TO HEALING WITH FAMILY MEMBERS

The mother of the young woman was too upset to tune out the "noise" of her daughter's cries, and get into the meditative state necessary for a healing interaction. That is wholly understandable, of course. I have the same problem when my own daughter is in pain. In addition, my daughter wants me present as her mother, sympathetically responding to her feelings when she is sick or in pain. None of this detached healer stuff! These scenarios illustrate the difficulty of doing healing on one's own loved ones. Even if the parent is able to get into the appropriate mind-state, the patient must also be receptive. Role confusion presents potential barriers for both healer and patient in many family situations.

HEALING WHEN I AM ILL DOES NOT DIMINISH THE HEALING EFFECT

Shortly after I learned that it was not necessary for me to use my hands or even stand near the patient for the healing connection to be made, I learned that I could act as a channel for healing even when I was feeling exhausted and sick. Now I know the key is my willingness to be used as an instrument of help to an ailing friend.

A woman who had recently had a mastectomy told me that the discharge from her lymph glands, and the pain that she experienced, was especially uncomfortable at night. When she told me that her husband was out of town, I asked if she would like to spend the night at my house, and she gratefully accepted my offer. I was feeling quite sick and lethargic at the time, with a sinus infection, bronchial congestion, and intermittent fever. Later in the evening when my friend told me she was experiencing great discomfort, she asked if I might be able to help her with her pain, as I had done in the past. I told her I was afraid that I might sap her energy because I felt so tired, but I was willing to help if I could.

I held my hands over her chest and silently asked to be used as an instrument of healing, and we both began to experience sensations of heat, tingling, and a sense of inner weightlessness. All of my aches and stuffiness disappeared, and I felt filled with a peaceful energy that opened my lungs and sinuses, enabling me to breathe freely. I felt wonderful, but I was afraid that my friend might feel worse. Quite the contrary. She also felt peaceful and free from pain, and we both slept soundly, and later awakened feeling quite well. I began to suspect that whatever was occurring was beneficially available to the healer as well as the patient in a healing interaction. Whatever healing "energy" was being attracted seemed to be truly limitless, just as spiritual healing traditions taught.

SOMETIMES HEALING ATTEMPTS DO NOT SEEM HELPFUL

As I think back over the variety of my healing experiences, I am able to recall a number of occasions when the patient's symptoms were not relieved, or the course of their disease did not seem to be affected. Sometimes, but not often, people's pain increased temporarily before they felt better. Russell's theory about these occurrences (and healing in general) is that the patients' vascular flow is stimulated, and the result can be experienced as painful. This is similar to how a person sometimes feels after he has been lying on his arm and the circulation is obstructed. When he moves and the circulation returns, it hurts before it feels better.

Sometimes I intuitively feel that a person will die, but spiritual healing is often able to relieve some or all of their discomfort during that process anyway. At other times, I have felt that I could have been more helpful by administering a series of treatments, but it was not possible for some reason. And very often, people become sleepy and fall into a deep sleep, when they had desired to feel activated. From my point of view, this surprisingly deep sleep is often a sign that a treatment is being effective. People are often more willing to allow time for their cars to be fixed than for the healing of their body.

It is important to recognize that the purpose of spiritual healing is not the indefinite extension of a person's life. Such extension is neither desirable nor possible. I enter every healing situation with hope for healing, but without any prejudgment as to what the physical outcome is going to be.

I most clearly realized that helping ease someone's pain is not always healthful when I once held my hands over a professional runner's painful foot. His pain ceased, and he felt wonderfully energized. I learned afterwards that he had gone out and run another ten miles. Later in the night he was awakened by excruciating pain, and he discovered, when taken to the hospital's emergency room, that he had a torn Achilles tendon.

Reflecting back, I believe that often when a patient is not helped, it's related to an inability to get either the patient or me into the requisite state of mind. This can result from one of us feeling self-conscious, or due to lack of privacy, or time pressure. Once a longtime friend was experiencing great pain, but was unwilling to even try participating in a healing interaction. I asked why, and she said that if nothing happened, she would feel embarrassed for me. "Even if I were not embarrassed?" I asked. "Then I'd feel you were foolish, and I wouldn't respect you." "And what if you were helped?" I asked. "We'll never know," she said, "because then *I* would be embarrassed, and I don't want to deal with it."

Another somewhat humorous experience, when healing results were not appreciated, happened when I worked in the typesetting department of a newspaper. I had an ongoing personality conflict with my supervisor, and the unspoken tension in the office was stressful for both of us.

In any case, one day my supervisor had a very bad headache, and no one in the office had any aspirin. I asked her if she'd like to try healing with me, and she was in such pain that she agreed. She removed her glasses, and I positioned one hand in front of her head and one hand behind. In a few minutes her pain had disappeared, and she was ready to resume her job specifying typefaces and sizes for the ads. She put on her glasses and discovered that she couldn't read with them anymore! She became intensely agitated. She was so disturbed about the phenomenon that I couldn't ascertain whether or not she was able to read *without* her glasses.

My co-workers and I were amazed — but my supervisor was so angry that she left and went home for the day. When I arrived at work the next morning, she was busily designing ads with her glasses on. She never mentioned the incident to me, and I never offered healing to her again, despite her frequent headaches. Nearly every week after that, however, someone else at work asked for my healing help.

DISTANT HEALING OVER THE TELEPHONE

I spent many years unable to confront many of the paradoxes of healing. My self-doubt and my reluctance to deal with other people's reactions to spiritual healing were familiar companions to me. Today those feelings are usually outweighed by my gratitude for being able to help people, and by my curiosity. My most unusual experience with healing occurred when I awakened one morning feeling a strong inclination to telephone a woman with metastasized breast cancer, whom I had met only briefly. I had not had any contact with the woman for many weeks, but I had heard from her friends that she never answered her telephone, as she was very weak and wanted to conserve her energy.

Nonetheless, I felt compelled to telephone her. I expected to be greeted by her answering machine, so I was surprised when the woman answered the phone after just one ring. Immediately after she said hello, I began to experience the sensation of an energized current vibrating through my body. I identified myself to the woman, and asked her how she was doing. She said she was more frightened than she had ever been, because her lungs were filled with fluid and blocked by a tumor, and she could barely breathe. She was waiting for her doctor to call her back, so she wanted to get off the phone right away. I told her I would do a healing meditation for her, and said good-bye.

I continued to sit in that vibrating altered state of consciousness until the feeling of a current flowing through me ceased. At that point about twenty minutes had elapsed, and I phoned the woman again. She again answered the phone after the first ring. She said that her doctor had still not telephoned her, but the emergency had passed. Her lungs now felt unobstructed, and she was able to breathe fully again.

Before I hung up, I told her that I hoped she continued to feel better. I later heard that it had been a holiday, and her doctor never returned her call that day. I was gratified to have been called upon to help — in a way that surpasses my understanding.

The last story I'll relate is about the healing of my co-author, which resulted in our collaboration on this book. It was another remarkable adventure in which I was glad to participate.

THE HEALING OF A PHYSICIST

As mentioned in the introduction, my co-author, Russell, was diagnosed with metastatic cancer of his liver in the winter of 1992. Spots appeared on the CAT-scan plates of his liver and intestinal cavity, and the radiologist told him that it was a recurrence of a cancer that he'd had eight years before. He looked sickly pale and had been losing weight when I began to work with him. Nonetheless, I told him he was not sick, and he should not *say* he was sick, or that he had cancer. All we knew, I declared, was that there were spots on some film. By that time, I was aware of the self-hypnotic effects that repeated affirmations of illness could produce in a person. I taught him to reframe the situation to one which posed a problem that he was learning to solve. He was not powerless: There are always many things a person can do differently to enhance the activity of his or her immune system, and strengthen the body's resistance to disease.

I wrote out a five-page prescription for Russell, based on everything in the research literature concerning immune-system enhancement. In addition, I did many healing meditations with him, and taught him to do self-healing imagery, loving affirmations, and even prayer, which was entirely new to him. Foremost among my recommendations was that he should get reconnected with his friends, and also join a group involved in some sort of spiritual practice, in order to create invigorating emotional and spiritual stimuli. Nourishing oneself with optimistic attitudes and goals; directing one's attention outward through creative projects for which one has passion, or through acts of service to others; and the cultivation of social and spiritual connections, can disrupt the course of disease and invigorate the immune system even more than the physiological changes stimulated by megavitamins and fresh, whole foods, deep breathing exercises, and physical activity, which I also recommended.

The basic idea was to change the host, physically, mentally, emotionally, and spiritually, so the disease would not recognize him. We reduced or eliminated known sources of stress and depression in his life and replaced them with hopeful, peaceful, and empowering activities and environments. I recommended new clothes, new glasses, a new haircut, and new behaviors to postulate a healthy future for a different person. These changes may seem to be superficial, but they are not at all. After these changes, Russell often did not recognize himself as he glanced in the mirror. He *felt* like a new person, and this sensation initiated unfamiliar attitudes and perceptions. In addition, co-workers and friends noticed the changes, and commented on them. The attention from others stimulated by the changes, and the conversations that followed, provided subtle psychological energy boosts to Russell, and enhanced his social connections. Another important activity in his healing was beginning to write this book together; it stimulated his creative juices, and promoted his extension of himself as he shared his ideas and experiences. I wanted him to reconnect to his spiritual essence, in any way he could, and express those aspects of himself that re-enthused him with purpose and aliveness.

Although the doctors were planning to start chemotherapy in two weeks — at the start of the new year — Russell had surmised from reading the scant treatment literature that chemotherapy is rarely effective for tumors in the liver. After his last CAT scan, he felt he had a decision to make — he could either go home and get ready to die, or he could take this time to change everything in his life that could possibly need changing. Russell did the latter. In the following pages, he relates what he experienced as a frightened cancer patient trying to understand the world of nontraditional therapies.

In the healing literature, I (Russell) found many different holistic and imaginative paths offering promising treatments for cancer. Some researchers described remarkable cures from the use of Laetrile from apricot pits. There were opportunities for coffee enemas in Mexico, and a healing retreat in the Alps run by the followers of Rudolph Steiner, where the doctors played string quartets for the patients after dinner. A highly regarded healing center in Texas was operated by Dr. Carl Simonton, who reported many remarkable cures of patients who took an active part in their healing through the use of self-healing visualizations.[5]

In California, the Commonweal Foundation offered a variety of supportive and nurturing therapies.[6] There was also the healing imagery approach of Jean Achterberg.[7] One that seemed the most appealing to me had the patient mentally picture the bad cancer cells being consumed by the good white blood cells. From the patient's point of view, the good news was that each of these approaches offered a few examples of people with very advanced cancer who followed these procedures and were cured. From the scientists' point of view, the bad news was that not a single one of these healing modalities supplied any statistics describing what fraction of the very sick people who were treated actually survived. It looked as though coffee enemas, string quartets, and visualization could each claim a few astonishing cures, but the odds didn't look very good. Given the choice, as I sat in my easychair surrounded by books, I thought that I would go with the string quartets. I've always loved Mozart.

The only researcher who offered encouraging data was H.J. Eysenck in England, who was a pioneer in supportive therapy for cancer.[8] His treatment was similar to Dr. David Spiegel's Expressive-Supportive Therapy that appeared, in research carried out at Stanford University, to be successful in helping women with breast cancer.[9] Eysenck convincingly showed that people who were socially isolated, or who rarely expressed their emotions — especially the so-called negative feelings of fear, anger, grief, or sadness — were significantly more likely to get cancer than emotionally expressive people. He found that repressed feelings were even more hazardous to your health than alcohol or cigarettes. To deal with these negative emotions, he created an approach that he called Creative Novation Therapy, in which he helped the patient to remake himself and change his attitudes and outlook on the world.[10]

Surgeon William Nolan wrote a book entitled *Healing: Doctor in Search of a Miracle*, in which he describes a patient who had metastatic abdominal cancer that was so advanced and invasive that it was impossible to remove.[11] Nolan sewed the man up and sent him home, without telling him that he expected him to die. A year later he saw the man shoveling snow outside his home in New York, where they both lived. Nolan was shocked to see the man alive. When the doctor asked him about his health, he thanked Nolan for taking such good care of him. He reported that he had been feeling fine ever since the operation! This miraculous cure stimulated Nolan to travel all over the world in search of other nontraditional healing. He visited many famous healers and healing centers, but always came away disappointed. His book chronicles his unsuccessful search for nonmedical cures, although he still believed that his personal miracle had occurred, because he had witnessed it himself.

The Institute of Noetic Sciences recently published an encyclopedic volume called *Spontaneous Remission*, written by O'Regan and Hirshberg, which catalogues several hundred well-documented cases in which people recovered from metastatic cancer, despite having truly been at death's door.[12] The following quotation by Dr. Lewis Thomas is from the introduction of that book, and summarizes the healing opportunity:

The rare but spectacular phenomenon of spontaneous remission of cancer persists in the annals of medicine, totally inexplicable but real, a hypothetical straw to clutch in the search for a cure. From time to time, patients turn up with advanced cancer far beyond the possibility of cure. They undergo exploratory surgery, the surgeon observes metastases throughout the peritoneal cavity and liver, and the patient is sent home to die, only to turn up again ten years later, free of disease and in good health. There are now several hundred such cases in world scientific literature, and no one doubts the validity of the observations.... But no one has the ghost of an idea how it happens.[13]

When the appointed time arrived for my chemotherapy to start, I was already feeling much better under Jane's encouragement. The doctors decided to take higher-resolution CAT scans to determine more precisely the nature and extent of my illness. The spots that had seemed so alarming from the initial pictures now appeared differently, and there seemed to be a question as to the correct diagnosis. They wanted to do a biopsy of my liver. I declined to do that, and preferred to wait for further developments, as I was feeling much better.

I have been well for the five years since Jane did healing treatments with me. We will never know if I actually had metastatic cancer, or if it was a misdiagnosis. What we do know for sure is that Jane's interactions with me saved me from chemotherapy, which quite likely would have killed me. The hospital is left with a similar pair of possibilities: Did they tell a well man that he had a terminal disease, or did a man with a terminal disease recover through the ministrations of a spiritual healer and immune-system coach? Neither outcome is attractive to medical science at the present time.

chapter nine

Minding the Body:
Significant Mind-Body Experiments

Science is not meant to cure us of mystery,
but to reinvent and reinvigorate it.
— Dr. Robert Sapolsky
Professor of Biology, Stanford University

Let knowledge grow from more to more,
Yet more of reverence in us dwell;
That mind and soul, according well,
May make one music as before....
— Alfred, Lord Tennyson

Throughout history, from the earliest of times, communities of people have recognized certain individuals in their midst who possessed a special gift of healing. In ancient Egypt, healers became revered advisors to the Pharaohs; in other cultures, they became founders of the world's great religions. Gautama Buddha, Jesus of Nazareth, and the prophet Muhammed were all known to be gifted healers.[1] The Hebrew prophets Elijah, Elisha, and Isaiah were acknowledged as healers as early as six or seven hundred years before Christ, and it is told that Moses healed many in Israel from serpent bites before that.[2] The first generations of Christians functioned primarily as a healing community.[3] Throughout Africa, Asia, and the Americas, tribal peoples have held their medicine men and healing shamans in highest esteem. As we look back in history, we see that the progression of thought in the Western world has not incorporated the broad range of knowledge, involving mind-to-mind healing connections, that has been effective in other cultures. We have much to learn about the role of consciousness in healing.

In the following pages, we describe several pioneering experiments that explore the role that one person's consciousness may have on another person's health. These studies demonstrate that focused mental attention can influence both the physical and mental processes of another person. Dr. William Braud, the director of research at the Institute of Transpersonal Psychology in Palo Alto, California, has referred to this intentional mental activity as "direct mental interaction." One interesting aspect of Braud's research is that the magnitude of the psychic benefit to the person being affected or helped is related to the degree of his or her need or acceptance of help.[4]

This chapter includes evidence for the effectiveness of remote mental suggestion, and the idea that distant hypnosis may account for some cases of distant psychic healing. This is not to say that all psychic healing derives from hypnotic influences, however.

Early research in hypnosis led to healing of psychogenic ailments and a wide variety of illnesses; hypnosis has been used for anesthesia during surgeries and amputations. The contemporary data for hypnosis at a distance shows that one person's mental processes of attention, intention, and imagery have the potential to interact with another distant person's psychological and physiological functioning.

In the Book of Exodus, God told Moses, "I am the Lord that healeth thee." Jesus told the Apostles to "heal the sick…and say unto them, the kingdom of God is come nigh unto you," and the Koran states that the Islamic revelation given to Muhammed "is a guidance and a healing for those who believe."[5] Prayer for healing is a central tenet of Christianity, Judaism, Islam, and even Zoroastrianism, a religion that has endured for over 2,500 years.[6] Indeed, the concept of healing body and soul has formed the essence of religious beliefs of tribes and cultures the world over. It is the foundation of some of their core attitudes about powers in the universe. We might even conjecture that if it were not for the healers and shamans from our earliest history, religious thought, as we know it today, might never have evolved.

For millennia, shamans and medicine men from Siberia to the Amazon have known and used healing practices, although the effectiveness of these practices was not discovered in Europe until the eighteenth century. Through all these years, a parade of shamanic drummers, dancers, diviners, herbalists, bone setters, trance mediums, spirit communicators, ritualizers, chanters, incanters, and exorcists have pursued their healing arts, about which we still have much to learn.[7]

In 1993, psychiatrist Dr. Daniel Benor brought together a compendium of over 150 controlled studies of psychic, mental, and spiritual healing on organisms as diverse as enzymes, cell cultures, bacteria, yeasts, plants, animals, and humans. More than half of the studies in his book *Healing Research* demonstrate significant effects of healers.[8] Nonetheless, the very possibility that nonlocal healing might offer valid therapy continues to challenge our prevailing worldview, especially in the United States.

In an article entitled "Healers and a Changing Medical Paradigm," Benor tells us that in the United Kingdom today, over 8,000 registered healers are officially recognized in the health-care system, and are certified to treat patients in over 1,500 government hospitals.[9] Physicians in private practice in Great Britain refer patients to healers, invite healers to practice in their clinics, and in some cases are themselves giving "paranormal" healing. The nonlocal healing therapies are known there as "spiritual," "faith," or "pranic" healing, or "bioenergy therapy." Healers in England regularly treat patients in government hospital centers for cardiac rehabilitation, pain, and cancer.

According to Benor, who founded a Doctor-Healer Network that publishes a newsletter in the United Kingdom, complementary healing therapies are being integrated with conventional treatment in Eastern Europe and Russia.[10] Some medical schools in Russia and Poland teach homeopathy and other alternative approaches to healing, and in Bulgaria, a government-appointed commission of scientists assesses healers' abilities and oversees their licensing. In fact, experiments investigating the efficacy of these nontraditional nonlocal healing modalities actually began in Europe in the eighteenth century.

MESMERISM AND HYPNOSIS

The charismatic German physician Franz Mesmer was, in 1779, the first person to systematically and scientifically investigate the healing of one person through the healing intentions of another. Although this sort of healing had been going on since the dawn of mankind, it appears that Mesmer was the first doctor to recognize the importance of strong rapport with his patients, as well as the relationship of psychological trauma to illness. In doing so, he led the vanguard of many courageous, unconventional, and effective healers to antagonize the medical establishment. He was also the first to utilize the trance-inducing techniques that have become the foundation of modern-day hypnosis therapy. He recognized the therapeutic benefits of human interactions for the treatment of nervous disorders, which he treated successfully.[11]

Mesmer had a theory that an invisible magnetic fluid flowed through the human body, animating it and promoting its health and vitality. He believed that sickness resulted from any blockage of the flow of this fluid, and that his therapeutic technique, known as Mesmerism, was able to restore the harmonious flow. This concept approximates the theories underlying the Hindu concept of prana, the Chinese concept of chi or qi, the Japanese ki, the mana of the Polynesian Kahuna healers, and the concepts underlying current ideas of bioenergy, which we discuss further in Chapter 10.

TRANSFUSION OF ENERGY OR TELEPATHY?

When Mesmer did his healing, he moved his hands up and down over the patient's body in a manner very similar to that of present-day practitioners of "energy" healing. Mesmer's charismatic personality, and his conception of transmitting magnetic fluid from his hands to the bodies of his patients, also have much in common with some twentieth-century religious healers who transfuse believers with the power of the Holy Spirit. Until a reliable "chi-meter" becomes available to document the actual transfer of this unusual energy, an alternative explanation may be that part of the healing effects of these processes is the result of a dynamic mind-to-mind interaction process.

The scorn and violent opposition that Mesmer encountered from the medical establishment of his time kept most doctors from experimenting with Mesmerism, despite its apparent efficacy. In the 1840s, the British doctor James Braid discovered that the hand passing over the body, the use of magnets, and Mesmer's magnetic fluid theory weren't necessary for healing. Braid found the process, which he named "hypnosis," to be a mind-to-mind phenomenon, and he was able to use mental suggestion to successfully anesthetize his patients for amputations and surgeries.[12]

Dr. James Esdaile also performed hundreds of surgical operations in India in the 1800s, using what he termed "magnetic sleep" to anesthetize his patients.[13] However, the British Royal Society continued to fervently reject ideas concerning the reality of either hypnosis or mind-to-mind communication in the field of medicine. Today, thousands of members of the American Society for Clinical Hypnosis help obstetricians and dentists perform painless operations without drugs, but it took over two hundred years for the utilization of these mind-to-mind therapies to be incorporated into medical treatment.

Franz Mesmer was the first physician to understand the remarkable healing potential of mental suggestion. He recognized that mesmeric-hypnotic phenomena were genuine and important, that they were essentially psychological in nature, and that they were valid subjects of scientific research.[14] Hypnosis as a face-to-face interaction has been studied for more than two centuries, demonstrating that a practitioner can affect a profound influence over his or her subject's health and physical functioning. These studies place hypnosis on a continuum with contemporary laboratory demonstrations of mind-to-mind interactions that are important analogs to psychic healing. It appears that the kind of mind-to-mind healing connections that we study today come to us with a two-hundred-year-old heritage of research by inspired investigators.

Hypnosis is described as a psychological state of an individual wherein functioning is at a level of awareness that differs from the ordinary state of consciousness. A hypnotized person's receptiveness and responsiveness to both positive and negative suggestion is heightened. The subject also gives as much significance to inner perceptions as they generally would to external reality.[15] It is well-known today that hypnotists are even able to cause functional blindness, deafness, and paralysis in hypnotized people.[16] Although Mesmer was able to cure many of these same afflictions in his patients, he was unaware of the potential negative aspects of hypnosis, the phenomenon of post-hypnotic suggestion, or of self-hypnosis.

We now recognize the potential danger of persons suffering adverse post-hypnotic reactions. For example, doctors have come to realize that pessimistic forecasts can have injurious effects on some patients. We are confident that a doctor's announcement that a patient has only a few months left to live, and that he should "put his affairs in order," might be as likely to cause the death of a suggestible patient as is the disease he is supposed to be suffering from.

Positive aspects of hypnosis have been effective in the removal of warts (which are actually small tumors) and for self-modification of blood flow, inflammation, burns, skin and musculoskeletal disorders, and asthma. This self-regulation of blood flow has allowed countless migraine sufferers to take personal charge of their disease. Hypnosis can also produce changes in a person's body temperature, enzyme secretion, learning ability, memory, and athletic performance.[17] It reveals potentialities within us that are ordinarily unavailable in our day-to-day lives. It's like finding a tool kit that we didn't even know we owned, and opening it to discover all kinds of tools within it that we unfortunately have no idea how to use.

A successful relationship between a healer and patient is very similar to that of the relationship between a hypnotist and his or her subject: Both patients of healers and hypnotic subjects must be willing, cooperative, and trusting. They must be relaxed, and believe that they can be healed (or hypnotized), and that the healer or hypnotist is competent and trustworthy.

Healees, as well as hypnotic subjects, must also believe that the process is safe, appropriate, and in agreement with his or her wishes.[18] Above all, the concept of rapport is primary for both processes.

These concepts were not so well understood, but they were used by the French physician Jean-Martin Charcot and the Viennese doctor Josef Breuer, who are acknowledged as the founders of modern psychoanalysis, as well as the teachers of Sigmund Freud.[19] Our interest in these practitioners is that they were the first healers to use suggestion in a clinical setting. Their experiments beginning in 1879 — 100 years after Mesmer — led them to discover that neurotic symptoms result from unconscious processes, and can be healed when they are brought to consciousness through the use of hypnosis. However, they thought that being in a hypnotized state was itself a diseased condition, and that hypnosis could only be used to cure extreme hysterical symptoms. Today we know that all illnesses have psychogenic components, so the term "neurotic symptoms" takes on new meaning.

We are aware that unconscious or autonomous processes affect our immune system, endocrine system, endorphins, blood flow, and muscle tension. We know from psychoneuroimmunology that we are often the victims of our own stray thoughts. Thus far in this chapter, we have been describing healing processes in which a healing practitioner was in proximity to the patient. However, the data from laboratory parapsychology experiments convincingly indicate that healers, doctors, or shamans can promote healing for a wide variety of illnesses and afflictions using distant mind-to-mind connections.

SUGGESTION AT A DISTANCE

Hypnosis is, of course, generally practiced in a face-to-face encounter, with the hypnotist talking directly to the patient. However, hypnosis research indicates that almost any person can cause another to become entranced, and that this effect can apparently be induced from a distance.

Hypnosis at a distance has been studied in the laboratory in Russia since the early part of the twentieth century. During the 1920s and '30s,

Russian physiologist and professor at the University of Leningrad, L.L. Vasiliev, conducted hundreds of hypnosis experiments with the direct support of Josef Stalin. Vasiliev researched hypnotic inductions done without words and often carried out at a distance from the hypnotized individual.[20] His work, along with some telepathy experiments carried out by J.B. Rhine, are among the best laboratory data we have for pure mind-to-mind connections that do not involve precognition or clairvoyance. His theory about "magnetic sleep," as it was named by his teacher Velinski, was that the mental commands given by the hypnotist traveled by way of electromagnetic fields that were generated when human muscles contracted, either voluntarily or convulsively. Vasiliev's book, *Experiments in Mental Suggestion*, first published in England in 1963, summarizes his and his colleagues' forty years of hypnosis studies at the Leningrad Institute for Brain Research.[21]

Official Soviet psi research in this century has prominently featured pain induction and behavioral manipulation from a distance. Vasiliev's most famous experiment was conducted between Leningrad and Sevastopol, with a distance of more than one thousand miles between the experimenter and the female subject, whom he could telepathically put to sleep and awaken.[22]

Vasiliev's research in the 1930s gave Western parapsychologists their earliest evidence that neither distance nor electromagnetic shielding reduced the accuracy or reliability of psychic functioning. Government-funded research of ESP and "biological imposition" from a distance in the Soviet Union began again in earnest in 1965, and frequently involved two experienced psychics who were able to communicate quite well with each other telepathically over long distances.[23]

STRANGULATION FROM A DISTANCE

The Russian actor Karl Nikolaev and his biophysicist friend Yuri Kamensky were well-known for their ability to telepathically transmit visual images to one another. Our friend parapsychologist Larissa Vilenskaya discussed with Kamensky the remarkable long-distance experiments he did with Nikolaev involving the transmission of feelings between Moscow and Leningrad.[24]

Vilenskaya told us that in one study, Kamensky transmitted feelings of severe pain; and in another, he even imagined that he was strangling his friend! He was so successful in his effort to distantly suffocate Nikolaev that the physicians monitoring the study became concerned that Nikolaev might actually die, so they stopped the test!

Interviews with Nikolaev in the 1970 book *Psychic Discoveries Behind the Iron Curtain* revealed how he had spent many years teaching himself Raja Yoga methods of breathing and relaxation, so that he would be more receptive to telepathic communication.[25] He was proud of his psychic capabilities, and welcomed the opportunities to demonstrate his ESP connection with Kamensky. However, he was greatly surprised when his partner sent him intense negative feelings instead of the images he was used to perceiving. When Vilenskaya asked Kamensky why he would want to transmit feelings of pain, strangulation, and physical blows in his research, he answered that he believed that negative emotions were transmitted more reliably and more strongly than happy or positive feelings.[26]

We don't necessarily agree that Kamensky's assessment is true in general, but in any case, this experiment clearly demonstrates the existence of telepathic connections independent of clairvoyant or precognitive perception.

In our opinion, this anecdote illustrates some fundamental differences between psychic and spiritual connections in general, and specifically between distant hypnosis and distant spiritual healing. They are alike in that they both involve nonlocal mind processes and exchange of information in ways we don't understand. In our opinion, distant hypnosis involves a fundamental *separation* of people on a psychic or mental level — one person doing directed mental activity, exerting personal effort, and willing a specific outcome for another that is not necessarily in accord with the other's wishes. In contrast, distant spiritual healing occurs as a manifestation of a *joining of minds*, resonance, and entering into a universal consciousness. It involves a surrender of individual will on the part of the healer, with no personal effort exerted, no specific outcome designated on the physical level, and a state of being that is characterized by a "letting" instead of a doing. This letting is a willingness to be an instrument of the general well-being of another in an impersonal, nonemotional way. That state has been called a state of compassion or love, and it activates spiritual healing, which we believe is the manifestation of spiritual consciousness in human awareness.

RECENT MIND-BODY RESEARCH IN THE FORMER SOVIET UNION

Larissa Vilenskaya and Dr. Edwin May did parapsychology research together for several years at May's government-funded laboratory in Menlo Park, California. While employed at Scientific Applications International Corporation, they spent two months in Russia in 1992 and 1993, investigating current parapsychology research in the former Soviet Union.

May and Vilenskaya report that the Russians continue to emphasize distant mental effects on living systems in their research.[27] Most Soviet parapsychologists have little doubt that a person's focused mental attention can influence the responses of living organisms. That belief is a long-standing part of the Russian folk tradition and culture. Government-funded parapsychological research continues to be carried out at the state universities of both Moscow and St. Petersburg, as well as at the Russian and the Ukrainian Academies of Science.

The most provocative research being done are studies showing distant telepathic interference in people's thinking and brain wave processes, and retarding their mental and physical reaction time. They report that distant psychic influences have also been observed to affect changes in the structures of animal cells that are responsible for neurotransmitter secretions. These changes in nervous system secretions affect animals' stress levels, and disrupt their health and immune-system activity, as well as their social behavior. Soviet researchers have demonstrated distant mental effects on the eating behavior of white mice, and remote mental interference of people attempting to solve math problems, or do memory-related tasks.

Dr. Sergei Speransky, a Russian biologist with a specialty in toxicology, told parapsychologist Larissa Vilenskaya, who has known him for over twenty years, that he has been studying ESP among social groups of mice, as well as humans' ability to affect animal ESP. In double-blind experiments, electronic engineering specialist Leonid Porvin, in Moscow, was able to significantly affect the eating behavior of mice 1,700 miles away in Novosibirsk, using photographs of the target mice, and a special technique for achieving altered states of consciousness conducive to distant influence. In another experiment, when mice from certain social groups were starved, their litter mates, who had been separated for the study, reacted by eating significantly more.

The Russians have apparently done research that involves the poisoning, irradiating, injuring, and stressing of a variety of animals. This research then calls for a healer-type of distant influencer to successfully block some of the threatening effects. They use these animals to study the injurious effects that a distant mental influencer can have on humans. They also use animals as biological detectors of when distant humans are psychically attempting to harm other people's mental and physical processes (similar to underground miners' use of canaries to indicate when the air supply is inadequate). Research is also being done on the disorienting effects of electromagnetic fields on animal and cell behavior, and on the ability of a trained distant influencer to block these injurious effects.

The focus of much of the Russian psi research is certainly highly disturbing. We are not at all surprised, however, that their research shows that a distant mental influencer can have great effect on people and other living systems. This is because their data are in line with the results of many well-conducted experiments of distant telepathy done in the United States over the past forty years. Our interest in this type of research is on healing, of course, but there has never been either a human or mechanical capability or element that can't be used for both good and evil. The same glass of water that can nourish a goldfish can drown a mouse.

The Russians have reported many diverse experiments involving distant mind-to-mind connections, but the majority of the studies are carried out by solo researchers. From a scientific point of view, what is lacking in the vast body of Soviet research — besides reverence for consciousness and life in all its forms — are systematic series of experiments replicated between laboratories. Each of the mind-body studies that we describe below was conducted in coherent experimental series. Together, the research presents a significant body of data supporting the concept of distant healing effects.

MIND-TO-MIND OR MIND-TO-BODY?

In 1965, Douglas Dean, at the Newark College of Engineering, showed conclusively that the autonomic nervous systems of subjects in his laboratory responded to the thoughts of a distant person.[28] Participants lay quietly in a darkened room, while a plethysmograph optically measured changes in their fingers' blood volume. These changes provide a measure of autonomic nervous activity. The sender, seated in another room, looked at randomly ordered cards with names on them, and tried to mentally transmit the names. The distant participants' autonomic activity increased markedly when the sender focused his or her attention on names that had personal significance for the participant (mother, sweetheart, stockbroker, etc.), as compared with random phone book names. At the same time, the participant was unaware of when the significant names were being observed by the experimenter.

UNDERWATER TELEPATHY

Because the experiment just described took place during the Cold War, Dean thought that his demonstration of a robust mental telegraph might be useful for communication with submerged submarines. He proceeded to conduct a successful underwater experiment where an experimenter was given a slate on which the significant target names were written in grease pencil, and then she went scuba diving to a 35-foot depth. The emotional content of the key names was successfully transmitted to a distant percipient connected to a plethysmograph. The experiment showed that seawater was not a barrier to psi.[29]

Rather than assuming that the agent somehow directly affected the subject's vascular system, we interpret the changes in the subject's blood volume to be an example of mind-to-mind interaction.

An interesting note about Dean is that his success with plethysmographic telepathy led him to examine the ESP of business executives. His remarkable finding was that in precognition tests, the managers from companies that were having major growth showed statistically significant ESP, while those from failing companies had significant negative ESP, or "psi-missing."[30] That is, they may well use their psychic ability to determine the right answer, but then do something different.

CALMNESS OR AROUSAL INFLUENCE FROM A DISTANCE

For over two decades, Dr. William Braud has conducted more than 30 experiments, involving over 650 testing sessions, examining the "direct mental influence of living systems." Braud has demonstrated that it is possible for one person's mental processes to telepathically affect those of another person, both directly and from a distance. With surprising reliability, his research, along with that of his associate Marilyn Schlitz, has shown that a subject in the laboratory can influence the physiological reactions of distant people by using methods of focused mental attention.[31]

Many of these studies were done by Braud, or by Braud and Schlitz, at the Mind Science Foundation in San Antonio, Texas. They measured people's attempts to affect other distant persons' autonomic nervous system processes, as measured by changes in their galvanic skin response (GSR), blood pressure, or slight, unconscious muscle movements. The influencer did not need to know whether or not his or her attempts to interact with the other person's system were successful for the galvanic skin responses of the distant people to be affected.

In all of these studies, two participants who had met each other briefly were situated in separate rooms for twenty-minute research sessions. During randomly determined periods, the influencer used mental techniques that had been found by Braud to be successful in previous experiments to affect a distant person's mental or physical reactions. Some of these strategies that he had studied include relaxation, centering or focusing attention, imagery or visualization, prayer or effortless intentionality, and evocation of strong positive emotions.[32]

The autonomic activity of the recipient was monitored (via electrodes connected to a computer system) when the influencer was using these techniques. The person being influenced did not know anything about the timing of the randomly interspersed influence or noninfluence periods.[33]

In fact, I (Jane) was an influencer in one of Braud's experimental series to see if one person could mentally affect another isolated person's electrodermal activity (GSR) from a distance. William Braud himself was the subject to be influenced. We had both realized that we had good rapport with one another during my initial intake interview. I had volunteered for the study, because I had been doing healing work off and on for ten years by that time, and had often experienced psychically merging my consciousness with another person.

Braud had asked me during the interview, "What does it feel like when you are doing healing?" I closed my eyes as I answered him, so that I could more precisely describe the vibrating light, heat, and colors that I experience during a healing interaction. I created an image of colored light in my mind's eye that was similar to what I would experience during what seemed like "a good connection" with a patient. Just as I started to describe the indigo and rose colors in the blue-centered target configuration that I was imagining, he asked me, "Are you seeing a target-like image, with dark blue in the bull's eye?" I was impressed, and answered yes. He asked again, "Is there pink around the perimeter?" "Uh-huh," I agreed.

I was shocked, but then I gathered my composure, and thought to myself, "Of course, he knows all about this, he has hundreds of subjects in his research, it's entirely routine for him...." So I said, "I guess this is all old hat for you. You probably do this with lots of people, all the time." And he surprised me by answering, "Oh, no. This is a first for me!" I was amazed. Then he told me that he would be the subject to be influenced in my experimental trials.

During the research sessions, Braud relaxed in a comfortable, overstuffed chair in a dimly lit room on the other side of the building from where I was. His chair was facing a fantastic color organ that he had constructed, which generated a variety of stimulating colors in syncopation with music coming through his earphones. There were electrodes attached to his wrists, and I could tell, from the fairly even recording of his GSR that was within my view, that he was very skilled at maintaining a relaxed state during the control and rest periods.

A computer-generated noise signaled to me when to start and stop trying to influence Braud. There were 30-second intervals of either influence or control times, which were randomly interspersed between 120-second rest periods. Those rest periods were most welcome! I was amazed at how much effort I put forth, very intently trying to arouse him, silently, with my mind.

Back then, I believed I needed to work very hard to excite someone from a distance. I broke out in a sweat, as the intensity of my effort would build. And then, after thirty seconds of strenuous concentration, I was to break off all connection with him, instantaneously. That was the most difficult task of all! For that, I tried all sorts of tactics, such as reciting the alphabet backwards to myself, in various rhythms, while I tried to pat my head and rub my tummy in a different rhythm, alternating directions clockwise and counterclockwise, while I marched around the room. If anyone had observed my antics, it would probably have been very entertaining.

I tried many different strategies to alarm, excite, startle, or bother him, as I continuously checked the instrument recording his reactions to learn which tactics were most effective. Writing about it now, I can understand how an experienced and effective stage actor, as was the Soviet psychic Nikolaev, would be successful at evoking and projecting such emotions to another person. It was difficult for me to self-monitor my "connectedness" to Braud, while simultaneously trying to startle him. I rarely feel highly angered or stressed, so it was unfamiliar for me to engender such intense feelings of arousal and agitation within myself. The experimental task did not at all resemble the peaceful, blissful feeling I was used to experiencing from connecting with people in healing interactions.

Overall, the experiment was successful. Now I know that the quality of the mind-to-mind connection and one's intentions are the important factors in distant mental influence, rather than the energy exerted in the trying and "doing."

Later, while relating our experiences to one another after each day's experimental series, we found that on many occasions, Braud had perceived the very same images and feelings that I had been trying to immerse and surround him with telepathically. When I sent him creepy crawly spiders, he felt them! For that particular experiment, I was asked to try to raise the GSR of the subject, so my intention was to startle, excite, or disturb him. Increasingly, in the past years, Braud has conducted experiments in which the agent tries to be helpful, or tries to promote peaceful experiences or improved mental functioning of the subject.

KNOWING YOU'RE BEING STARED AT FROM A DISTANCE

Additional studies by Braud and Schlitz showed that if a person simply paid full attention to a distant person whose physiological activity was being monitored, he or she could influence that person's autonomic galvanic skin responses. In four separate experiments involving seventy-eight sessions, one person stared intently at a closed-circuit TV monitor image of the distant participant, and influenced the remote person's electrodermal (GSR) responses. No intentional focusing or mental imaging techniques were used by the influencer, other than staring at the "staree's" image on the video screen during randomly interspersed staring and nonstaring control periods.[34]

In these studies, Braud and Schlitz discovered something even more interesting than this telepathically induced effect on our unconscious system. They found that the most anxious and introverted people being stared at had the greatest magnitudes of unconscious electrodermal responses. In other words, the shy and introverted people reacted with significantly more stress to being stared at than did the sociable and extroverted people.[35] This experiment gives scientific validation to the common human experience of feeling stared at and turning around to find that someone is, indeed, staring at you.

DISTANT MENTAL INFLUENCE VIA TV?

Marilyn Schlitz and Stephen LaBerge, at the U.S. government-funded laboratory of Science Applications International Corporation in Menlo Park, California, successfully replicated Braud and colleagues' experiments, making some interesting changes in the protocol. In 1993, they measured the extent to which people unconsciously sense the telepathic influence of a distant person who is looking at their video image.[36] Again, the two participants were only briefly acquainted. In these studies, however, the observer was instructed to attempt to excite, arouse, or startle the person whose video image they were staring at. Schlitz's and LaBerge's work differed from the previous work by Braud and Schlitz, because in the earlier studies, the influencer simply stared at the video image, without trying to influence the staree directly. Also, in the Schlitz and LaBerge experiment, the influencer was specifically trying to increase the arousal response of the recipient.

Parapsychologist Larissa Vilenskaya was one of the starers in the successful Schlitz and LaBerge experiment. She describes her experience in the video staring experiment to the authors in the following paragraphs:

> When there was someone whom I met only briefly before the test, I always asked the person's first name — somehow, it seemed important to me. During the "staring" periods, I called the person silently by his or her name and tried to draw their attention by mentally communicating some urgency. I imagined that the person turned his or her head to look at me, while I silently projected the message, "Look at me! I need to talk to you!" This was done mostly in images, rather than words.
>
> Other urgent messages I sent with the intent to elicit the attention of the person were, "I'm very cold! Please help me and bring a blanket!" or "I'm in danger! Help!" I sometimes also imagined that he was the one in danger needing my help. I tried to get his attention, so I could help him.

This body of mental influence research carried out primarily by Braud and Schlitz used to be called biological psychokinesis, or Bio-PK. Today it has the more descriptive title of Distant Mental Interaction with Living Systems (DMILS). The effect of systematic manipulation of a distant person's physiological responses by video observation has obvious important implications. Governments, both at home and abroad, have been investigating whether world leaders could be influenced by a psychic practitioner watching a video image — an idea often exploited in science fiction.

An additional implication for us as a community of spirit is the influence that the violence in films and TV has on all of us, and not just on those doing the viewing. Violent imagery engenders fear and distrust, which in turn promote psychic defensiveness, and separation from unity-consciousness. As the amount of gratuitous violence we tolerate as a society escalates, the mind-to-mind connections that are our natural inheritance will diminish. It becomes increasingly difficult to maintain trusting, open hearts in daily life within a community of disconnected, fearful people. Our thoughts as well as our defensiveness have far greater effects than most of us realize.

More recently Schlitz carried out a landmark experiment, showing the great importance of the state of mind and expectations of the researchers on the outcome of the experiment. Skeptical English psychologist Richard Wiseman had unsuccessfully conducted three careful attempts to replicate the staring experiments we have just described. Their failure was completely in line with his view of psi. On hearing of his failure to replicate her experiments, Marilyn proposed a collaborative study with Wiseman. Using the same laboratory, a common protocol, and the same subject pool that Wiseman used, Schlitz again demonstrated a successful outcome. The participants whose video image was being stared at showed significant physiological responses, as opposed to when they were being ignored. Wiseman again fulfilled his negative expectation and found no effect, clearly demonstrating that the consciousness of the experimenter profoundly affects what he or she gets to observe.[37]

THOUGHTS AFFECTING DISTANT HUMAN BLOOD CELLS

Dr. William Braud also did remarkable experiments that reveal connections between the thoughts and mental images of an individual and the activities of distant cells. We reported this study previously in Chapter 4, when we described some of the greatest ESP experiments of the century. Braud demonstrated that people were able to significantly affect the rate of hemolysis, or bursting, of red blood cells in a test tube of water, situated in a distant room. The participants were able to mentally protect the cells by directing their attention to them, and by visualizing the cells remaining intact, in spite of the pressure on their membranes to rupture. In blind studies, there was a slight tendency for people to be able to protect their own blood cells better than the cells of another person.[38]

Braud has discussed the implications of his experiments for the existence of distant healing, and suggests that these same mind-to-cell interactions may take place within one's own body, either some or all of the time. He postulates that similar mind-to-cell interactions may be occurring during the staring and electrodermal experiments he conducts.

Physician and author Deepak Chopra has presented the idea that living cells respond to consciousness. In his classic books *Quantum Healing* and *The Seven Spiritual Laws of Success*, Chopra addresses many aspects of mind-to-mind connections in healing that are related to Braud's research, as well as to concepts considered in this book.[39]

HELPING DISTANT PEOPLE TO FOCUS THEIR ATTENTION

Braud's more recent work investigated telepathic effects on people's emotional, social, and cognitive activities. In research reported in 1995, subjects successfully concentrated their attention on helping isolated participants in a distant room to stay focused on an object.[40] In addition, Braud found that the subjects who had the most difficulty in focusing their attention at the beginning of the experiment showed the most significant improvement with telepathic help. He notes that this effect is similar to those discovered by Bernard Grad in his research (which we discussed in Chapter 4), where healing resulted only with stressed plants, not healthy ones.[41] Braud's latest experiment involving people psychically helping others from a distance suggests that meditation by a critical number of people may be able to calm the minds of others in the local geographic vicinity. Isn't that a hopeful thought?

SUCCESSFUL HEALING PRAYER IN A HOSPITAL

In 1983, physician Randolph Byrd carried out a large clinical experiment at San Francisco General Hospital to test the efficacy of prayer for healing.[42] Over a period of 10 months, he studied the effects of intercessory or helpful prayer on 393 patients hospitalized with heart disease. Byrd's study showed that the patients who had received prayer experienced fewer medical complications, including a lower incidence of pneumonia. The prayed-for group also required significantly less ventilatory assistance, and fewer antibiotics and diuretics, than did the patients who had received no intercessory prayer.

This study illustrates how difficult it is to separate distant healing effects from outcomes that may be due to other causes. For instance, the research did not include any method of determining whether the people who were assigned to pray actually did pray, or if the people who got better had better coping styles, or other psychological characteristics that would account for their improvement. On the other hand, the control group may also have received helpful healing prayers from friends or family members, which could have masked an even greater distant healing effect.

We recognize that there is no perfect research: It is always possible to criticize a study after the fact. We feel that in this work, however, the principle variables have been well balanced between the prayed-for and the control group. This pioneering investigation by a courageous researcher will go down in history as a landmark study. The apparent effectiveness of healing prayer as demonstrated in this experiment would be advertised on television, just like Bufferin and Excedrin, if prayers were a profit-making drug.

DISTANT PSYCHIC HEALING IN ISRAEL

In Israel, Zvi Bentwich and Shulamith Kreitler reported research in 1994 indicating that patients in Kaplan Hospital who received distant healing recovered faster from hernia operations than patients who did not.[43] Fifty-three patients recovering from hernia operations were randomly assigned to one of three groups: one group received verbal suggestions that they would recover rapidly, another group was the focus of distant healing, and the third group served as controls. The healing procedure was determined by the healer herself, who asked only to be informed as to the time of the operation. No other contact between the patients and the healer took place, and neither the experimenters nor physicians knew which group the patients had been assigned to.

The "healed" patients did significantly better in four ways than the other patients: their surgical scars, as evaluated by the doctor, healed faster; they had fewer cases of elevated temperature; and they experienced less pain, and more improvement in other attitudinal factors.

DISTANT HEALING WITH AIDS PATIENTS

In 1995, Dr. Elisabeth Targ of the California Pacific Medical Center and Fred Sicher of the Sausalito Consciousness Research Laboratory conducted a double-blind pilot study of the effects of distant healing intention with twenty AIDS patients. They wanted to examine whether there would be any difference in outcome from working with "psychic healers" rather than with a prayer group such as Dr. Byrd used in his earlier healing experiment. In this six-month study, the goal was to examine whether the healed group would live longer, feel better, and have improved T-cell concentrations compared with the control group. Results of this pilot study were considered encouraging enough to attract funding for a larger replication study, with forty AIDS patients, completed in 1997. Dr. Targ reports that the results strongly bolster those of the first study.[44]

CONCLUDING THOUGHTS

It is clear to the authors from more than thirty years of investigations that one's physiological functioning can be affected by the thoughts of another person. We do not yet know the causal mechanism involved, but the results are indisputable.

The experience that psychic, spiritual, and energy healers have in reducing the pain and stress of a patient may be the best evidence we have in all of psychical research for a direct mind-to-mind connection between people. Of course, not every case of a healer's interaction with a person spontaneously recovering from pain is evidence of a psychic event. There are several possible explanations that must be considered in any situation where a healing professional interacts successfully to decrease the pain of a suffering person.

Psychiatrist Elisabeth Targ delineates three hypotheses for healing outcomes. The first is that when a healer is present with the patient, the healer's presence may cause a distraction from the pain, or psychologically enhance relaxation of the patient. Relaxation of the musculature of a distressed person almost always produces a reduction in pain, and this process need not involve any ESP whatsoever.

Secondly, a healer (either distantly or in the presence of a patient) may psychically guide the patient in using naturally endowed self-healing capabilities. Stimulation of the endocrine system, endorphin production, or a psychoneuroimmunological response may be promoted psychically, in that all of these systems are known to be susceptible to ordinary mental and psychological influences.

A third factor to be considered in healer-patient interactions is psychokinesis. This term refers to a possible direct interaction between a healer's mind and a patient's body.

I (Jane) add a fourth hypothesis for healing outcomes. That is, healing information may be manifested through the focused consciousness of a caring person or healer who surrenders his or her individuality, and is willing to be used as a vehicle of spiritual healing. Such a healing message would involve a greater consciousness, different from what an individual healer alone could provide.

As stated previously, we don't assume that every case of surprising spontaneous recovery from pain or illness has a psychic or spiritual component. However, we feel those cases that do appear to involve some form of distant healing make a strong argument for a mind-to-mind hypothesis, rather than that the healer directly affects the physiological processes of the patient.

In this chapter we have discussed the relevant research in the field of healing that suggests a relationship between a healer's focused intention and physical changes in human patients. Our feeling is that a spiritual healer may facilitate a connection between an organizing and purposeful principle (which some people call God) and the healee. Jane's sense is that the experience she has in healing interactions may enable an influx of information that "activate[s] the healee's self-healing capabilities in the direction of balance, and away from previously distorting or interfering influences."[45]

In addition, some healers may well have the potential for changing the electrostatic charge and temperature of their hands. This effect might create a type of local field that is effective for healing, such as in promoting muscle relaxation, and affecting the vasculature of the patient, which would, in turn, promote the reduction of pain, itching, and swelling of tissues. In a comprehensive review of mental healing experiments, psychologist Dr. Jerry Solfvin concluded that such healing probably involved both interpersonal as well as transpersonal elements, or what we are calling local as well as nonlocal processes.[46]

William Braud has written that the effort to isolate the type or source of the psi in psychic healing is misguided. "In short," he says:

> I don't think it is a useful question to ask. Indeed, the "bottom line" of all psi findings seems to be a lesson that such questions about who's doing the psi, what type of psi is it, etc. are not appropriate ones, and that such questions presuppose a worldview that is different from the one that psi findings are presenting to us.[47]

The emerging view of psi is that it is a "dynamic *process* that involves *a field of persons and events* — a field that is transspatial, transtemporal, and transpersonal (to again quote Braud)."[48]

We have described the evidence that makes us believe that the interaction between healer and healee in distant healing is primarily mind-to-mind rather than mind-to-body in nature. The reason is at least twofold: In the

field of parapsychology research, there has been high-quality, well-repli-
cated laboratory evidence for over forty years documenting the existence of
a mind-to-mind connection. The evidence for mind-to-body influence is
much less robust at this time. In addition, there is much uncontested evidence that both hypnosis and placebo effects can alleviate pain and enhance
healing, and that they both can be, and are, stimulated by mental activity
and can be seen as forms of mind-to-mind connections.

It is possible that the nondistant healing that Jane and others have done
may be due to the power of suggestion, even though they have not been
trained in hypnosis. It's important to point out that no one really understands how "hypnosis" or "suggestion" actually works. Founding member
of the British Society for Psychical Research and prominent psi-researcher
Frederic Myers wrote in 1903 that such words are by no means explanations, even though they may help us describe the conditions under which
the phenomena occur. He said they are "mere names which disguise our
ignorance" concerning the nature of mind and consciousness.[49]

We have not explained all or even most of the mysteries of healing. I
(Jane) do not believe that research experiments explain the role of prayer, or
what seem to be spirit helpers, in healing. We certainly don't know the
mechanism for clairvoyant diagnosis and prescription. Scientists have not
yet proved or disproved the existence of a life energy that millions of people
for twenty-five centuries have called prana, chi, ki, or bioenergy. Nor have
they shown that the intention to harm is greater or less than the power of
loving intentions to help or heal.

What is true for me is that the research we have described here has
inspired me to continue to practice healing interactions, despite the skepticism of our times. My deepest belief is that there is meaning in illness, and
that a primary element inherent in our physical and emotional dis-ease has
to do with the opportunities it presents for expanded awareness of our
mind-to-mind connections. This idea been beautifully expressed in a quotation from Larry Dossey's *Meaning & Medicine*:

> We tend to think that the purpose of prayer [or healing] is to termi-
> nate sickness, but we forget that the purpose of sickness may be to

initiate prayer, or, more generally, a consciousness of the infinite.[50]

— Brad Lemley

I am grateful to the researchers we have cited, and to all the others we have not mentioned, for their dedication to a field of inquiry that provokes much scorn and fear. They have given me the courage to continue to express an attribute that I do not understand, with the hope that it continues to be of value to those in need of healing.

In words expressed by the nineteenth-century poet, A.H. Clough, I ask,

That true results may yet appear,
Of what we are, together, here.

chapter ten

W a y s   o f
H e a l i n g

A little science estranges men from God, much science leads them back to Him.
— Louis Pasteur

That they all may be one; as thou, Father, art in me, and I in thee, that they also may be one in us. . . .
— John 17:21, Holy Bible

VARIETIES OF HEALING EXPERIENCES

Although my (Jane's) invitation to healing came to me in a dream — as described in Chapter 7 — I believe anyone can learn to heal, though some people may have more talent than others. Some would say I gave myself permission to do healing in my dream, but I say I received a "calling." Receiving the instructions while sleeping, as I did, merely made the inclination to practice spiritual healing more compelling.

In any case, I believe the kind of healing I do — spiritual healing — differs from remote viewing and psychic or energy healing, in that it entails the belief in a unifying force in the universe that transcends the healer's (or any other individual's) separate identity. For me, spiritual healing involves a belief in a nonlocal primary consciousness; and this consciousness expresses itself or unfolds through a channel created when a healer shifts his or her attention from self-consciousness to helping another, and from separateness to joining together.

223

I do not refer to spiritual healing as "faith healing" because openness, or suspension of disbelief, rather than faith, is necessary on the part of the patient. I participate by surrendering my own will and entering a nonordinary state of consciousness, so that a transpersonal mind may express itself through the opening provided by my willingness to be its vehicle. This merging of consciousness for the purpose of healing entails trust by both patient and healer. In my practice, it also embodies the concept that giving is receiving. I believe that my participation in a healing interaction lifts my consciousness as well as the consciousness of the patient. We make contact with a universal consciousness together, and I believe that connection permits a spiritual power to affect human activity.

I give my attention, and receive an experience of an expanded state of awareness during healing — my very being becomes activated with consciousness, and my body feels infused with light. Doing healing feels much like the life-changing dream experience that I described in Chapter 7. I begin each healing interaction with faith that something lawful, but as yet unexplainable, will occur; and then I experience it occurring. I perceive its activity by inner sensations of vibrations, movement, and colors; and overwhelming feelings of inner bliss and peace. Observable changes in a patient's physical symptoms are made possible by our mind-to-mind connection.

Spiritual healers are primarily concerned with a way of being, whereas other types of healers attend to the sick person's body, and try to heal the patient's physical symptoms. They direct their attention outward, and concentrate on replenishing or manipulating the sick person's "energy flow." Energy healers do this in the presence of the patient, using their fingers or the palms of their hands. Reiki, Therapeutic Touch, pranic healing, and Chi Gong are examples of this type of subtle energy healing. Psychic healers, on the other hand, are able to manipulate symptoms with their minds from a distance. I believe that psychic healing, energy healing, and spiritual healing belong in different experiential categories, though each of them involves nonlocal mind connections, and each may promote healing. I have participated in both spiritual and so-called energy healing, and some recent healing experiences I have had with family members illustrate the differences.

A DAY IN THE LIFE OF A HEALER

My older brother realized that he was seriously ill when he collapsed on the tennis court in exhaustion, after failing to catch his breath during a coughing spell. Until then he had played tennis and golf regularly. He thought he had the flu, because of his weakness, coughing, and dizziness, so he went to bed. After many days of rest, he felt weaker than before, and his coughing jags were longer and more intense. So he went to the doctor, and after some tests, he learned that one of his heart valves was damaged. As a result of congestive heart failure, fluid had gathered in his chest cavity and was crowding his lungs, causing his coughing. My brother then had open-heart surgery to replace the faulty heart valve. But his heart muscle was still so weak that he was unable to regain his energy, and he failed to recuperate.

He experienced long bouts of coughing and pain, he had difficulty catching his breath, and he felt tired and dizzy most of the time. Attempting to talk wore him out, and chewing and swallowing food was so difficult that his weight dropped to 125 pounds. I lived a thousand miles away from him and I had gone on vacation after his surgery, so I was not aware of his condition. On the day I found out about it, I had just returned and was too tired to make the trip to visit him. So I got very serious about distant healing.

I went to bed in the early evening and entered into a deep state of prayer. I asked God to let my heart beat for my brother's heart. I willed that my strength be his, to give a boost to his system. "Jump-start his heart," I thought, as I drifted down through a dark tunnel of mind, and floated into an ocean of light. Then my prayer changed into a state of surrender — a prayer asking to join in being of service to the highest good for my brother.

A great sense of peace enveloped me, and I remember thinking that maybe I was the one who needed to accept any outcome for my brother. I don't believe that death is the end, or a tragedy. But I do believe impending death is an opportunity to express love. I knew that not enough loving words had been expressed to my brother, or among *any* of my family members. I became so tranquil that I had no wish to move my body, and didn't even seem able to. I don't know how long I lay on my bed in that deep, loving silence, but I will never forget what shocked me out of the reverie.

I was jolted to waking consciousness by the thumping of my own heart-beat! Whump! Whump! Whump! My whole upper body pulsed with each throb. I could hear my blood being pumped out of my heart and into my arteries, and incoming blood surging into an empty heart chamber before the muscle contracted to squeeze it out again. Thrr-ump! Thrr-ump! Thrr-ump! The beats were so loud that they echoed in my ears. The force of my heart contracting so violently took my breath away, and it almost hurt. "Am I having a heart attack?" I wondered. I was frightened. I unbuttoned my shirt and uncovered my chest so I could watch this amazing phenomenon. I was able to see my heart muscle contract and rise as it throbbed under my skin, all the while emitting dull thumps. After many minutes, the thumping sub-sided, and my chest stopped pounding. I lay in my bed in silence once again.

I wanted to believe that my experience was somehow related to the improved functioning of my brother's heart, but I never thought I would receive any sort of confirmation about it. I knew that if my brother died, and I hadn't done absolutely everything I could to help him live, I would have a difficult time forgiving myself. I also knew that part of his failure to recuperate had to do with his social isolation — he had moved to a distant state, and had become out of touch with most of his longtime friends. He had, in fact, been deeply troubled — failing to thrive for quite some time before his heart failed.

I knew that I needed to let my brother know he was loved. I decided to do one of the riskiest things I've ever done in my life. It was also for me an ultimate act of love. I decided to telephone my brother's friends from the distant past, and ask them to pray for him. I told them that if they pre-ferred, they could call him on the phone. Although he was too weak to speak, he would be able to hear their voice and feel their caring.

This experience proved to be so powerful for both my brother and myself, that, when someone comes to me for spiritual healing, I now often suggest asking for prayers from friends. In my brother's case, I did not expect that many of his friends would act on the suggestion, thinking that most of them probably did not pray, or believe in any community of spirit.

To my surprise, my colleague Russell encouraged me. "I don't pray as you do," he said. "But if someone asked me to pray for my friend, I would do it. Give people the chance to know how sick your brother is, and let them decide for themselves." So I did. And it was definitely worth the risk.

I went to see my brother the next day. When I arrived at the house where he was resting, his girlfriend Sandy came outside to meet me. She said he seemed better, but he was still very tired. She told me it was wonderful that I had called his friends — several of them had telephoned, and their caring voices really cheered him up. Then she told me that the previous night, something very remarkable had happened. I include her story here in her own words:

> He went to bed right after dinner, before I did. I was getting ready for bed, and he called out to me that he could hear his heart suddenly start to pump, and that he could actually feel his heart valves working. He exclaimed, "It's so loud, it's going to keep me awake!" I became very concerned, and wondered if he was all right. I went over to him, and I was going to put my head on his chest. Before I even got there, I could hear his heart pounding! Boom-boom; boom-boom. Like a tom-tom drum. My face was still at least twelve inches from him. It was that loud — I didn't even have to put my ear on his chest! It was fast and loud.
>
> We went to sleep, and we could still hear his heart pounding. When we woke up, we didn't hear it anymore. It was just that one night that we heard his heart beat so loud.

This was my most profound experience of distant healing to date — and it seemed to be the turning point in my brother's recovery. What my brother and I experienced that day during a healing interaction was also quite amazing.

My brother felt comfortable watching a football game on TV as I began my healing meditation sitting cross-legged on his bed. He continued to watch the game while I held my hands near to his body and cleared my mind to attune to him. It took many minutes to calm my mind because I had been so shocked by his pale, thin appearance. He seemed like a shrunken skeleton to me. In short, I was very upset, which is not usually the case when I begin a healing session.

In a very few minutes, however, I felt the familiar peace and light flow through me, and I felt intimately connected to my brother. I was at one with him, in a deep, loving space. He closed his eyes, his head fell back on the pillow, and he seemed to enter into a peaceful state of reverie. I turned down the TV with the remote control and ran my right hand above the front of his body, which was clothed and under the covers. When my hand, about six inches above him, came to his left chest area, it was blocked from continuing down over his torso. My palm felt as if it were being deeply scratched by jagged splinters sticking out of the end of a rotten board. I had never before experienced such a strong sensation as that during healing. It shocked me out of my peaceful state. I was so surprised that I repeated the move with my hand, and I felt the same painful scratching sensation in my palm.

I felt a natural inclination to smooth over the jagged splintered-feeling area with my hand, still six inches over the bedclothes. I continued to do that with my eyes closed, feeling very peaceful once again. I felt enclosed in light, even infused with light. I felt transparent, and highly energized. After a few timeless minutes, my hand slipped past where the sharp splinters had been. Again I was startled out of my dreamy state. I opened my eyes, and repositioned my hand a few inches over my brother's upper chest. As I brought my palm over the area, my hand again slid rapidly past the place where it had previously been scratched and blocked.

At that very moment, my brother said, "I just felt my blood flowing through my heart — I felt my heart valves start working. It felt clogged there, and now it's flowing through. I could feel it. You did it. I would never have believed this if I hadn't experienced it!"

I withdrew my arm, and expected him to become alert and continue talking to me. Instead, to my great surprise, without opening his eyes or saying anything more, he went into what seemed to be a very deep sleep. He began to make such loud noises that I was shocked and dismayed. The rhythmic noises were a combination of loud snoring and intense choking when he inhaled; and moaning, choking, and fluid bubbling when he exhaled. I was afraid he might be choking to death. It was so loud that I couldn't understand why he didn't wake himself up. And then I thought with great trepidation that maybe this was the death rattle I'd heard about. I watched him, frightened, yet fixated. Horrified, yet curious. The very loud, unpleasant sounds continued for what seemed like over five minutes, and then they ceased. I was relieved to see him still breathing! Now, surely he'll wake up, I thought.... But he didn't.

So I closed my eyes, and sat peacefully enveloped in the light beside him for what could have been minutes or hours. The next thing I remember was his voice asking, "How long do you do this?" I opened my eyes, saw him looking at me, and answered, "Any time.... We're done." And he sat up and said, "Good. I'm hungry. Let's go keep Sandy company." And he got up and I followed him into the kitchen for a short visit before leaving.

What a day that was! I experienced sensations that "ran the gamut" of healing experiences I'd had over the past twenty years.... Was it energy healing? Spiritual healing? Or coincidence?

Spiritual healing can bring an influx of life force to a person with diminished energy — but ultimately we all have to figure out how to live our lives so that the energy coming into us at least equals that expended. We can do this by increasing acts of self-love (through positive internal dialogue, and activities that enhance our feelings of joy, connection, and self-worth) and minimizing feelings of resentment, guilt, hopelessness, or helplessness. Giving caring attention to others, and participating in meditation and prayer are also ways to enhance our vitality and immunity to disease. Prayer from others is another avenue of love that can assist in the nonlocal mobilization of life force through mind-to-mind connections.

EXTENDING OUR VIEW OF THE MIND

Just as contemporary physicists have been grappling with the role of consciousness in the physical world, health practitioners have been debating the extent to which the mind affects the health of the body. Let us explore how one person's mind, directed with healing intentions, may affect another person's health; how mind-to-mind connections can facilitate "energy healing," as well as distant psychic and spiritual healing. Physician Larry Dossey asks:

> How do prayer, noncontact therapeutic touch, extended effects of meditation, effects of transpersonal or distant imagery, and diagnosis at a distance fit into modern medicine? *Can* they fit? I believe the answer is yes, if we are bold enough to extend our views of the mind.[1]

Recently, Dossey's commitment to the study of mind-body healing has led him to become executive editor of the new journal, *Alternative Therapies in Health and Medicine*. In his inspiring books *Recovering the Soul, Meaning & Medicine*, and *Healing Words*, Dossey describes three distinctively different types of healing methodologies that have been used throughout the course of medical science.[2] Since they generally fall into historical sequence, he referred to these categories of healing as "Eras." Dossey's ideas provide a helpful framework for understanding the relationship of remote viewing to healing, so we describe the three types of methodologies here.

In medical Era I, all forms of therapy are physical, and the body is regarded as a mechanism that functions according to deterministic principles. Classical laws of matter and energy, as described by Newtonian physics, guide these approaches to healing, which focus solely on the effects of material forces on the physical body. The Era I approaches to healing encompass most of "modern" medical technology and include techniques such as drugs, surgery, and radiation. They also include CPR, acupuncture, nutrition, and herbs, but mind is not a factor of healing in this era.

Dossey extols the accomplishments of Era I medicine in the history of healing, just as modern physicists acknowledge the contribution of Newtonian physics to our understanding of the laws of the physical universe. "These achievements are so significant that most persons believe the future of medicine still lies solidly in Era I approaches," says Dossey, despite the fact that "all the major diseases of our day — heart disease, hypertension, cancer, and more — have now been shown to be influenced, at least to some degree, by the mind."[3] A similar analogy may be drawn in the field of physics, where the classical models persist, even though they are unable to account for the data of relativity, quantum physics, or remote viewing.

Era II, according to Dossey, describes the kind of mind-to-body approaches to medicine that involve the psychosomatic effect of one's consciousness on one's own body — the idea that "what you think affects your health." Era II medicine does attribute a causal effect of mind, but the mind is still seen as a function of brain chemistry and anatomy. Era II acknowledges the connection between an individual's brain, mind, and organs. Its therapies involve psychosomatic medicine, and include counseling, hypnosis, biofeedback, and self-healing imagery and relaxation techniques, as well as psychoneuroimmunology. Eras I and II are similar in that the mind is still considered to be localized in one's body, as well as in present time.

In the 1990s, we have entered the third era of medical therapies. Despite the important advances of Era II medicine, researchers recognize that it is still incomplete. In Era III medicine, mind is seen as unconfined by either space (brains or bodies) or time (present experience). We recognize that *our nonlocal mind may affect healing* both within and between people. *Non-contact healing modalities between people in each other's presence, as well as between people distant from each other, become possible with nonlocal mind.* It is this latter element that distinguishes Era III medicine.

Healing modalities from all three of these categories can be highly efficacious in certain situations and under the right conditions. The greater range of therapies that has become available with each new era of medicine has not extinguished the value of the healing methodologies of another era. Instead, each era's healing therapies complement the approaches used in the others. Many people don't understand this, and think that one mode must be sacrificed in order to use the other.[4]

In my (Jane's) practice as a healer, I have experienced the disappointment and antagonism that clients express towards Era I medicine, once they discover the efficacy of self-healing imagery, for instance, or the healing power of herbs, or of a particular energy healer. As we discover more about nonlocal healing, we are not required to eliminate the physically based treatments of Era I, or discard the mind-body therapies of Era II. Rather, our lives become enriched with the extended range of healing choices available to us. Thus, I consider myself as practicing a complementary healing method, within a comprehensive system of health-promoting choices. Our choices for treatment are especially enhanced by the possibilities of Era III medicine.

This third Era is distinguished by the active nature of unbounded consciousness. Physical processes within the brain are recognized as influencing mental and emotional content as well as states of awareness. But we know that *mind is not limited to the brain*. Our mind-to-mind connections facilitate healing across distances, and allow us to gain information in nonordinary ways, such as remote viewing and distant clairvoyant diagnosis. Since this book is concerned with the nonlocal aspect of mind, this chapter includes discussion of the noncontact and distant healing modalities that characterize Era III medicine.

PSYCHIC HEALING

Psychic healing and spiritual healing are similar in that they both involve nonlocal mind, and they both may affect a person's health from a distance. Psychic healing as described here requires the healer to exert mental effort directed toward the patient's mind or body with a goal of "trying to heal." In general, psychic healing modalities involve training, trying, directing one's attention to a particular part of the patient's body, and logical decision-making on the mental level of the practitioner.

Psychic healing involves human judgment and skill, as does the practice of medicine. Since human decision-making is fallible, inappropriate psychic healing can result in imbalance in the affected system, and possible injury to the patient. Of course, the same potential for imbalance or disharmony may derive from medical treatment, physical therapy, or psychotherapy as well.

Psychic healing is similar to remote viewing in that they are both examples of our extended capacities on the mental plane of awareness. Because misjudgment or misuse of psychic healing ability is possible, some people fear and condemn it. However, I believe psychic healing, as well as spiritual healing, will both be rightfully acknowledged in the future, right along with surgery, pharmacology, botanical medicine (herbs), and nutrition. The expertise and integrity of the practitioner are as important in psychic healing as they are in those we choose to anesthetize us or cut us open and stitch us up again.

SPIRITUAL HEALING

It is my belief that Dossey's Eras of Medicine should be amended to reflect refinements in our understanding of nonlocal healing methods. Psychic healing, energy healing, and spiritual healing may one day each be in their own categories in Era III.

As mentioned earlier, one distinction between psychic and spiritual healing is that spiritual healing involves active compassion, in the presence of surrendered egos. It cannot occur without this aspect of service, which some Biblical translations call "charity." A spiritual healer operates from the perceptual foundation of which Martin Heidegger wrote:

> A person is neither a thing nor a process, but an opening or clearing through which the Absolute can manifest.

Spiritual healers enter a different state of consciousness from that of psychic healers. Their methods — what they experience while in the healing interaction — and the source of knowledge about how to do healing, are not the same as those of psychic healers. Spiritual healing occurs from the healer "letting" spirit work through him or her to assist the sick person's innate self-balancing, harmonizing, and healing capacities. In my experience, it involves the activation and expression of transpersonal love. It is not a mental function or a "doing" — *it is an experience of one universal mind unifying with itself, which is the main aspect of love.* As such, it is as unlikely for spiritual healing to disrupt a person's health as it is for someone to be too balanced.

It is also impossible for a spiritual healer to attempt to kill specific cells in a test tube for the sake of research. It's not that killing a form of life goes against our morality — it is because spiritual healing doesn't operate that way. It is not a type of mental force exerted willfully and selectively — it is a *letting*, which promotes coherence, rather than the healer's killing separate cells, or undesirable parts of a living system.

Dr. Stanley Krippner, a leader in the field of consciousness studies, has been studying the spiritual and psychic dimensions of healing for more than three decades. As described in Chapter 4, Krippner's research showed that the thoughts of one person could directly influence the mental state of another.

More recently, Krippner has been inspiring students in South America, as well as in San Francisco at Saybrook Graduate School, which he founded, and at California Institute of Integral Studies. In his 1976 book *The Realms of Healing*, co-authored with Alberto Villoldo, Krippner discusses the question of how nonlocal healing happens.[5] He outlines many paradigms or sets of beliefs shared by both psychic and spiritual healers. These sets of beliefs differ markedly from orthodox Western scientific assumptions, because both psychic and spiritual healers share worldviews that incorporate nonlocal mind.

According to Krippner, Western scientists and healers have divergent concepts of the way the universe relates to local and nonlocal views of consciousness. Krippner's first distinction that sets healers apart from scientists is that spiritual healers typically believe the universe includes some sort of deity or "higher consciousness." They generally see the universe as being "purposeful," and they perceive people to be evolving toward an expanded or higher level of consciousness or awareness.

The second distinction between Western scientists and psychic and spiritual healers is that nonlocal healers from many cultures report that they see and sense a variety of nonphysical things that cannot be seen by most other people, and cannot be detected by any known physical instruments. Among these phenomena are auras of light that surround living organisms, spirits of various entities, and a type of life energy that flows through and emanates from living creatures. The vibrations and fluctuations of this life energy, which is essential to one's health, can ostensibly be sensed and manipulated by healers. These nonmaterial phenomena are just as real to healers as are the physical characteristics that can be perceived by ordinary sense perception, and detected by current instruments.

In the worldview of spiritual and psychic healers, according to another of Krippner's distinctions, death is not the end of human life — some immortal part of the human spirit endures. For healers as well as mystics, the human nervous system does not produce consciousness — rather, the brain and nervous system are viewed as instruments of perception, through which awareness of consciousness becomes possible for humans. As a result, says Krippner, healers perceive all human consciousness as being connected; and people are not seen as being isolated individuals, but rather as interconnected.[6] So, we would say that healers are aware of mind-to-mind connections that occur over spatial distances and across time. A physicist would call such connections "nonlocal mind."

Psychical research pioneer William James, author of the classic *Varieties of Religious Experience*, has said that the concept of "spiritual" entails a process that "establishes the self — however briefly — in a larger power and sufficiency."[7] Joel Goldsmith was one of the great spiritual healers of this century. He wrote thirty-some books on healing and spiritual mysticism, and described the spiritual healing process this way:

> Treatment is a technique employed to lift consciousness to such an elevation that a contact with God is established, which permits spiritual power to flow into human activity.... This realization on the part of the person giving the treatment reveals the spiritual identity of the one who has asked for healing....[8]

Goldsmith went on to explain that attempting to do good things or to think virtuous thoughts was helpful for people in their life, but these things would not lead to an ability to do spiritual healing. It is the opening to another realm of consciousness that allows healing to occur.

In the spiritual healing interactions in which I participate, what *feels like* a flow of energy being transported through me to the patient is wholly independent of any good deeds I may have done before, or anything I do with my body or to the body of a patient. Healing occurs through a joined state of consciousness. I surmise that the drumming, chanting, dancing, and rhythmic breathing that is part of healing ceremonies in other cultures has to do with a similar entraining of minds in a nonthinking realm. Joined minds, combined with intentions to help heal, can have real effects on the body.

ENERGY HEALING

Although spiritual healing differs in practice and experience from so-called energy healing modalities such as Reiki healing, Chi Gong, Therapeutic Touch, pranic healing, and the Barbara Brennan and Rosalyn Bruyere healing techniques, the successful results may actually derive from some similar principle involving joined minds and helping intentions. Theories of energy healers regarding the life force coincide with the practice of spiritual healing, if one thinks of the energy as being a manifestation of consciousness.

We have attempted to summarize the similarities among different energy healing techniques. These overall descriptions are not meant in any way to judge the effectiveness of any particular school of healing, or subtle energy modalities of healing in general. All nonlocal healing is controversial. Whether or not one method or another involves "energy transfer" is still very much an open question. One of the purposes of this book is to explain why the authors believe that "information transfer," or more precisely, "information access and sharing," is an inherent aspect of both energy and spiritual healing modalities. In this way, remote viewing and healing connections are related. They both reveal aspects of coherence, or our mind-to-mind connectedness to one another.

The various schools of subtle energy healing teach their own stylized theories and techniques, which usually involve some combinations of physical and mental exercises and practice. These methods of healing often require study and memorization by the healer-in-training concerning hand positions to be used during healing, or specific points on the healee's body toward which to direct energy for particular ailments. Breathing exercises, visualizations and meditations, and some process of initiation by a master healer are involved to varying degrees, depending on the particular school of healing. The experienced healer-teacher may transfer healing abilities and/or energies to the student, which theoretically open the energy centers and "raise the vibration level" of the student. These students are then able to channel greater amounts of the universal life energy to another person to facilitate healing.

The concept of an invisible life force that permeates and activates all living systems, including the earth and the universe, is central to energy healing modalities. This vitalizing life force, variously called bioplasma, chi, qi, mana, prana, or subtle energy "is impossible to grasp, measure, quantify, or isolate... [and is] known only by its effects," according to Beinfield and Korngold, authors of *Between Heaven and Earth: A Guide to Chinese Medicine.*[9] Subtle energy healing techniques are based on the belief that this life force flows along nonphysical channels or meridians (called *nadis* in Sanskrit) in the body.

Theoretically, we are born with a certain amount of innate life energy or chi, and throughout life we continue to replenish it by absorbing varying amounts from the earth, sunlight, the air, food and drink, and through positive interactions with other living creatures. Conversely, we can become drained of our prana or chi by excessive muscular activity or improper breathing, as well as by our undisciplined thoughts and intentions.

According to energy healing theory, our life force can become blocked in various parts of our bodies when we experience physical, mental, or emotional trauma, or when we either consciously or unconsciously withhold our emotional expression associated with trauma. Being surrounded by crowds of people or being in the company of depressed, ill, angry, or fearful people is said to deplete our supply of essential life energy as well. On the other hand, nutrition and herbs, physical training and breathing exercises, touch and massage, acupuncture, rest, meditation, and manipulation or restoration of the energy field by a healer are all thought to have restorative effects on the flow and supply of our body's vital life force.

Both energy healers and spiritual healers conceive that imbalances, depletion, or blockages in the flow of our life force (or consciousness) precede and cause physical symptoms of illness. Invigorating, balancing, and unblocking the flow of this life energy becomes the goal of energy healing. The authors believe that an essential aspect of both energy and psychic healing is actually the transfer or access of healing information through mind-to-mind connections.

Energy healers generally share a system of beliefs that includes the existence within the body of energy centers, called "chakras," which transduce "universal life energy" into human energy. The seven main chakras situated along the spinal cord are said to rotate and generate a field or aura of light that surrounds and interpenetrates the body. The word "chakras" comes from the Sanskrit word meaning "wheels of light," and although the concept of chakras came from the Upanishads and other Indian texts, many other energy healing systems adopted the concept.

Many schools of energy healing base their principles on occult or "hidden" esoteric teachings from ancient societies. Therapeutic Touch derives from the pranic healing of India, Kahuna healing from ancient Polynesia and Egypt, Reiki and Joh-Rei healing from Japan, and Chi Gong from traditional Chinese medicine. Some schools of energy healing freely admit that their techniques are derived from the healing methods of other cultures, while others maintain that their methods are unique.

Rosalyn Bruyere is a well-known energy healer and teacher in Southern California, as well as the author of a book entitled *Wheels of Light: Chakras, Auras, and the Healing Energy of the Body.*[10] As a child, Bruyere was encouraged by her great-grandmother to pay attention to the light (or aura) that she saw surrounding plants. The elderly lady maintained that plant cuttings imbued with vivid light were far more likely to regenerate into vigorous new plants than were the dimly lit plant parts. Bruyere found that her great-grandmother's assertions were true. However, when the older woman began to have conversations with her dead husband, Bruyere's family had the grandmother hospitalized, where she was subjected to electroshock therapy. So Bruyere learned at a young age that visions of auras and other psychic abilities were best not discussed. Years later, after Bruyere had been trained as an engineer, she began to redevelop her clairvoyant abilities, influenced by

Native American, Egyptian, Hindu, and Tibetan traditions. She became a widely respected energy healer.

Healer Bruyere uses the term "channeling" to describe a common energy healing technique in which:

> ...one person (the healer) acts as a channel to transfer various frequencies of energy to another person (the client) for the purpose of rebalancing chakras (stabilizing the energy field), thereby facilitating stress reduction, regeneration of tissues, and healing.[11]

Bruyere and other energy healers use a variety of techniques to assess a client's aura or energy field so they can make diagnosis and treatment decisions. Prominent New York healer Barbara Brennan teaches her students to scan their clients' energy field to find "imbalances, tears, stagnations, and depletions" in their flow of energy.[12]

THERAPEUTIC TOUCH

Students of Therapeutic Touch, another form of energy healing, learn to move their hands a few inches over the body of a patient from head to feet, become aware of changes in sensory cues in their hands, and redirect areas of accumulated tension in their patients' energy fields by movement of their hands.[13] They also learn to sense with their hands differences in temperature and pressure, pulsations, "tingles," and feelings similar to slight electric shocks as they run their hands a few inches over the client's clothed body from head to foot.[14]

Therapeutic Touch was derived from the ancient practice of the laying on of hands, and today it is used by nurses in hospitals and clinical settings throughout the world. Its theoretical principles and techniques were first taught in 1972 to nursing professor Dolores Krieger of New York University by clairvoyant healer and Theosophist Dora Kunz. According to Kunz, Therapeutic Touch (hereafter shortened to TT) actually came from the pranic healing methods described in ancient Yogic texts. The Sanskrit terms were changed to generic English so the technique could be taught to Western health professionals. After learning the TT principles, Krieger began to conduct research on the healing method at New York University School of Nursing, and to write books and journal articles reporting her findings.

Russell has an interesting story to tell about an early encounter he had with Dora Kunz. She demonstrated her clairvoyant abilities to him forty years ago at the New York Theosophical Society, by psychically locating magnets that Russell had hidden. Kunz told Russell that she could sense the location of the magnets by the auras of light that she saw emanating through the physical objects behind which the magnets were hidden. She was also able to correctly distinguish from a distance which poles of the magnets were north or south by the different colors of light that they radiated.

Targ, then a young graduate student, was so impressed with Kunz's ability that he was led to further investigate human perception of magnetic fields. He talked with researchers at Cambridge University who were investigating the production of "visual phosphines," which are colored lights seen by people exposed to very high magnetic fields. While at Cambridge, he had an opportunity to work with a type of blind African fish, Gymnarcus, that navigates by perception of magnetic fields. Russell theorizes that these kinds of short-range magnetic interactions could be relevant to the short-range effects of energy healing or noncontact methods of Therapeutic Touch, although he does not see them as relevant to distant healing.

Therapeutic Touch originally involved some laying on of hands, as well as the manipulation of the energy fields that are believed to surround the body. What makes TT unique among the schools of energy healing is its use internationally among the entire spectrum of health care professionals, and the extent to which its effects have been the subject of clinical research. Such research on the effects of Therapeutic Touch has shown remarkable evidence for the elevation of human serum hemoglobin, alteration in EEG (electroencephalograph), EKG (electrocardiograph), galvanic skin response, and decreases in people's anxiety, diastolic blood pressure, headache pain, and pain after surgery.[15] Therapeutic Touch has been taught to more than 36,000 health care professionals, at more than 80 colleges and universities in the U.S., and in more than 70 countries throughout the world.

FURTHER DIMENSIONS OF THERAPEUTIC TOUCH

In 1984, Janet Quinn, a doctoral candidate in nursing at NYU, published landmark research in the field of ostensible energy healing. Her work was the first to show that *physical contact was not necessary for the healing effects of TT to occur*. More important, Quinn's research demonstrated *the pivotal role of the healing intentions* of the healer, using a modified version of Therapeutic Touch that did not involve physical contact with the patient. Quinn's study involved sixty cardiovascular patients hospitalized at St. Vincent's Medical Center in New York. Her randomly assigned control group received sham but realistic-looking noncontact treatments, and they had no change in their physiologic measures of anxiety. The group of patients receiving noncontact Therapeutic Touch from practitioners intending to heal in a mind-centered state had dramatic decreases in physiologic measures of anxiety following their treatments.[16] Quinn considers it possible, as we do, that through a shift in consciousness, Therapeutic Touch practitioners in some way facilitate a "repatterning of the recipient's energy field through a process of resonance, rather than an energy exchange or transfer."[17]

Quinn admitted to me (Jane) that she was highly skeptical of the whole process when she was a student in the first accredited TT class at NYU School of Nursing in 1975. Quinn's life at that time was inordinately stressful, since she was working full-time while being a graduate student. She said she had only signed up for the class in Therapeutic Touch because it looked like an easy elective. "But when Krieger did Therapeutic Touch on me, it blew me away!" Her full statement was:

> As Krieger began to do Therapeutic Touch on me, I could feel all the tension in my body being drawn to my center. Then I had intense chest pain. When Krieger did Therapeutic Touch over my chest, it was as if the pain was drawn out of me. My whole body relaxed. I felt grounded and centered. Even my mind became clear and focused. It blew me away! I stayed clear and relaxed and focused like that for more than a week.[18]

Quinn told me that her most profound experience with Therapeutic

Touch occurred when she was caring for her mother, who was ill with cancer. She had been sitting at her mother's bedside for many hours and decided to see if she could do TT without going through the motions. Quinn said she began to imagine that she was sending healing energy to her mother from her hands:

> An important part of Therapeutic Touch is that it is done with the intention to help or heal. So I centered myself, and imagined myself in a cocoon of peace and calm and total well-being with my mother. I visualized that I was projecting energy from my hands, but I kept my hands and body completely still. I did Therapeutic Touch without the movement.
>
> My mother had been lying there silently without moving for quite awhile before this. Just when I was visualizing myself in this cocoon of peace and calm with her, she opened her eyes, turned her head, and looked directly at me. "You make it so much easier," she said.
>
> For me, that was a turning point. It was life-changing. It was clear to me that there is another dimension to reality that we don't know much about.[19]

This sounds to me very much like spiritual healing. That experience compelled Quinn to return to graduate school to conduct research on non-contact Therapeutic Touch.

More recently, Quinn's colleagues have been interested in measuring immune system effects of TT *on both the practitioners as well as the recipients of the treatments*.[20] Since other research has demonstrated that positive emotions can have a beneficial effect on one's health, Quinn reasoned that the feelings of compassion and unconditional love, that are the focus of TT practitioners, should enhance the healer's immune system as well as that of the recipient.[21]

THE MEDIUM, THE MYSTIC, AND THE PHYSICIST

Psychotherapist Larry LeShan is another researcher with a passion for understanding how healing works. LeShan has a wealth of over forty years' experience in both teaching and practicing nonlocal healing, and he has written more than fifteen books and eighty articles on the subject. He was one of the first clinical researchers to write about the importance of "resonance" or "merging of consciousness" between healer and client in what we now call nonlocal healing. In his classic 1974 book *The Medium, the Mystic, and the Physicist*, LeShan discusses how most people's ordinary sensory reality is profoundly different from other ways of perceiving reality as described by healers, psychics, physicists, and mystics throughout history.[22] He postulates that nonlocal healing, precognition, and remote viewing are possible in the same nonsensory state of merged consciousness that mystic poets and psychics describe.

LeShan realized he had been grouping together two distinctly different categories of nonsensory awareness that were somehow related to different types of healing. He sums up the two types of healing consciousness this way:

> In Type 2 the healer tries to heal; he wants to and attempts to do so through the "healing flow." In both Type I and Type 2 he must (at least at the moment) care completely, but a fundamental difference is that in Type I he unites with the healee; in Type 2 he tries to cure him.[23]

SPIRITUAL HEALING AND PSYCHIC HEALING FURTHER DEFINED

Thus, LeShan discovered two different modes of healing from observing his experiences in different states of awareness. In one type of healing, the healer aims for a unity state of consciousness, and merges his or her mind with the All or Infinite One or God, as well as with the recipient of healing. There is no focus on hand positions or symptoms, no sensing of auras or energy flow, and no diagnosis of the health problem.

LeShan's Type I healing is what the authors call "spiritual healing." It involves a sense of surrender of individual desires and thoughts, a relinquishing of all distinctions between healer and patient — a sense of "letting healing happen," as opposed to "I am doing something to this person's body to make healing happen."

> Let then the motive for action be in the action itself, not in the event.
> — The Bhagavad Gita[24]

All of the ostensible energy healing modalities we have described fall under LeShan's category of Type 2 healing. We call them modes of "psychic healing," because they involve physical or mental actions done with the intention of manipulating another person's physiology or energy flow. In our terminology, psychic healing involves decision-making processes, learned concepts and diagnoses, the consideration of body functions and symptoms, or a focus on "doing something" to someone else with the intention to affect changes in a body. Psychic healing may be done distantly, or in the presence of the patient.

Psychic, or energy healing, originates from an assumption that a practitioner is acting upon a recipient. As long as the practitioner is focused on doing something to the patient's body, a separation of consciousness between healer and patient is maintained, and this division distinguishes these modes of interactions from spiritual healing. In actuality, psychic and spiritual healing can be complementary to each other, as well as to the other physical and mental healing modalities described by Larry Dossey in Eras I and II of medicine.

When physicians realized the efficacy of mind-body healing techniques that had formally been the domain of psychologists, health educators, and nurses, they began to incorporate them into their practice. Drs. Larry Dossey, Deepak Chopra, Jerry Jampolsky, Bernie Siegel, and Norman Shealy are some of the physicians who have written about their conscious use of nonlocal mind in their therapies. It is possible that most successful physicians use nonlocal mind in their healing practice, even though they may be unaware of it.

Historically, some spiritual healers possessed psychic abilities that complemented their spiritual healing capabilities and allowed them unusual flexibility in interacting in the nonlocal domain. Olga Worrall, one of this country's most renowned and researched spiritual healers, referred to her gift as "spiritual healing" rather than "psychic healing." She said that although her psychic abilities enhanced the healing she did, spiritual healing is usually accomplished by people who are neither clairvoyant, clairaudient, nor psychically mediumistic in any way. She stated that, "The 'healing' current flows through every clear channel available, whatever the 'healer's' psychic abilities, or, for that matter, religious beliefs."[25]

It is likely that many energy healing practitioners from time to time access states of awareness that allow the principles of spiritual healing to manifest. However, they themselves may be unaware of the distinction in states of consciousness, or of their mind's transitions between these states. Reiki healing and Therapeutic Touch are two energy healing modalities in which the training of practitioners involves concepts of altruism and compassion. I believe that the inclusion of universal love is an important factor that distinguishes these methods of healing from others that mainly manipulate energy, such as acupuncture. Where there is trust and merging of minds, combined with intentions to help or heal, and surrender of individuality, spiritual healing can occur.

CHANGING THE PATIENT'S REALITY

LeShan's concept of spiritual healing involves "changing the construction of the reality that the patient is in" and feeding a part of the patient that's undernourished. He explains it simply and poetically:

> We need to live both in the world of the One and the world of the many. But we're ... undernourished in our need for being in the world of the One.... [The healer] feeds that undernourished part of the ... [patient], and their self-healing abilities [are assisted to] operate at a higher level.[26]

HEALING MESSAGE OR HEALING ENERGY?

So, if a healer is actually sending a healing message, does that mean that he or she is not sending any healing energy? Not necessarily — it's just that no one has reliably measured this "energy" yet, though many have tried. The existence of a nonlocal consciousness does not necessarily mean that some sort of energy exchange is not occurring when people are near each other. It is possible that healers have the ability to change the distribution of electrical charge in their hands, or of the local space surrounding them, at will.

One researcher investigating that idea is Dr. Elmer Green at the Menninger Foundation in Topeka, Kansas. He is best known for his work investigating the physical feats of meditating yogis, who could prodigiously slow their heart rates and go into a state resembling hibernation, with greatly reduced metabolic functioning.[27] Recently, Green reported that while working with energy healer Mietek Wirkus, he was able to measure a surge of 80 volts on the wall of the electrically shielded room when Wirkus initiated a healing procedure. It would not be at all surprising if a patient experienced or showed physiological changes in response to such changes in electrical potential of a healer's hands.

There are ample reports of the successful detection of a variety of *effects* of energy healing modalities. Healing practitioner Paul Dong, who has co-authored a book on Chi Gong reports that Chinese scientists have detected a wide spectrum of effects from Chi Gong masters generating external chi.[28] They include infrared radiation, static electricity, changes in magnetic fields, light waves, neutrons, beta rays, and two-way radiation of electromagnetic energy.[29]

Eventually, we may be able to document the existence of some flow or transmission of extremely low frequency (ELF) radiation that promotes healing by evoking resonance among minds in living cells (DNA). Such resonating effects in healing interactions may derive from wave properties and fluctuations, rather than the intensity of the radiation. At this time, we believe that mind-to-mind connections and loving, caring intentions on the part of the healer are the primary precursors to healing effects.

SPIRITUAL SURGERY

There are evidently many different states of consciousness that affect healing interactions. Chi Gong, Therapeutic Touch, and spiritual healing all involve aspects of transpersonal mind connections that are not understood at this time. Still another approach to psychic healing was done by Arigo, the Brazilian healer known as the "Surgeon with the Rusty Knife." He was a peasant with a third-grade education who successfully operated on thousands of patients who experienced no pain, trauma, or infection. He treated hundreds of patients a day in the 1950s and 1960s in a shed by his house, doing surgeries with his rusty jackknife, and correctly diagnosing patients' ailments and writing medically correct prescriptions. Arigo was known to stop the blood flow of his patients with a verbal command, though he was unable to control his own blood flow.[30] He believed that the spirit of a dead German doctor whom he had never met, and whom he called Dr. Fritz, guided him in the surgeries, and told him the names of the medicines to prescribe.

Both the Brazilian Medical Association and Catholic church officials sued Arigo for illegal practice of medicine and witchcraft. He was jailed in 1958 and 1964, despite the fact that he was revered by multitudes of people whom he helped, and despite the fact that he worked for free, accepting donations. Friends of mine in the Peace Corps watched Arigo do his amazing surgeries over a period of years. Russell's friend, the American physician and psychic researcher Dr. Andrija Puharich, led a team of doctors to Brazil to investigate and film the healer. Arigo removed a tumor from Puharich's arm with his jackknife, while Puharich felt nothing and didn't bleed. Puharich believed that Arigo controlled some unknown form of life energy. The phenomenal healer died in a car accident in 1971. Arigo apparently functioned on an entirely different level of nonlocal mind than the healers we've been discussing thus far.

OTHER TRANSPERSONAL APPROACHES

Historically, many different types of practices have been used by people to alter their state of consciousness, and to enable them to access a nonlocal transpersonal realm. These include Buddhist and Yoga meditation methods, as well as techniques involving sound or rhythmic body movements. Examples of these are the chanting of mantras, prayers, or songs; the beating of drums; and the movement practices of Yoga, Tai Chi, Anthroposophist Eurythmics, and Hassidic and Sufi Dervish dances. Other more physiological methods of consciousness-altering techniques have been used, such as fasting; the use of hallucinogenic and other pharmacological agents including LSD, psilocybin, and MDMA; various methods of asceticism; and ritualistic breathing patterns such as the Pranayama Yoga breathing techniques. These consciousness-altering methods have proven valuable for self-inquiry and self-exploration, but they have yet to prove themselves useful for healing others.

Therapeutic Touch and Reiki healing both involve a type of mind-centering that resembles Buddhist or Yoga meditation. Such centering or meditation, combined with a healer's helping intent, seems to facilitate an occurrence that feels like a flow of physical force or energy to both healer and patient.

CHI GONG

Chi Gong healing is related to a Chinese martial art called "Empty Force," which involves the seeming transmittal of energy through space by means of thought. Both Chi Gong healing and Empty Force are traditional Chinese practices based on the concept of learning to direct one's external life energy by means of training one's breath, thought, and body.[31] Mind-to-mind connections are recognized as playing a part in both disciplines. Chi Gong practitioner Paul Dong reports that "The response to external chi [healing] treatment depends not so much on the nature of the disease as on the degree of the patient's receptivity to chi."[32]

Four scientists investigating chi at the Chinese Academy of Sciences issued a report summarizing their understanding of the complex role of mind in chi (which is here spelled qi):

> It appears to us that qi is a much more complicated matter than we originally supposed it to be. Qi is probably a complicated organic combination of substance, energy, and message. At present, substance, energy, and message are studied separately in science. Scientists are very unfamiliar both in theory and in experiments with what conditions will occur when these three produce effects at the same time.[33]

Mind is also known to be a factor in pranic healing, the forerunner of many contemporary modalities of subtle energy healing. Twentieth-century scholar of Indian philosophy Ernest Wood discusses the role of mind in pranic healing:

> Each teacher has his own variations, but in all cases it is agreed that there is no deliberate manipulation of these "airs." What does happen in cases of psychic healing, is that the healer gives some of his own "vitality" by a process resembling thought-transference....[34]

This essential life force that healers and patients alike perceive as energy seems to act as an interface between mind and matter. It seems to respond to information from a healer's focused intentions, and to affect the physiology of a patient's body. Some individuals have a highly developed psychic sense that allows them to perceive flowing colors around a person's body that give information pertaining to one's health. Some psychic healers possess an uncommon ability to do psychic diagnosis, and believe that the process of psychically diagnosing and treating illness can be taught to others, just as if it were another medical specialty.

PSYCHIC DIAGNOSIS

Prominent New York healer Barbara Brennan teaches students at the healing school she founded to use a "High Sense Perception" to observe their clients' auras. Students learn to watch the client's constantly changing flow of energy, which is undetectable by normal vision.[35] Brennan attempts to teach this clairvoyant perception to her students, so that they may use it in their healing practice to diagnose clients' problems, and rebalance and recharge their clients' energy field or aura.

Brennan was formerly employed as a physicist at NASA, where she studied the reflection of solar light from the earth. Her knowledge of spectroscopy allows her a rare specificity in talking about people's auras. When she described a person's energy field as measured in hundreds of nanometers, she got laser physicist Russell's attention.

When Russell and I did a remote-viewing demonstration for her, she described seeing a beam of light going from his head to wherever his focus of attention was. While Russell had his eyes closed during the remote-viewing process, Brennan correctly reported when his attention was on her, or me, or when it was focused on the adjoining room where the target object was hidden. When the "light beam" from Russell's forehead finally contacted the target object, Brennan called out, "That's it! You've got it!" before he had even said a word!

Brennan contends that all disease originates from psychological and spiritual problems. She sees the effects of a person's negative thoughts, wrong beliefs, and difficult relationships in his or her auric field. Toxic emotions and thoughts, as well as childhood traumas and injuries, manifest as blocks in the flow of energy in a person's aura, or distortions in the rotating colors of the chakras as they pull vital energy into a person. She explains her detailed theories and instructions for manipulating and recharging the human energy field in her two books, *Hands of Light* and *Light Emerging*, much of which were channeled to her from her spirit guide Heyoan.[36]

Caroline Myss is another person who has the ability to do psychic diagnosis by observing a patient's energy field. She has teamed up with physician Dr. Norm Shealy to give workshops on "Energy Anatomy" and "How One's Biography Becomes One's Biology: Learning the Language of the Human Energy System." Myss, like Brennan, also believes that illness stems from harmful perceptions, attitudes, and stress patterns. She says that there are specific target areas of the body that she sees in the aura as being affected by specific patterns of toxic attitudes and emotional scar tissue. For example: "Fears regarding financial stress affect the health of the lower back; emotional barriers to experiencing love undermine the health of the heart;" and a strong need to control others influences the health of the body's sexual area.[37]

Myss adds another important concept to the notion of mind affecting health: She says that *interfering with developmental change, or trying to prevent spiritual growth, forms a type of energy pattern that can and does create disease.* In the language of energy, she says, "A heart attack is an explosion of energy attempting to break through or break down an emotional barrier that a person has created."[38]

Myss describes herself as a medical intuitive, and believes that we all have such capabilities. She describes intuition as our "emotional apparatus upgraded to a perceptual skill" working as a vehicle for gathering information.[39] She says that intuition is our birthright, and it is a "natural by-product of the flowering of a mature self-esteem and sense of empowerment — *not power over, but power to be* (italics ours)."[40] In the book *The Creation of Health* Myss teaches that all response patterns created by human attitudes and affecting our health essentially fall into four basic areas: issues of power, responsibility, wisdom, and love.[41] Myss and Shealy conducted research from 1985 to 1987 in which Myss did her intuitive diagnoses over the telephone, given only the name and birthdate of Shealy's patients. The patients were with Shealy in his Missouri office, while Myss diagnosed from twelve hundred miles away with a 93 percent accuracy rate.

Both Myss and Brennan are able to do psychic diagnoses from a distance. This suggests that the aura of prana or chi surrounding our bodies consists of information rather than energy. It may be that some people access this information field most easily through psychic sight or clairvoyance, which is analogous to remote viewing. Others may experience the information kinesthetically, which allows them to "feel" the emotional scar tissue that Myss "sees." The renowned early-twentieth-century American psychic Edgar Cayce diagnosed illness and prescribed remedies to over thirty thousand people from a distance while in an unconscious state. He attributed his reputed high degree of accuracy to the consciousness of each of his patient's body cells, which he said communicated with his unconscious mind, and told him what was troubling them.[42]

DISEASES AS UNHEALTHY CONVERSATIONS

We know from the work of neuroscientist Dr. Candace Pert, the former head of the brain biochemistry section at the National Institute of Mental Health, that surface molecules on the walls of our bodies' cells, called receptors, regulate physiological functions as well as brain communication in the body.[43] Our brains, affected by our feelings and ideas, promote the production of chemical messenger molecules, called neuropeptides. These messenger molecules attach themselves to cell receptors, and allow us to experience euphoria and painlessness.

We could think of the messenger molecules as little skeleton keys, which fit into the keyhole-like receptors on the membranes around certain body cells. The same kind of messenger molecules that are produced in our brains and affect our levels of pain and euphoria, as well as their keyhole like receptors, are found on immune system cells. Our immune system cells can be activated by these chemical messengers to destroy cancer cells, or to stimulate the production of new cancer-fighting cells. The rate at which our bodies produce the chemical messenger molecules is determined by our emotions, and the field of knowledge concerning this relationship is known as psychoneuroimmunology. There is no longer any doubt that a person's stress, fears, resentments, anger, love, grief, and coping style affect his or her cellular defense against the spread of cancer.[44]

EMOTIONS CONVERTING MIND TO MATTER?

These discoveries over the last twenty years have led Pert to propose a theory that *emotions are the key element that effects the conversion of mind to matter in the body.*[45] Emotions are not just in the head or the brain: They are part of the body, and we can no longer make clear distinctions between the brain, our mind, and our body. In fact, Pert refers to white blood cells as "bits of the brain floating around the body."[46] She says, "Brain and body make and receive the same messenger molecules in order to communicate effectively. They 'speak' the same language — the language of neuropeptides."[47] MIT neuroscientist Dr. Francis Schmidt calls neuropeptides "informational substances."[48] Psychologist Dr. Lydia Temoshok, head of the U.S. Military's Behavioral Medicine Research Program on HIV/AIDS, also tells us that:

> Neuropeptides are a universal language by which cells from different biological systems interact and alter each other's behavior. They are a medium of exchange, and *what they share is information* [Emphasis added.][49]

There is no such thing as a purely psychosomatic or purely physical illness: *Diseases are conversations, or events involving the exchange of information among cells within a living system.* And scientists have documented that mind and information travel throughout the body, not just in the brain or nervous system. If this is so, and if one accepts the reality of shared mind-to-mind exchanges of information discussed in this book, then it does not seem so far-fetched to believe that spiritual and psychic healers are able to promote healing in another person by caring, connecting, and sending a healing message.

chapter eleven

Prayer and the
Healing Connection

In order to arrive at what you are not,
You must go through the way
in which you are not.

— T.S. Eliot
The Four Quartets

Love is not a product
to be given away,
but a process to be allowed
to flow through us.

Author Unknown

In Chapter 8, I [Jane] have described experiences that taught me mind-to-mind connections were involved in healing. In this chapter, I describe the mindset that I and many others have found helpful in initiating the practice of spiritual healing. Because the path of the spiritual healer is a way of being, rather than a way of doing, I cannot provide a set of rules that will lead to the ability to do spiritual healing. Spiritual healing is a nonanalytical practice, and unlike psychic healing or energy healing, there are no specific mental or physical moves that lead to success. Instead, I shall describe how spiritual healers *feel* about their practice, since I believe it is through the feeling path that healing will occur. Spiritual healing could be said to be the way of the mystic, rather than of the scientist, because it is about a state of awareness, rather than a system of thoughts and actions.

Only recently have I fully realized that I am a spiritual healer with psy-chic abilities. I have been reluctant to call myself a "spiritual" healer because my concept of God is more generic than that of other spiritual healers. Also, my beliefs don't fit the mold of any one religion or mode of healing. Although it is common for me to access psychic information about my clients when in a merged consciousness with them, I do not see clients' auras or do clairvoyant diagnoses by observing them, as some psychic and energy healers do.

It is clear to me that these energy healers are doing some other kind of nonlocal healing than I practice. I have not learned any particular method, but my clients and I are both aware of a feeling that we describe as a flow of energy during healing interactions. I never feel energy flowing into me; I only feel it well up inside me during a healing "treatment." I often experi-ence tears flowing out of my eyes, though I am not at all sad during healing. When I hold my hands a few inches away from a client's body, we both feel sensations of heat, tingling, and vibrations during treatments. Sometimes my face, neck, and upper body feel very hot to me, though my skin seems to be of normal temperature. Other times patients feel heat in particular places in their bodies, despite the fact that my hands feel cold. It has never seemed to matter where I place my hands during the healing session. I follow an inner guidance or intuition at times, and at other times it is as if my hands are pulled or drawn to an area of the patient's body.

From my perspective, one aspect that makes spiritual healing different from other forms of so-called energy healing is that no particular hand movements over the patient's body are necessary. I am not in a thinking or decision-making state. It feels like I am absorbed into an active process of transcendent intelligence and expansive light. When this occurs, I am unaware of the passage of time or the weight of my body, though I am fully conscious and able to converse with the client. The feeling of being bathed in light, and having my consciousness enveloped in a presence of love, feels so peaceful that I prefer not to talk during healing sessions. My sense of hearing becomes extremely sensitive in this state, and even very soft music becomes too loud for me.

I feel so good that I imagine I am in a state of what has been called "bliss" in ancient wisdom teachings. I have never experienced this extended elated state in any other activity of my life, though sexual orgasm brings on a state of consciousness that feels somewhat like a preview to a healing connection. In both states, I feel open and transparent, floating, and filled with light shining through me.

In spiritual healing, a mind-to-mind "attunement" between healer and client is the most important aspect. This attunement can be established at a distance, over the phone, or in the same room as the patient, who may be conscious or unconscious, sleeping or awake. The process is enhanced when I bring my hands near to the client's body, but after I enter into a deep state of healing consciousness, my hands are not necessary. However, holding my hands near to the patient is helpful in assisting both of us to relax and open to the attunement — and this is essential for healing.

Spiritual healing can only occur when the healing information transmitted by the healer is not blocked by a patient's conscious or unconscious barriers to the message. A patient has to be open or receptive to a new experience of consciousness, and to receiving help from a nonlocal source that we don't understand. Helping a patient to become receptive can take a healer a few seconds, many minutes, or many sessions. It takes patience and caring, as well as trust.

Physical barriers between patient and healer do not impede spiritual healing power. I have participated in healing interactions with positive results despite the physical obstructions of wheelchairs, hospital beds, body casts, and medical machinery.

Recently, I experienced a healing interaction with a patient, before I consciously initiated it. It occurred because we had just finished meditating together with a group that meets regularly for that purpose. I had not yet adjusted my attention to sensory reality, and was still in a prayerful state. However, a woman in pain was standing next to me, and waiting for me to open my eyes so she could ask me to do healing with her. Her silent asking apparently initiated the exchange of healing information. It felt to me like a vibrating surge of energy flowing through me to her.

The sensation was so unexpected, before she had even vocalized her request, that I was startled, because I didn't understand why I was experiencing such a feeling. After we had finished the healing session, she told me that her pain had started to subside while she was standing, and it disappeared during the treatment. Her pain returned the next day, but it was not as severe as it had been since she fell and injured herself.

This surprising interaction made more sense to me after I read Olga Worrall's concept of what happened when she did healing:

> Energy from the universal field of energy becomes available to the healer through the act of tuning his personal energy field to a harmonious relationship with the universal field of energy.... He acts in this way as a conductor between the universal field of energy and the patient.[1]

For a person to be able to regularly access this "harmonious relationship" with the "universal field of energy," he or she is likely to lead a simplified life, unencumbered by multiple activities or numerous stressful interactions. I, myself, prefer not to be responsible for maintaining a lot of possessions, or a lifestyle that distracts my attention from a harmonious relationship with my own mind. I try to avoid scheduling a lot of activities that create barriers to my awareness of being present in the moment. I do what I can to promote mind-to-mind connections with others. They are their own reward.

Olga and Ambrose Worrall, whom I have mentioned previously, were among the most well-known spiritual healers in the United States in the mid-twentieth century. Ambrose was an engineer by day, but he and his wife held weekly healing services at their New Life Clinic, in a Methodist church in Baltimore, Maryland. Sometimes more than three hundred people would come to them for healing each week. During their morning healing sessions in the church, they administered laying on of hands healing, which Olga said was an important part of a neophyte spiritual healer's development.[2]

However, the Worralls were probably best known for the distant healings they did in the evenings from their home. Every night at 9:00 p.m. the Worralls observed a period of silence for absent healing. They encouraged people in need of healing to "tune in" and join these prayer times. Thousands of people who believed they were helped by the Worralls' distant healing prayers wrote them letters of thanks, and these letters have been saved for the rest of us to ponder at the Worrall Institute in Springfield, Missouri.

When I heard Olga Worrall speak in the 1970s, I was moved by the conviction she had about the reality and effectiveness of the distant healing in which she participated. At that time, I wondered how one could be so sure of something no one understands, and few people believe. I knew then that I had a talent for laying on of hands healing, but I was skeptical of the distant healing concept. Now, in part because of the remote-viewing work I've done, and also the parapsychological research related to healing that we discussed in Chapter 9, I am able to believe in the reality of distant healing, and I practice it occasionally.

Regarding the role of so-called "faith" in her practice, Olga Worrall said that prayer on the part of the patient was not an essential ingredient, but prayer on the part of the healer was a necessity. I especially like Worrall's description of prayer as a "form of attention" that creates "a carrier wave" for healing.[3] Her prayers were in the form of a request to be used as a healing channel, and an expression of gratitude for being used as an instrument of healing. They were not prayers asking for any particular outcome regarding the patient's symptoms, or of petitioning, urging, or bargaining for healing to occur.

HEALING PRAYER

I used to think that prayer was something other people did, something that involved communication (usually pleading) to some great, all-pervasive mind that could somehow hear our thoughts. I didn't realize that what I did during healing is what some people call prayer. Now I believe that healing prayer is neither action, nor healing thoughts, nor any communication at all done by a healer. For me, prayer is not about getting any *thing* — but it usually involves getting filled with peace, which in turn melts the barriers between one person and another. I like the concept that prayer is the fulfillment of oneness. It is an experience of being loved.

My concept of God is infinite consciousness, with aspects of power, truth, love, and presence. I do not ask this nonlocal mind that I know as God to heal a patient's body, or to save his life. I do not ask for any specific outcome on the physical plane of form. Instead, I seek to be in the same state of awareness that Buddha, Ramakrishna, Lao-tzu, and Jesus spoke of. When acting as a healer, I ask to be used as a window or channel of this awareness, so that a patient might also experience it. I ask to be assisted in being helpful. I seek a state of both receptivity to God, and attunement to the patient.

LOVE

A healing interaction is initiated by an impersonal, nonemotional, caring intention of a spiritual healer — a willingness to help. I believe that this attitude of willingness to be used as an avenue of help by a primary healing consciousness is what spiritual masters have called "love," "compassion," and "charity." The motivation behind my willingness to practice as a spiritual healer is my belief that we are all connected at some level: We are one great mind that reveals itself through us when we allow it to do so. The practice of spiritual healing involves surrender, or the cessation, of my own desires and thoughts (self-less-ness), so that the harmonizing, balancing life force can flow through me. *Anyone can decide to do this.* I hope more people try it.

THE ROLE OF MEDITATION

I also believe that the practice of meditation is useful to other people as well as to the meditator. In meditation, a quiet, thoughtless mind creates an opening for expanded consciousness or wisdom, or what some people call the "light of God," to be released into our world of physical forms. The regular practice of quieting my mental noise and directing my attention within also promotes confidence that I will be able to achieve that mind state in the presence of patients experiencing stress and pain.

THOUGHTS ON PSYCHIC ABILITIES, SPIRITUAL HEALING, AND ENERGY HEALING

Remote viewing is similar to spiritual healing in that, for both of them, you have to be willing to have nothing happen in order for something *to* happen. They are undertakings with no guaranteed outcomes. For both, you have to be willing to appear foolish and be unattached to the results. Experience helps, because you know that previous outcomes have been positive. Both activities must be entered into with the expectation of success. The more often you consciously adjust your awareness to the nonlocal mind space, whether it is for remote viewing or spiritual healing, the more natural and easier it becomes. With practice, one develops trust in his or her own ability.

Spiritual healing and remote viewing are similar in another sense, in that the practitioner in both processes becomes involved in accessing extrasensory information that is only available to a quiet mind devoid of thoughts. A remote viewer is seeking specific information from her timeless, nonlocal mind. The message is translated into thoughts, drawings, and sensory impressions. A spiritual healer becomes involved in the transmission of nonspecific, nonlocal information to another person, without ever translating or analyzing the message. Changes in a patient's physiology would be the translation of the message into the sensory domain.

The issue of attachment to outcome brings up a clear distinction between psychic and spiritual healing. Psychic or energy healers have usually studied their methods of practice, and paid someone to teach them effective healing techniques. They then use what they have learned and practiced as a means to earn a living. When healing is an occupation, and money is exchanged for services, people are understandably concerned with having predictable outcomes. In this context, healers and patients are both likely to be more comfortable with the concept of "energy exchange" in healing than they are with the intimacy and mystery inherent in mind-to-mind connections. "People don't want you running barefoot through their mind and trampling on their ego boundaries," is the way Russell expressed his concern regarding mind-to-mind healing to me.

Spiritual healers, on the other hand, freely admit that they never know what will happen in a healing encounter. We try to get ourselves out of the way so healing may occur. Speaking for myself, I practice healing interactions because it is a "calling" that *chose me*. It was given in a revelation, and it is practiced from inspiration. I do not understand how it works, or why some people have instant relief from pain or other symptoms that lasts for years, while others experience only temporary or partial symptom relief, or no relief at all.

A SPIRITUAL HEALER'S CONCEPT OF A PATIENT

I view a patient as a person who has a temporary need for a boost in self-healing potential, or a person who is unable to tap the source of supply. A person who chronically suffers from stress or depression, for instance, often benefits temporarily from spiritual healing. However, such people may need to change the way that they interpret and experience their life events in order to maintain their vitality consistently. An experience of spiritual healing can bring on an essential transformation of consciousness that literally opens one's mind to new perceptions — a different way of perceiving and experiencing reality. This opening enables self-healing. We might never have learned about our mind-to-mind connections, or connecting to the Source, if we had never needed healing. So illness can be seen as an opportunity — an invitation to cease doing, be still, and see our relationships to others and to the world in new ways.

THE MIND OF A SPIRITUAL HEALER

I perceive myself as having some attribute or talent for achieving coherence with another person and boosting his or her self-healing energy. Somehow I am able to access a Source of healing information through a particular form of attention, psychically adapt my body-mind to another person, and act as a clear channel between the Source and the receiver, who is the patient.

A healing interaction with a spiritual healer promotes the unfolding of spiritual information, which includes an awareness of our interconnectedness, within the mind of the patient. Such opening in the consciousness of the patient allows access to a universal consciousness, which is called many names, including God. The information accessed may be perceived by the patient as an influx of energy, which seems to interrupt their train of thought. Healing often brings forth a creative potential within an individual, and evokes a deep, peaceful feeling. I believe this peace is related to feeling connected — to oneself, to me, to a universal spirit, and to some deep source of meaning in life that we rarely acknowledge. Spiritual healers call this connected feeling "love."

HOW TO LEARN SPIRITUAL HEALING

Although it is a rare occurrence for someone to decide that they want to become a spiritual healer, some people have done so. I would hope this book encourages many more people to practice spiritual healing. Some or all of the modalities of energy healing taught today may actually function by the same principles as spiritual healing, so the study and practice of any healing technique might offer access to spiritual healing. Since spiritual healing is an activity of consciousness available to all who are open to it, anyone can learn to do it; but the discipline and devotion involved may be discouraging. Helpful seminars on the LeShan approach to healing are taught in various locations in the U.S. by psychotherapist Dr. Joyce Goodrich, from the New York-based Consciousness Research and Training Project.[4]

Spiritual healing is a nonrational practice, and the decision to engage in the process is usually arrived at in some manner that is not logical. Revelations, dreams, and near-death experiences are the type of occurrences that move a person to become a spiritual healer. These experiences reveal the presence of a consciousness and power in the universe greater than one's own.

SPIRITUAL PRACTICE

How does one learn to do spiritual healing? I recommend taking up a spiritual practice that has *quieting the mind* as its goal. The purpose of learning to stop one's thoughts, and turn one's attention away from physical sensations, is to cultivate an awareness of a greater consciousness, and create a receptivity in oneself for it to manifest.

A spiritual practice for healing should help a person learn how to be fully present in a peaceful, timeless state of awareness. That state of being brings an individual an experience of our interconnectedness, so the practice inherently nurtures a willingness to help people, and a reverence for mind-to-mind connections.

Stay with your spiritual practice, and read books written by other spiritual healers to give you confidence that healing is really possible. Spiritual healers whose writings have encouraged me include: Joel Goldsmith, Larry LeShan, Agnes Sanford, Kathryn Kuhlman, Murdo MacDonald-Bayne, Edgar Cayce, Edgar Jackson, Harry Edwards, Malcolm Southwood, and Gordon Turner. Authors Sally Hammond, Hans Holzer, and Harold Sherman have also written books about spiritual healing that I found interesting. One of our goals in writing this book is to show that we are all able to be instruments of healing. It is part of our natural heritage. It's part of what Patanjali, as well as Jesus and other spiritual masters, were trying to teach us.

Spiritual practice is not an intellectual exercise, although any focused activity, including intense thinking, can transport one's mind to a nonlocal, unself-conscious, timeless state of awareness. A spiritual practice is any process that trains people to shift their focus of attention away from past experiences and worries, future fears, and current thoughts or sensations to an ever-present state of just being. A healer obviously isn't in that state all the time — rather, healers know how to get there. When you are able to focus your attention on the here and now, you will have a thoughtless, peaceful mind. You will be at ease with yourself, as well as with others who come for healing. The other part of being a healer is simply caring enough to want to help.

THE INFINITE WAY

One of the most inspired and prolific writers about spiritual healing was Joel Goldsmith, mentioned above and in Chapter 10. His ancestors were Jewish, though he had little training in religion. After completing the eighth grade, he left school to become a salesman. A sick colleague told Joel that he knew that if Joel prayed for him, he would be healed. Joel tried it rather than argue. The healing that his friend experienced led to a conversion experience for Joel that compelled him to devote his life to mystical studies, and to teach a spiritual path he named "The Infinite Way." Before his death in 1964, he wrote more than thirty books about "practicing the presence," in which he explained that learning to do spiritual healing is not about "being good." It is about sharing an experience:

> Prayer is a state of receptivity in which Truth is realized without conscious thought.... It is the expression of a desire for a greater awareness of God.... God is an experience [and prayer is an experience of God].[5]

The spiritual healing mind state is not something a person would necessarily learn during religious training. It isn't achieved by doing nice things for people, or by not swearing or coveting (I was relieved to learn). It is not about *doing* anything. The state is already accessible to each of us, and we can choose to be in that state of awareness at any time, although coveting is always a problem. It is not something that I am able to will with intensity — rather, I give myself over to it. That is what is meant to me by, in Christian terminology, "The kingdom of God is within," or "Tat tvam Asi" in the Sanskrit of the *Vedas*, meaning "That art Thou." The Christian mystic Meister Eckhart described it by saying, "God is an is-ness," and the Katha Upanishad, a sacred text of India, tells us in Sanskrit: "Finer than the fine, greater than the great, the Self hides in the secret heart of the creature." A spiritual healer quiets his or her thoughts, goes within to a silent, peaceful part of us that is connected to every other, and holds that space.

"True prayer must be done purely," says Lawrence LeShan.[6] By that, he means that the person praying for healing must hope for a nonspecific "best outcome" for the patient. Or, a person could pray for harmony to be manifested in another part of the All. Anything specific beyond this, LeShan thinks, would lead to a division and separation of the parts from the whole — disrupting the transpsychic (nonlocal) way of being in the world, and returning one to the sensory reality of the physical body.

A spiritual healer need not, and probably could not, consciously will the healing energy or information to flow. It's more about evoking an ever-present potential. *The connection is already there — if one removes the barriers to that awareness.* Some call this nonemotional state of awareness of our connectedness "love," or "compassion." My concept of love is unity consciousness, which cannot occur in the presence of fear, nor without trust.

Actually, the fastest learners of spiritual healing in my experience have been parents of injured or ill children who are suffering. When medical intervention is either unavailable or insufficient for healing, and people are in pain or failing to heal, their loved ones often become highly motivated to seek out a nontraditional healer, and to take part in a healing process to which they may not have been previously receptive. They already have a mind-to-mind connection with the patient, and their passion to help someone they care about directs their attention away from themselves, and enables them to focus their mind. They are surprised to find how effective their selfless, focused attention can be when they ask a power greater than themselves to use them as an instrument of healing. In Chapter 8, I describe an incident in which this occurred, and mention it again to show that in actuality, little or no study is needed to do spiritual healing.

CHANGE YOUR LIFE, CHANGE YOUR MIND

Psychiatrist Gerald Jampolsky has developed a system of mind-training that one could use to become a spiritual healer, because it's based on helping people to remove their mental barriers to the awareness of our inherent connectedness. In his classic book *Love Is Letting Go of Fear*, he describes a system of "Attitudinal Healing," which is an approach to consciously choosing to change attitudes of anger, conflict, fear, and resentment in order to heal relationships and experience peace of mind.[7] The core assumption of the program is that it's not actually other people or uncontrollable circumstances that cause our life's stress, but rather our own thoughts, feelings, and attitudes *about* people and events.

Jampolsky and his colleagues founded the first Center for Attitudinal Healing in California in 1975, to provide peer support groups to children with life-threatening illnesses.[8] Attitudinal Healing teaches that the source of our peace or distress is within us, and that while we can't change events or other people, we do have control over how we perceive them, and how we allow them to affect us. Attitudinal Healing became so meaningful to people from all around the world that an international network was founded to help people deal not only with their own illnesses and fears, but also with community conflicts.[9] Its concepts are now taught in more than 100 different independent programs throughout seventeen countries.

Attitudinal Healing concepts have been applied to a variety of sociological problems in communities involving conflict, grief, and violence. The ideas have been taught by volunteers to help children and adults break the cycles of fear, attack, and resentment in racially diverse school districts and neighborhoods, and to help war refugees in Croatia and Bosnia, cancer patients in Russia, and people experiencing post-traumatic stress syndrome in places such as Oklahoma City after the catastrophic bombing that occurred there in 1995.

This system for changing one's mind incorporates the Twelve Principles of Attitudinal Healing, which were developed by Jampolsky to help people address their painful emotional issues and assist them in making health-promoting changes in their lives. The essence of these principles is that "To change your life, you first change your mind."[10] Dr. Susan Trout, founder of the Washington, D.C. Center, and author of *To See Differently*, says Attitudinal Healing is about being of service to others as an extension of one's own healing.[11] It is related to love, as defined by author Scott Peck, who says love is "the will to extend oneself for the purpose of nurturing one's own or another's spiritual growth."[12] An act of giving creates an opening to receive love.

Since the Principles of Attitudinal Healing are relevant for anyone desiring to do spiritual healing, we have included them here:

THE TWELVE PRINCIPLES OF ATTITUDINAL HEALING

1. The essence of our being is love.
2. Health is inner peace. Healing is letting go of fear.
3. Giving and receiving are the same.
4. We can let go of the past and of the future.
5. Now is the only time there is, and each instant is for giving.
6. We can learn to love ourselves and others by forgiving rather than judging.
7. We can become love-finders rather than fault-finders.
8. We can choose and direct ourselves to be peaceful inside regardless of what is happening outside.
9. We are students and teachers to each other.
10. We can focus on the whole of life rather than the fragments.
11. Since love is eternal, death need not be viewed as fearful.
12. We can always perceive ourselves and others as either extending love, or giving a call for help.[13]

A SELF-TAUGHT HEALER

Alan Young made a great contribution to the field of spiritual healing when he relinquished his career as an attorney and corporate vice-president to devote himself to his spiritual practice. He read everything he could find about spiritual healing. After two years of intensive study, prayer, and meditation, he began to practice healing himself.

Young summarized his conclusions in a book, aptly titled *Spiritual Healing*. He is confident that "There are two key points to understanding the spiritual healing process itself, namely Unconditional Love and Complete Surrender."[14] Young also did a comparative study of channeled teachings on spiritual healing when he was investigating the phenomenon. These teachings in many ways coincided with his own experience, so he assembled excerpts from them into another book called *Cosmic Healing*.[15] The book is an anthology of channeled material by various psychics in England and the United States throughout the past century, and contains a fascinating compilation of descriptions of spiritual healing.

THE CONDITIONS FOR A HEALING ENVIRONMENT

Healer Ambrose Worrall said that spiritual healers and physicians are alike in that they both have to ensure the best conditions for successful operations on the patient.[16] Worrall prepared himself for healing treatments by maintaining personal cleanliness, and a relaxed, expectant state of mind.

Worrall described how he prepared the patient for spiritual healing by sitting with him or her and doing a "tuning-in operation." For this, he fixed his attention on the patient, but not on his or her body, or existing symptoms. His goal was to cause his patients to temporarily forget about their afflictions. He talked casually about sports, or any other topic that would build rapport and divert the mind of the patient away from their disease or symptoms. Bad hygiene on the part of the patient was, Worrall believed, an impediment to the tuning-in process, and made the task more difficult for Worrall.

When "attunement" was achieved, the "healing flow" occurred. "I am simply relaxed and let this strange power do the work," he said.[17] Books by and about the Worralls cited here attest to the many successful outcomes of their patients for over thirty years.

Ideal healing conditions are promoted in an environment that optimizes relaxation and rapport between client and healer. Many spiritual healers have preferred to work in a church, because the hallowed, peaceful ambiance promotes a sense of trust for those who are comfortable in a place of worship. Sometimes a neutral space that avoids the negative psychological associations that many people have of organized religion and religious institutions is preferable. Since people have complex thoughts and feelings associated with their homes, families, and workplaces, I often prefer to do healing treatments elsewhere.

The ideal space for spiritual healing should be devoid of any unpleasant sensory stimuli or mental associations that might promote psychological defensiveness, or detract from a client's ability to relax. I prefer to practice healing in a small, quiet, private room with soft, diffused light. I find quiet, inspiring music to be helpful in the attuning process. It relaxes both the patient and me, and helps divert the client's attention away from pain, symptoms, and self-consciousness.

A patient need not have faith or even believe that the treatment will be helpful for healing to take place. What is important is that the patient be relaxed and "open" to whatever may occur, and allow the process to take its course. Sometimes negligible results occur with the most prayerful people, and other times skeptical patients experience remarkable outcomes. It has taken me many years of healing practice to develop a nonattachment to the outcome. Most people are helped to some degree by spiritual healing, but the irony is that nonattachment of the healer is a crucial element for success.

The act of asking for a treatment or coming to the healer's treatment space is very important for the patient. It initiates the healing interaction by providing an opening for "new information" to come into their being. Spiritual healing is not obstructed if a patient is unconscious or asleep — in fact, the healing interaction often puts people soundly to sleep quite rapidly. Sometimes the effects of a treatment are not obvious until after a client has gone home, gone to sleep, and reawakened. It took me some time to realize that spiritual healing might occur best during sleep, possibly because a patient's mind, when awake, may block access to the healing information.

Often, a series of treatments over time are necessary, and other times, one treatment can result in the elimination of a person's pain or the restoration of function to an injured body part. Sometimes, the self-repair systems of patients are mobilized to heal different health problems than the one they had in mind when they came for healing treatment.

During healing interactions, both the patient and I often feel that we are bathed in a serene sea of warmth. It feels pulsating, peacefully invigorating, and wonderful. Sometimes, both the client and myself experience synesthesia, where we "sense" expanding or pulsating vibrations of colored light infusing the space around us. The experience is so overwhelming and unexpected when it occurs that it can be initially frightening. It sometimes leaves us speechless. Those times have been among the most profound and memorable of my life — they are a high like no other for me.

In a discussion about psychotherapy, psychologist Larry LeShan has said, "Therapists operate on different theories, but the thing they have in common is, they model."[18] By this, he means that therapists pay attention to the patient, and thereby teach the patient to pay attention to himself. This is true for healers as well. Healers have respect for the patient, and thereby teach the patient to respect himself. "What you're really trying to teach is an attitude, but attitudes can't be taught. They have to be caught."[19] What the patient can do, in turn, is to "set an example for his or her own immune system." We can mobilize our own self-healing potential by loving ourselves, says LeShan, and by treating ourselves as if we are worth caring for, and as if our life is worth fighting for.

I think this practice of psychotherapists is similar to that of spiritual healers. The healer provides access to a healing template or field of loving, harmonizing information for the patient, which then amplifies the patient's own self-healing knowledge. It could be that the healer provides clear access to a universal consciousness (which some know as love, or God) for the patient, and that this catalyzes the patient's *self-love*. I perceive that a spiritual healer opens a window of revitalizing information to the client. Spiritual healing provides a mental by-pass operation that allows new access to a nonlocal, spiritual mind for those who carry conscious or unconscious barriers to it.

I believe love, in the sense of caring about the well-being of others, is active information that organizes the substance of living forms (the body) when barriers to its expression or reception are removed. Such barriers are erected when individuals maintain or defend their psychic separateness. Resentment, guilt, fear, worry, and even grief create such barriers, whereas trust and gratitude dissolve them. Unity consciousness extends itself through space and time, seeking to amplify itself wherever minds remove the barriers to their connections.

It is the function of love to unite all things unto itself and to hold all things together by extending its wholeness.

— *A Course in Miracles*

Joel Goldsmith wrote that it didn't take courage for him to establish his healing practice — it took understanding. He believed that the main objective of spiritual healing is not physical. The purpose of healers is not to keep everybody alive on earth permanently. He said, rather, the goal of spiritual healing is spiritual regeneration and "soul expansion."[20] His writings have given me the courage to leave behind my previous work as a university professor and researcher, and give priority to work that no one really understands. Goldsmith taught that:

It becomes the responsibility and privilege of every person to lift the world in some measure above its present level of consciousness.[21]

I believe that spiritual healers are able to help others, not because they are "better" than others, or have powers someone else does not possess, but because they know the truth of that "responsibility and privilege."

chapter twelve

The Physics
of Miracles
and the Magic of Mind

The great strength of science is that it is rooted in actual experience. The great weakness of contemporary science is that it admits only certain types of experience as legitimate.

— David Bohm

We have now reached the end of our story. What have we learned? As scientists, the data have convinced us unequivocally of the reality of psi abilities. After twenty years of research, supported by the Army, the Navy, NASA, the CIA, and others, it is clear to us that the Indian sage Patanjali had it right when he wrote his famous sutras twenty-four hundred years ago.[1] Patanjali said that one obtains psi data by accessing the akashic records, which in the Hindu tradition contain all information past, present, and future. He taught that we can see into the distance and know the future by becoming what we wish to see, and creating a single-pointed focus of attention on our desired objective.

It is now clear that this is a goal ordinary people can achieve. We have seen remarkable results in hundreds of remote-viewing trials with dozens of viewers. Without a doubt, people can learn to use their intuitive consciousness in a way that transcends conventional understanding of space and time, to describe and experience places and events that are blocked from ordinary perception. The whole force of the data in this book shows this to be true. So, the phenomenon exists, but how does it work?

We, of course, don't know the complete answer to that question, although some things about the answer are known. For example, the data for more than a hundred years of psi research show that there is no significant decline in the accuracy of any kind of ESP with increasing distance between the viewer and the object viewed.[2] We also know it is no more difficult to look a short distance into the future, than it is to describe a present-time hidden target. Our SRI data supporting these two assertions is very strong and convincing. We can conclude from this that it is very unlikely that any kind of electromagnetic field is involved in carrying psi signals. That can be concluded because the very geometry of our three-dimensional space requires that signal strength decreases as you get farther from the source. In fact, the signal decreases in proportion to the square of the distance. That is, the radio signal you receive at ten miles' distance is 100 times weaker than the signal you pick up at one mile. At 10,000 miles' distance, such as in our Moscow-to-San Francisco experiments, the radio signal would be 100 million times weaker than one mile away. However, we do not see the slightest evidence of such a distance-related decrease in psi ability. Although the popular model for ESP involves some kind of mental radio, in which my mind "sends a signal" to your mind, we believe that this model is probably not correct.

Instead of signals being sent, the data suggest that the desired information is always present and available. In remote viewing as well as healing, the agent's focused intention calls the information forth. Both the healer and the remote viewer act as messengers. In remote viewing, the viewer translates impressions of the information into drawings and verbal concepts. In psychic healing, the healer interprets impressions from the patient and converts them into clairvoyant diagnoses and energy-manipulating actions to remedy a problem in the patient's body. In spiritual healing, the healer acts as a conduit to the patient of healing information from the community of spirit in which we all reside. The healer makes no translation of the healing template accessed from the nonlocal connection, which stimulates the patient's cells to reorganize themselves into a healthy, coherent pattern.

To paraphrase the distinguished physicist John Archibald Wheeler, we would say that the answer to the mechanism of psychic abilities will be found in the geometry of space-time, and not in the electromagnetic fields. What Wheeler actually said is, "There is nothing in the world except curved empty space. Matter, charge, electromagnetism...are only manifestations of the bending of space. Physics *is* geometry!" [Emphasis added.][3]

What Wheeler had in mind in 1957, when he made this assertion, is that in spite of the successes of quantum theory, a geometrical approach gives a more comprehensive model of space-time. In addition, the physical laws that we experience, such as the laws of gravity and force, derive principally from symmetry laws and from the underlying geometry of space-time. What symmetry laws mean is that a given physics experiment conducted at different places or at different times must give the same result. The law of conservation of energy, which is the foundation of physics, can be derived explicitly from these symmetry laws. We similarly think that since psi must be compatible with physics, its explanation will also be derived from the geometry of space-time.

When we say that the eventual description of the physics of psi will come from geometry, we mean that psi is often seen as paradoxical because we presently misconstrue the nature of the space-time in which we reside. The naive realist picture of our reality says that we are each separate creatures sitting on our own well-circumscribed points in space-time. Modern physics, for the past thirty years, has been asserting that this concept is not correct.

The quantum physicist's view is that we live in a "nonlocal" reality, which is to say that we can be affected by events that are distant from our ordinary awareness. This is a very alarming idea for an experimental physicist, because it means that laboratory experiments set up on an isolated table are subject to outside influences that may be beyond the scientist's control. In fact, the data from precognition research strongly suggests that an experiment could, in principle, be affected by a signal sent from the future! David Bohm has called this web of connections "quantum-interconnectedness." So, the short answer to the question, "How is it that I can describe a distant object?" is that the object is not as distant as it appears. To us, the data suggests that all of space-time is available to your consciousness, right where you are.

In 1935, Albert Einstein, together with Boris Podolsky and Nathan Rosen (hereafter referred to as EPR) published a now-famous physics paper entitled, "Can Quantum Mechanical Description of Physical Reality be Considered Complete?"[4] It pointed out that quantum theory (which they found very aesthetically unsatisfying), predicted that under certain conditions, photons sent off in opposite directions at the speed of light might still have a connection with each other. Einstein was concerned that this correlation between photons traveling away from each other, which he described as "ghostly action-at-a-distance," would allow the possibility of messages to be sent faster than the speed of light. Message sending could occur if we could make changes in a beam of photons coming toward us, and observe *reliable* corresponding changes in another beam traveling away from us. According to relativity theory, it is impossible for an informational connection to be maintained between two points that are receding from each other at the speed of light. Einstein therefore concluded that there must be something fundamentally wrong with quantum theory.

In 1964, physicist John Bell at the European Organization for Nuclear Research (CERN) proved the far-reaching inequality theorem now known as Bell's Theorem, and rigorously described the consequences of the EPR conjecture. Bell's Theorem implied that if an EPR-type of experiment involving photons going off in opposite directions were actually carried out, then, according to Nobel prize-winning physicist Brian Josephson, "there must be a mechanism whereby the setting of one measuring device can influence the reading of another instrument, however remote."[5]

The appropriate physics experiments testing this conjecture have now been carried out in several laboratories worldwide: by Freedman and Clauser in Berkeley in 1972, by Aspect and his colleagues in Paris in 1982, and by Gisin at the University of Geneva in 1997.[6] All of these experiments show that the widely separated photons do indeed appear to be correlated with each other, even over kilometer distances. However, since they fluctuate randomly, the person at the receiving end of the system has no way to determine whether the sender did or did not change the state of the photons the receiver is presently observing.

Einstein was correct in his analysis showing that there was a correlation between these photons receding from each other at the speed of light. At this time, however, it seems that he was mistaken in his concern about the correlation violating relativity theory, because it does not appear that the photons can be used for message sending. Therefore, it is the EPR analysis from the 1930s, together with the contemporary experiments cited above, that have given scientific support to the current view of nonlocal connectedness. We do not believe that EPR-type of correlations are the explanation for mind-to-mind connections, but we think that they are an unequivocal laboratory example of the nonlocal nature of our universe which makes these connections possible.

If this explanation does not seem to be entirely clear, it is probably because even though Einstein published these ideas sixty years ago, the smartest physicists in the world still do not agree on all of the implications of these nonlocal connections. In fact, Josephson wrote of these experiments, "The existence of such remote influences or connections is suggested more directly by experiments on phenomena such as telepathy (the connection of one mind to another) and psychokinesis (the direct influence of mind on matter), both of which are examples of so-called psi functioning." Josephson went on to write:

> One may imagine that life may exist from the beginning as a cooperative whole, directly interconnected at a distance by Bell-type nonlocal interactions, following which, modifications through the course of evolution cause organisms to be interconnected directly with each other.... One can see conceptual similarities between psi skills and ordinary skills, e.g., between perceptual skills of hearing and telepathy on the one hand, and between the forms of control of matter involved in control of the body, and in psychokinesis, on the other.[7]

In addition to the theories of physicists, writings of poets and philosophers that originated even before Biblical times have articulated the idea that physical separations are more illusory than real. Buddhist teachings, following from the earlier Vedic tradition, postulate that human desires and attachments arising from distinctions such as "here and not here, now and not now" are the cause of all the world's suffering. This concept is beautifully and clearly delineated in Ken Wilber's book on the Buddhist worldview, appropriately called *No Boundary*.[8] He describes the many levels of awareness associated with the Perennial Philosophy, which is a term Aldous Huxley used for the highest common factor present in all the major wisdom traditions and religions of the world.[9] The Perennial Philosophy has as its first principle that consciousness is the fundamental building block of the universe — the world is more like a great thought than a great machine. We human beings can access all of the universe through our own consciousness and our nonlocal mind. This philosophy also maintains that we have a dual nature, both local and nonlocal, both material and nonmaterial. Finally, the Perennial Philosophy teaches that the purpose of life is to become one with this universal, nonlocal consciousness that is available to us. That is, to become one with God, and to help others to do likewise.

In this worldview, one experiences increasing unity consciousness through meditation, as one passes "upward" through physical, biological, emotional, mental, spiritual, and aetheric levels of awareness. Through meditation one experiences the insight that one is not a body — one *has* a body. The idea that separation is an illusion has been spelled out by mystics for at least twenty-five hundred years. Hinduism teaches that individual consciousness (Atman) and universal consciousness (Brahman) are one. Patanjali taught that the realized being achieved a state of awareness in which "the Seer is established in his own essential and fundamental nature."[10] Plato called such people who had transcended the boundaries of their separate selves "the spectator[s] of all time and all existence."[11] The view of life in which we are all connected with God, and in which the kingdom of God is within us all, awaiting to be realized and experienced, is part of both the Jewish and Christian traditions as well.

In Judaism, the local community of spirit is often referred to as *HaShem* (the Name), while in Christianity it is called the Holy Spirit, or Emmanuel, the immanent or indwelling God of all. This view of a community of spirit arose, very likely, from mystics of every sacred tradition whose meditations led them to have oceanic mind-to-mind feelings of one-ness and love. "Such realization may be fleeting or lasting, spontaneous or the product of religious practice, but it is an enduring feature of human life," to quote Leonard and Murphy.[12]

Russell once had a conversation with Margaret Mead in which he expressed disappointment about the lack of general acceptance of the exis-tence of ESP in the scientific community. She sternly told him that he shouldn't complain, because after all, Giordano Bruno had been burned at the stake in the sixteenth century during the Inquisition, for espousing ideas not very different from ours. Bruno believed in the unity of all things, and strongly opposed Aristotelian dualism for separating body and spirit. He exhorts us all to achieve union with the "Infinite One" in an infinite uni-verse. Baruch Spinoza in the seventeenth century had a similar worldview, but he was luckily spared the Inquisition because he was Jewish. He was, however, banished from his own synagogue because of his pantheistic model of God being in all things, including himself.

The philosophy of a universal connection among all things was taught in the 1750s by Bishop George Berkeley, who could be considered an early Transcendentalist. He felt that the world was greatly misapprehended by our ordinary senses, and that consciousness was the fundamental ground of all existence. In the nineteenth century, Ralph Waldo Emerson and Henry Thoreau believed in a strongly connected spiritual community, which Emerson called The Oversoul. Their Transcendentalism gave rise to many New Thought churches in the U.S., such as Christian Science, Science of Mind, and Unity. The famous Viennese psychiatrist Carl Jung described our mind-to-mind connections in terms of a collective unconscious. The coher-ent theme among all of these is that *there is an essential part of all of us that is shared.* Contemporary Judaism teaches a similar view of our interconnected-ness. The revered Jewish theologian Rabbi Lawrence Kushner tells us that:

> Human beings are joined to one another and to all creation. Every-thing performing its intended task doing commerce with its neigh-bors. Drawing nourishment and sustenance from unimagined other individuals. Coming into being, growing to maturity, procreating.

Dying. Often without even the faintest awareness of its indispensable and vital function within the greater "body...." All creation is one person, one being, whose cells are connected to one another within a medium called consciousness."[13]

Historically, the belief in our connected nature has been largely based on the personal experiences of the people who shared this view. Today, we recognize that just because large numbers of people have believed something (such as the flat earth) for several millennia, it does not by any means make it true. How are we to decide if we should consider this view of community of spirit to be deep nonsense unrelated to nature, or a valid concept of the workings of the world? The usual scientific approach is to see if the model offers testable predictions.

A contemporary nonreligious model of this connectedness has been presented by physicist David Bohm in his last book, *The Undivided Universe*.[14] This physics text has great contemporary credibility, because Bohm derives quantitatively correct answers to some of the most puzzling questions at the ragged edges of modern physics. Bohm provides a compelling ontology (or model) encompassing all the data that we have been examining. He does this through the use of a holographic model of the universe. This model is especially appealing for the psi researcher at this time, because the defining property of the hologram is that every tiny piece of the hologram contains a complete picture of the whole.

English biologist Rupert Sheldrake developed a "hypothesis of formative causation," based on the existence of organizing fields very similar to Bohm's "active information" wave functions. Sheldrake's theory was published in his 1981 book, *A New Science of Life*, which introduced the idea that some sort of organizing fields that transcend space and time determine the characteristic forms and behavior of living organisms, as well as physical systems of all levels of complexity.[15] He called these fields of formative causation or "morphogenetic fields." According to Sheldrake, once such fields become established through some initial behavior of an organism, that behavior then becomes facilitated in others through a process called "morphic resonance."

The authors of this book feel that there has been an exponential increase in human intellectual evolution over the past hundreds of years, which can be partly explained by Sheldrake's hypothesis, which we liken to global mind-to-mind interactions. The relation between these interactions and Sheldrake's model is explored by Peter Russell in the book *The Global Brain*:

> Applying Sheldrake's theory to the development of higher consciousness [or expanded awareness], we might predict that the more individuals begin to raise their own levels of consciousness, the stronger the morphogenetic field for higher states will become, and the easier it would be for others to move in that direction. Society would gather momentum toward enlightenment. Since the rate of growth would not be dependent on the achievements of those who had gone before, we would enter a phase of super-exponential growth.[16]

In summary, we believe that Patanjali's akashic records, Sheldrake's morphogenetic fields, and Bohm's active information are all directly accessible by consciousness. Bohm and Josephson make it clear that consciousness must be considered as influencing the physical universe, if there is to be a solution to both the psi and the EPR measurement problem.

If you look at a hologram on a photographic plate, the imbedded three-dimensional image is invisible. It is entirely dispersed in the optical interference pattern spread throughout the plate, even though these fringes cannot be seen or measured directly. Bohm calls this the implicate, or enfolded, order in the holographic plate. The explicate order is the three-dimensional picture that you see when you illuminate the hologram with a laser beam. The important idea is that each of us has our mind in our own small piece of the space-time hologram, containing all the information that exists, or ever was. Imagine that you had a large sheet of postage stamps, where the whole sheet showed a picture of a flag, and each small stamp showed a picture of the same flag. As you break off smaller and smaller pieces of the hologram, the three-dimensional field of view decreases along with the spatial resolution, but you still get the whole picture. It's as though you start with a big piece of matzoh. No matter how small a piece you break off, you still have matzoh. Bohm says:

The essential features of the implicate order are, that the whole universe is in some way enfolded in everything, and that each thing is enfolded in the whole.[17]

This is the fundamental statement of a holographic ordering of the universe. It says that, like a hologram, each region of space-time contains information about every other point in space-time. And our data indicate that this information is available to consciousness. Bohm continues:

...all of this implies a thoroughgoing wholeness, in which mental and physical sides participate very closely in each other. Likewise, intellect, emotion, and the whole state of the body are in a similar flux of fundamental participation. Thus, there is no real division between mind and matter, psyche and soma. The common term psychosomatic is in this way seen to be misleading, as it suggests the Cartesian notion of two distinct substances in some kind of interaction.[18]

This is Bohm's rejection of any kind of mind-body dualism. Bohm considers physics to be comprehensive enough to embrace consciousness. And moreover, it is consciousness that comes to the fore to solve many of the so-called observational paradoxes in quantum mechanics:

Extending this view, we see that each human being similarly participates in an inseparable way in society and the planet as a whole. What may be suggested further is that such participation goes on to a greater collective mind, and perhaps ultimately to some yet more comprehensive mind, in principle capable of going indefinitely beyond even the human species as a whole.[19]

In the holographic universe of David Bohm, there is a unity of consciousness, a "greater collective mind," with no boundaries of space or time. Similarly, we believe that our psychic abilities offer us one way of experiencing this world of nonlocal mind, or community of spirit. Remote viewing reveals to us a part of our spiritual reality, but it is only a tiny part of the total spiritual spectrum.

Michael Talbot, author of *The Holographic Universe*, has described this model more poetically:

> And so we have come full circle, from the discovery that consciousness contains the whole of objective reality — the entire history of biological life on the planet, the world's religions and mythologies, and the dynamics of both blood cells and stars — to the discovery that the material universe can also contain within its warp and weft, the innermost processes of consciousness. Such is the nature of the deep connectivity that exists between all things in a holographic universe.[20]

According to this model, remote viewers find what they are looking for in one small piece of the total hologram, just as we are able to extract and remember data from the past. The smallness of our holographic mental image accounts for the lack of resolution in remote viewing, because we experience only a fraction of the total hologram. The nonlocal holographic model illustrates how we can describe and experience distant points in space-time. We illuminate the hologram of space-time with our coherent consciousness, as we do when recovering a memory. These views of collective unconscious are called by many names, and have been with us for millennia.

This model of psi functioning suggests that the information is always with us and available, and that psi is not some kind of mental radio. This is not a new theory, but it seems to fit the data much better than most information or energy-transmission models. Similarly, in the case of distant healing, we believe that the positive effect of the healer is achieved through making available a healing message or information, rather than a healing ray or energy. We recognize that as more data is collected in the coming years, we will be able to create more appropriate models than the one described here.

We have previously recalled the aphorism, "What experiments are to the scientist, experience is to the mystic." In Chapter 7, Jane has written of her intense pain, prayer, and dream experience that led to her subsequent experiences involving spiritual healing. Now that we have discussed analogies of the physics and mathematics of mind-to-mind connections, we can address the implications of the many spontaneous experiences of psi that people are having outside the laboratory.

The most recent research in the field of near-death studies has focused on the aftereffects of the NDE. These aftereffects include a pattern of changes in the NDEr that psychology professor Kenneth Ring has interpreted to be "indicative of a generalized awakening of higher human potential."[21] Research data of Ring, Greyson, Kohr, and Morse indicate that a significant number of near-death experiencers have at the same time convincing validated psychic experiences.[22] They see not only the light at the end of a spiritual tunnel, but also verifiable events that occurred during their period of unconsciousness.

George Gallup, Jr. reports in *Adventures in Immortality* on the results of a Gallup Poll on the prevalence of near-death experiences.[23] The apparent remote-viewing capabilities that accompany many NDErs during their out-of-body experiences are particularly interesting. Gallup tells us that of the approximately 160 million adult Americans alive at the time of his survey, one in twenty, or an estimated eight million adult Americans, have likely had an NDE. The spontaneous experience of remote viewing that occurs to a sizable number of NDErs is increasing the awareness of psi abilities for countless people who never would have given ESP a second thought.

Near-death researcher Ring points out in his book *Heading Toward Omega* that even if Gallup's estimate were off by millions of people, the near-death experience is becoming a "very significant and pervasive phenomenon" in our society, occurring to millions, and indirectly touching the lives of millions of others.[24] Gallup reports that slightly more than a third of those adults who come close to death today in our country undergo an NDE, in addition to an unknown number of children. Ring adds, "Because of the highly developed state of our resuscitation technology, we can safely assume that millions more will have this experience themselves in the years to come...."[25] NDE statistics are included here because we believe this enduring phenomenon will be significant to the field of psychic research in the coming years.

Although the actual cause of the near-death experience needs clarification, researchers agree that a common outcome is the transformation of consciousness that occurs for people who have NDEs: the realization that "the true value of existence is the connectedness that you have going with every other living thing."[26] Another frequent feature of NDEs is an out-of-body experience (OBE) wherein the NDEr has verifiable visual perceptions and knowledge of events that are highly similar to the remote-viewing episodes that we have described in this book. Researcher Michael Sabom, in his book *Recollections of Death*, provides impressive evidence of NDErs, resuscitated in hospitals, who were able to describe events they could not possibly have seen or known by ordinary sense perception, given the positions of their bodies and their physical condition.[27] Other psychic experiences reported to have occurred during the unconscious state of NDErs, and which are more difficult to study and verify, include precognition of future events, the comprehension of foreign languages never previously understood by the NDEr, and clear visual perception by nearsighted individuals during a remote-viewing experience.[28]

Dr. Ring is interested in the meaning of the near-death experience, just as we are interested in what the existence of remote viewing can tell us about the nature of reality, mind, and who we really are. He has postulated that the NDE may be an indication of our potential for expanded awareness. Remote-viewing research is providing additional evidence of our extended abilities. A near-death experience is too high a price to pay for psychic development, but it is nonetheless exciting that so many people are having these kinds of experiences.

With this book, we hope to inspire others to reach outside the restrictions of our previously held assumptions, and experience our greater potential of mind. In doing so, we can enable each other to expand our mutual trust, imagination, creativity, and love. We can help each other to express more fully the true dimensions of our being. George Leonard and Michael Murphy, two of the founding figures of the human potential movement, have written a book entitled *The Life We Are Given*, in which they outline a long-term program of consistent practice for realizing our fuller potentials of body, mind, heart, and soul.[29] We believe as they do, that "Most of us realize just a fraction of our human potential. We live only part of the life we are given." They tell us that:

> The culture we inhabit reinforces only some of our latent capacities, while neglecting or suppressing others. In the contemporary West, for example, there is great support for high-level athletic development, but relatively little for advanced meditation and the metanormal capacities it evokes.[30]

Our old friend Patanjali, at least three hundred years before Christ, described a litany of "metanormal" abilities available to those who practiced meditation consistently. We list them in their entirety in Chapter 6, and only reiterate here that contemporary research involving remote viewing, near-death studies, psychic diagnosis, and distant healing are confirming that many of the extended abilities known to Patanjali are becoming manifest today. Some of them include: "Knowledge of past and future; perception of the small, the concealed, and the distant; knowledge of other inhabited regions; knowledge of the interior of the body; and general intuition."[31]

A central aim of the practice of Yoga, as expounded by Patanjali, was the understanding and experience of our true nature of oneness with God and each other. Emotional equanimity, nonantagonism to any situation that might arise, expanded awareness, joy, fulfillment, and psychic abilities were the by-products of such understanding. The development of every human faculty — rational, intuitive, physical, emotional, and ethical — which may be conducive to that end of perfect knowledge, and union with the Divine, were part of Yogic practice.

We said at the outset that this was a book about psychic abilities and healing connections. We believe that psi's greatest value will be found in its ability to help us discover a deeper understanding of who we are, to enable us to experience our most intimate relationship with each other, and to learn to more fully appreciate the wonder of the universe and our place in it. As we look toward the future, it is our hope that our investigations of remote viewing and healing will make a contribution toward achieving a more peaceful and compassionate world.

The Nobel Peace Prize of 1989 was awarded to His Holiness the Dalai Lama, the Tibetan spiritual and political leader. While head of the Tibetan government in exile during the Chinese occupation of his country, he has become a revered spokesperson for healing and peace in the world. In an interview with the Dalai Lama on the subject of facing the future with hope, he said:

> All we have is education. It's our only weapon, along with the example we can set. And this education, from the Buddhist viewpoint, begins with the notion of interdependence.... This has to be said and explained: above all, it has to be proved....
>
> This shared awareness is essential if we want to improve, however little, our own attitude toward the world, our own relationship with it. We must overcome the isolation of our mind, we must renew our ties with the rest of the universe. Otherwise we are lost. Lost because separate. We have to show people, indefatigably, that our interest is the interest of others, that our future is the future of others.[32]

The Dalai Lama went on to say that we must find a new spirituality apart from any religious dogma, one that promotes a secular morality based on the connectedness and interdependence of all life, and the cultivation of peaceful-mindedness and compassion for all. "We ought to promote this concept with the help of scientists," he said.[33] We want to be part of such a movement, and this book is offered in the hope that it serves that end.

In our own experience, we have found the approach of *A Course in Miracles* to be one of many useful and practical tools for cultivating peaceful-mindedness.[34] It says that our primary misperception in need of correction is our belief in our separation from one another. It teaches that, "A universal theology is impossible, but a universal experience is not only possible but necessary."[35] This necessary experience refers to the experience of our connection and oneness with others. The Course tells us, just as the Dalai Lama said, that a truly wise person, no matter what the path, is one who "has seen in another person the same interests as his own."[36] The acceptance of our shared awareness is, for us, the bridge between nonlocal perception and spiritual healing. It is in this context that we understand spiritual healing as "loving your neighbor as yourself."

So we have indeed come full circle — from governments using our mind-to-mind connections for defense, to the Dalai Lama's promotion of the research and knowledge of our interdependent nature as a "weapon" for survival. We believe that the data for our interconnected consciousness is just the sort of evidence that the Dalai Lama was looking for.

We've traveled through time, from ancient scriptures to modern physics. We have journeyed through the space of our nonlocal universe of interconnectedness. *A Course in Miracles* reiterates what the ancient sages have told us, and instructs us to pay attention to the here and now:

> Your task is not to seek for love, but merely to seek and find all of the barriers within yourself that you have built against it.[37]

Similarly, we would say that we don't have to search for psi, but our task is rather to seek to remove the barriers that we and our society have erected against it. Our understanding of mind-to-mind connections derived from experience, as well as science, offers us ongoing opportunities to achieve this goal.

The Persian mystic Jelaluddin Rumi of the thirteenth century knew:

> *I've heard it said there's a window that opens*
> *from one mind to another,*
> *but if there's no wall, there's no need*
> *for fitting the window, or the latch.*

Chapter Notes

INTRODUCTION: THE ILLUSION OF SEPARATION

1. David Bohm in Renèe Weber, "Meaning as Being in the Implicate Order Philosophy of David Bohm: A Conversation," in B.J. Hiley and F. David Peat, eds., *Quantum Implications: Essays in Honor of David Bohm.* (New York: Routledge, 1987), p. 436.
2. Larry Dossey, "Healing Happens," *Utne Reader*, Sept./Oct. 1995, pp. 52–59.
3. Norman Friedman, *Bridging Science and Spirit: Common Elements of David Bohm's Physics, The Perennial Philosophy, and Seth* (St. Louis, MO: Living Lake Books, 1994).
4. The Dalai Lama in Jean-Claude Carriere, "Facing the Future," *New Age Journal*, Nov./Dec. 1995, p. 146.
5. Alan H. Batten, "A Most Rare Vision: Eddington's Thinking on the Relation Between Science and Religion," *Journal of Scientific Exploration*, vol. 9, no. 2, Summer 1995, pp. 231–234.

CHAPTER 1: WHAT I SEE WHEN I CLOSE MY EYES

This chapter is based on a talk given at the 1993 Annual Convention of the Parapsychological Association, Toronto, Canada. *Exceptional Experiences of Psi Investigators: Their Meanings and Implications*, symposium with William Braud and Rhea White (co-chairs), Russell Targ, and Montague Ullman.

1. Alfred J. Ayer, *Language, Truth and Logic* (New York: Dover Publications, Inc., 1952).
2. Ibid.
3. Brian Inglis, *Natural and Supernatural* (London: Hodder and Stoughton, 1977).
4. William Nolan, *Healing: Doctor in Search of a Miracle* (New York: Random House, 1974).
5. René Warcollier, *Mind to Mind* (New York: Collier, 1963); and Upton Sinclair, *Mental Radio* (New York: Collier, 1971).
6. Robert McKim, *Experiences in Visual Thinking* (Monterey, CA: Brooks/Cole, 1972).
7. Russell Targ, William Braud, Marilyn Schlitz, Rex Stanford, and Charles Honorton. "Increasing Psychic Reliability," A panel discussion presented at the 33rd annual conference of the Parapsychological Association, Chevy Chase, MD, Aug. 16–20, 1990. *Journal of Parapsychology*, vol. 55, 1991, p. 59.

8. Ken Wilber, *No Boundary* (Boston: Shambhala, 1979).
9. Gerald Feinberg, "Precognition — Memory of Things Future," in proceedings of a conference on Quantum Physics and Parapsychology, Geneva, Switzerland (New York: Parapsychology Foundation, 1975), pp. 54–75.
10. Larry Dossey, *Recovering the Soul* (New York: Bantam Books, 1989).
11. Swami Prabhavananda, *How to Know God*, translated by Christopher Isherwood (Hollywood, CA: Vedanta Press, 1983).
12. Ibid.
13. Ernest Wood, *The Glorious Presence* (Wheaton, IL: The Theosophical Publishing House, 1974).
14. Jessica Utts, "An Assessment of the Evidence for Psychic Functioning." Prepared for the U.S. Central Intelligence Agency through the American Institute of Research, Division of Statistics, University of California, Davis, 1995.
15. Lois Duncan and William Roll, *Psychic Connections* (New York: Delacorte Press, 1995).

CHAPTER 2: OUR ASTONISHING NONLOCAL MIND

1. Harold Puthoff and Russell Targ, "A Perceptual Channel for Information Transfer over Kilometer Distances: Historical Perspective and Recent Research," *Proceedings of IEEE*, vol. 64, no. 3, March 1976, pp. 329–354.
2. Russell Targ, Elisabeth Targ, and Keith Harary, "Moscow–San Francisco Remote Viewing Experiment," *Psi Research*, vol. 3, no. 3–4, Sept./Dec. 1984.
3. Russell Targ and David Hurt, "Learning Clairvoyance and Precognition with an ESP Teaching Machine," *Parapsychology Review*, July/Aug. 1972.
4. Edgar D. Mitchell, "An ESP Test from Apollo 14," *Journal of Parapsychology*, vol. 35, no. 2, 1971.
5. Sheila Ostrander and Lynn Schroeder, *Psychic Discoveries Behind the Iron Curtain* (Englewood Cliffs, NJ: Prentice Hall, 1970).
6. Arthur C. Clark, *Childhood's End* (New York: Ballantine Books/Random House, 1953).
7. C.A. Robinson, Jr., "Soviets Push for Beam Weapon," *Aviation Week*, May 2, 1977.
8. Harold Puthoff and Russell Targ, "Perceptual Augmentation Techniques," *SRI Final Report*, (covering the period of January 1974 through February 1975), Dec. 1, 1975.
9. Russell Targ and Harold Puthoff, *Mind-Reach: Scientists Look at Psychic Abilities* (New York: Delacorte, 1977).
10. Russell Targ, "Remote-Viewing Replication: Evaluated by Concept Analysis." *The Journal of Parapsychology*, vol. 58, September 1994.
11. Legion of Merit Award for Joseph McMoneagle (1984), in Edwin C. May, "The American Institutes of Research Review of the Department of Defense's STAR GATE Program: A Commentary," *Journal of Scientific Exploration*, vol. 10, 1996, pp. 89–107.
12. E.C. May, "AC Technical Trials: Inspiration for the Target Entropy Concept," in *Proceedings of the 1995 Parapsychology Association Conference*, Durham, NC, July 1979.

CHAPTER 3: WHAT WE HAVE LEARNED ABOUT REMOTE VIEWING

1. Roger Penrose, *Shadows of the Mind: A Search for the Missing Science of Consciousness* (New York: Oxford University Press, 1994), p. 419.
2. N.F. Dixon, *Subliminal Perception* (London: McGraw-Hill, 1971).
3. Paul Ferrini, "The Door to the House of Love," *Miracles Magazine*, vol. I, Autumn 1991, p. 53.

4. H.E. Puthoff, R. Targ, and C.T. Tart, "Resolution in Remote Viewing Studies," in *Research in Parapsychology 1979* (Metuchen, NJ: Scarecrow Press, 1980).

5. C.W. Leadbeater, *Occult Chemistry* (London: Theosophical Society, 1898).

6. James Spottiswoode, "Geomagnetic Fluctuations and Free-Response Anomalous Cognition: A New Understanding," *Journal of Parapsychology*, vol. 61, no. 1, March 1997.

7. Russell Targ, E.C. May, and H.E. Puthoff, "Direct Perception of Remote Geographic Locations," in *Mind At Large: Proceedings of IEEE Symposia on Extrasensory Perception* (New York: Praeger, 1979).

8. Edwin C. May, James Spottiswoode, and Jessica Utts, "Decision Augmentation Theory: Toward a Model of Anomalous Mental Phenomena," *Journal of Parapsychology*, vol. 59, Sept. 1995, pp. 195–221.

9. Jim Schnabel, *Remote Viewers: The Secret History of America's Psychic Spies* (New York: Dell Books, 1997).

10. Albert Einstein, *Ideas and Opinions* (New York: Bonanza Books), p. 12.

CHAPTER 4: THE MASTERS OF THE UNIVERSE AND THE MYSTERY OF PSI

1. Alfred North Whitehead and Bertrand Russell, *Principia Mathematica* (Cambridge, England: Cambridge University Press, 1910).

2. Patanjali, *Sutras*, in Swami Prabhavananda, translated by Christopher Isherwood, *How to Know God* (Hollywood, CA: Vedanta Press, 1983).

3. Ken Wilber, *The Spectrum of Consciousness* (Wheaton, IL: Quest Books/The Theosophical Publishing House, 1993); Ken Wilber, *No Boundary* (Boston: Shambhala, 1979); and Shankara, in Swami Prabhavananda, translated by Christopher Isherwood, *Crest-Jewel of Discrimination* (Hollywood, CA: Vedanta Press, 1975).

4. J.B. Rhine and J.G. Pratt, "A Review of the Pearce-Pratt Distance Series of ESP Tests," *Journal of Parapsychology*, vol. 18, 1954, pp. 165–177.

5. M. Ryzl, "A Model of Parapsychological Communication," *Journal of Parapsychology*, 1966, pp. 18–30.

6. J.G. Blom and J.G. Pratt, "A Second Confirmatory Experiment with Pavel Stepanek as a Borrowed Subject," *Journal of the ASPR*, vol. 62, 1969, pp. 28–45.

7. James Carpenter, "Toward the Effective Utilization of Enhanced Weak-Signal ESP Effects," A paper presented at the AAAS meeting in New York, 1975; and James Carpenter, "Prediction of forced-choice ESP performance, Part-3," *Journal of Parapsychology*, vol. 55, Sept. 1991, pp. 227–280.

8. Upton Sinclair, *Mental Radio* (New York: Collier, 1971).

9. Ibid., pp. 116–119.

10. René Warcollier, *Mind to Mind* (New York: Collier, 1963).

11. Louisa Rhine, "Frequency and Types of Experience in Spontaneous Precognition," *Journal of Parapsychology*, vol. 16, 1954, pp. 93–123.

12. S. Freud, "Dreaming and Telepathy," in G. Devereux, ed., *Psychoanalysis and the Occult* (New York: International Universities Press, 1953).

13. J. Eisenbud, *Psi and Psychoanalysis* (New York: Grune and Stratton, 1970).

14. M. Ullman, S. Krippner, and A. Vaughan, *Dream Telepathy* (New York: Macmillan, 1973).

15. S. Krippner, C. Honorton, M. Ullman, and M. Masters, "A Long-Distance 'Sensory Bombardment' Study of ESP in Dreams," *Journal of the ASPR*, vol. 65, 1971, pp. 468–475.

16. C. Honorton, "Meta-Analysis of Psi Ganzfeld Research: A Response to Hyman," *Journal of Parapsychology*, vol. 49, 1985, pp. 51–91.
17. D. Bem and C. Honorton, "Does Psi Exist? Replicable Evidence for an Anomalous Process of Information Transfer," *Psychological Bulletin*, January 1994.
18. M. Schlitz and C. Honorton, "Ganzfeld Psi Performance Within an Artistically Gifted Population," *Journal ASPR*, vol. 86, 1992, pp. 83–98.
19. James C. Terry and Charles Honorton, "Psi Information Retrieval in the Ganzfeld: Two Confirmatory Studies," *Journal ASPR*, vol. 70, 1976, pp. 207–219.
20. Ibid.
21. R. Hyman and C. Honorton, "A Joint Communiqué: The Psi Ganzfeld Controversy," *Journal of Parapsychology*, vol. 50, 1986, pp. 251–264.
22. M. Schlitz and E. Gruber, "Transcontinental Remote Viewing," *Journal of Parapsychology*, vol. 44, 1980, pp. 305–317.
23. K.R. Rao, *The Basic Experiments in Parapsychology* (Jefferson, NC: McFarland & Co, 1984).
24. R. Targ and H. Puthoff, "Information Transfer Under Conditions of Sensory Shielding," *Nature*, vol. 251, 1974, pp. 602–607; and Hansen, M. Schlitz, and C. Tart, "Remote Viewing Research 1973–1982," in R. Targ and K. Harary, *The Mind Race* (New York: Villard, 1984).
25. M.B. Eddy, *Science and Health*, 1875, and *Science and Health with Key to the Scriptures*, First Church of Christ Scientist, 1971.
26. Herbert Benson, *The Relaxation Response* (New York: William Morrow, 1975); Herbert Benson, *Beyond the Relaxation Response* (New York: Times Books, 1984); and Dean Ornish, *Dr. Dean Ornish's Program for Reversing Heart Disease* (New York: Random House, Inc., 1990).
27. John C. Eccles, *Facing Reality* (New York: Springer-Verlag, 1970).
28. W. Braud and M. Schlitz, "Consciousness Interactions with Remote Biological Systems: Anomalous Intentionality Effects," *Subtle Energies*, vol. 2, 1991, pp. 1–47; and W. Braud, "On the Use of Living Target Systems in Distant Mental Influence Research," in L. Coly, ed., *Psi Research Methodology: A Re-examination* (New York: Parapsychology Foundation, 1993).
29. W. Braud, "A Role of Mind in the Physical World," *European Journal of Parapsychology*, vol. 10, 1994, pp. 66–77.
30. W. Braud, "Direct Mental Influence on the Rate of Hemolysis of Human Red Blood Cells," *Parapsychology 1979* (Metuchen, NJ: Scarecrow Press, 1980), pp. 140–142.
31. Beverly Rubik and Elizabeth Rauscher, "Effects on Motility Behavior and Growth Rate of Salmonella Typhimurium in the Presence of Olga Worrall," in W.G. Roll, ed., *Research in Parapsychology 1979* (Metuchen, NJ: Scarecrow Press, 1980).
32. B. Grad, "A Telekinetic Effect on Plant Growth," *International Journal of Parapsychology*, vol. 6, 1964, pp. 472–498.
33. Douglas Dean, "Infrared and Ultraviolet Techniques to Test for Changes in Water Following the Laying On of Hands." Doctoral dissertation, Saybrook University, San Francisco, CA (1983), international microfilm number 8408650; and Stephan Schwartz, Rand DeMattei, James Spottiswoode, and Edward Brain, Jr., "Infrared Spectra Alteration in Water, Proximate to the Palms of Therapeutic Practitioners." *Subtle Energies*, vol. 1, 1990, pp. 43–72.
34. B. Grad, R.J. Cadoret, and G.I. Paul, "The Influence of Unorthodox Methods of Treatment on Wound Healing in Mice," *International Journal of Parapsychology*, vol. 3, 1961, pp. 5–24.
35. Dean Radin, *The Conscious Universe* (New York: HarperEdge, 1997).

CHAPTER 5: PRECOGNITION: TIME AND TIME AGAIN

1. Foundation for Inner Peace, *A Course in Miracles* (New York: Viking Penguin, 1996), p. 1.
2. Alfred North Whitehead and Bertrand Russell, *Principia Mathematica* (Cambridge, England: Cambridge University Press, 1910).
3. S.E. Braude, *ESP and Psychokinesis: A Philosophical Examination* (Philadelphia, PA: Temple University Press, 1979); and J. Eisenbud, *Paranormal Foreknowledge* (New York: Human Science Press, 1982).
4. Elisabeth Targ and Russell Targ, "Accuracy of Paranormal Perception as a Function of Varying Target Probabilities," *Journal of Parapsychology*, vol. 50, March 1986, pp. 17–27.
5. Charles Honorton and Diane C. Ferari, "Future-Telling: A Meta-Analysis of Forced-Choice Precognition Experiments," *Journal of Parapsychology*, vol. 53, Dec. 1989, pp. 281–309.
6. R. Targ, J. Katra, D. Brown, and W. Wiegand, "Viewing the Future: A Pilot Study with an Error-Detecting Protocol," *Journal of Scientific Exploration*, vol. 9, no. 3, 1995, pp. 67–80.
7. David Bohm and B.J. Hiley, *The Undivided Universe* (New York: Routledge, 1993).
8. Norman Friedman, *Bridging Science and Spirit: Common Elements of David Bohm's Physics, The Perennial Philosophy, and Seth* (St. Louis, MO: Living Lake Books, 1994).
9. Dean Radin, "Unconscious Perceptions of Future Emotions: An Experiment in Presentiment," *Proceedings of Parapsychological Association*, 39th Annual Convention, San Diego, CA, 1996.
10. Helmut Schmidt and Lee Pantas, "PK Tests with Internally Different Machines," *Journal of Parapsychology*, vol. 36, 1972, pp. 222–232.
11. Helmut Schmidt, "Random Generators and Living Systems as Targets in Retro-PK Experiments," *Journal ASPR*, vol. 91, 1997, pp. 1–14.
12. Honorton and Ferari, "Future-Telling: A Meta-Analysis of Forced-Choice Precognition Experiments."
13. G.R. Schmeidler, "An Experiment in Precognitive Clairvoyance: Part-1. The Main Results;" and Part-2. "The Reliability of the Scores," *Journal of Parapsychology*, vol. 8, 1964, pp. 1–14, 15–27.
14. S. Krippner, M. Ullman, and C. Honorton, "A Precognitive Dream Study with a Single Subject," *Journal of the ASPR*, vol. 65, 1971, pp. 192–203; and "A Second Precognitive Dream Study with Malcolm Bessent," *Journal of the ASPR*, vol. 66, 1972, pp. 269–279.
15. Russell Targ and Harold Puthoff, *Mind Reach: Scientists Look at Psychic Abilities* (Delacorte, New York, 1977).
16. H.E. Puthoff and R. Targ, "A Perceptual Channel for Information Transfer over Kilometer Distances: Historical Perspective and Recent Research," *Proceedings IEEE*, vol. 64, no. 3, March 1976, pp. 229–254.
17. J.W. Dunne, *An Experiment with Time* (London: Faber & Faber, 1969).
18. B.J. Dunne, R.G. Jahn, and R.D. Nelson, "Precognitive Remote Perception," Princeton Engineering Anomalies Research Laboratory (Report, August 1983).
19. Elisabeth Targ and Russell Targ, "Accuracy of Paranormal Perception as a Function of Varying Target Probabilities," *Journal of Parapsychology*, vol. 50, 1986, pp. 17–27.
20. Russell Targ, Jane Katra, Dean Brown, and Wenden Wiegand, "Viewing the Future: A Pilot Study with an Error-Detecting Protocol," *Journal of Scientific Exploration*, vol. 9, no. 3, 1995, pp. 367–380.

21. Michael Murphy, *The Future of the Body* (Los Angeles: Jeremy P. Tarcher, Inc., 1992).

CHAPTER 6: ARE PSYCHIC ABILITIES SACRED?

1. Arthur Koestler, *The Roots of Coincidence* (New York: Random House, 1972).
2. Rachel Naomi Remen, "Is Psi Sacred?" *Noetic Sciences Review*, vol. 35, Autumn 1995, p. 36.
3. Ibid., p. 34.
4. Kenneth Wapnick, *Forgiveness and Jesus* (Farmingdale, NY: Coleman Publishing, 1983), p. 136.
5. Rabbi David A.Cooper, in Eliezer Sobel, "Contemplative Judaism," *The Quest*, Winter 1995, p. 68.
6. *Holy Bible*. I Corinthians 12: 8–13.
7. Dean Brown, *Direct from Sanskrit: New Translations of Seven Upanishads, the Aphorisms of Patanjali, and Other Microcosmic Texts of Ancient India* (Los Angeles: Philosophical Research Society, 1996); Swami Prabhavananda, *How to Know God: The Yoga Aphorisms of Patanjali*, translated by Christopher Isherwood (Hollywood, CA: Vedanta Press, 1953, 1981); I.K.Taimni, *The Science of Yoga* (Wheaton, IL: Quest/Theosophical Publishing House, 1961), pp. 307–309; Ernest Wood, *Yoga* (Baltimore, MD: Penguin, 1962), pp. 76–79; Ernest Wood, *The Glorious Presence* (Wheaton, IL: Theosophical Publishing House, 1951), p. 215.
8. Taimni, *Science of Yoga*, p. 308.
9. Patanjali, *Yoga Sutras* iii: 36, in Wood, *Yoga*, pp. 78–79.
10. Patanjali, *Yoga Sutras* iv: 1, in Wood, *Yoga*, p. 78; and Patanjali, *Yoga Sutras* iii: 16–48, in Wood, *Yoga*, p. 78.
11. Patanjali, *Yoga Sutras* iv.
12. Shankara, *Ode to the South-Facing Form*, in Wood, *Glorious Presence*, pp. 214–216.
13. Shankara, in Wood, *Glorious Presence*, p. 122.
14. C. Norman Shealy and Caroline Myss, *The Creation of Health* (Walpole, NH: Stillpoint Publishing, 1988); and Caroline Myss, in Larry Dossey, *Meaning & Medicine* (New York: Bantam, 1991), p. 188.
15. Jeffrey Mishlove, *The Roots of Consciousness* (Tulsa, OK: Council Oaks Books, 1993).
16. The Intuition Network, 369-B Third Street, #161, San Rafael, CA, 94901-3581.
17. Stephan A. Schwartz, *The Secret Vaults of Time* (New York: Grosset & Dunlap, 1978); and Stephan A. Schwartz, *The Alexandria Project* (New York: Dell Publishing Co., 1983).
18. Shealy and Myss, *The Creation of Health*.
19. Ibid.
20. Shafica Karagulla, *Breakthrough to Creativity* (Marina del Rey, CA: DeVorss & Co., 1967).

CHAPTER 7: THE MAKING OF A HEALER

1. Foundation for Inner Peace, *A Course in Miracles* (New York: Viking Penguin, 1996).
2. Richard P. Hayes, "Nagarjuna's Appeal," *Journal of Indian Philosophy*, 1994, pp. 299–378.
3. Stanislav Grof and Christina Grof, in R. Walsh and F. Vaughan, *Beyond Ego: Transpersonal Dimensions in Psychology* (Los Angeles: Jeremy P. Tarcher, 1980); and S. Grof & C. Grof, eds., *Spiritual Emergency: When Personal Transformation Becomes a Crisis* (Los Angeles: Jeremy P. Tarcher, 1989).
4. Yvonne Kason, *A Farther Shore* (Toronto: HarperCollins, 1994).

5. Foundation for Inner Peace, *A Course in Miracles*, p. 1.
6. Richard M. Bucke, *Cosmic Consciousness* (New York: E.P. Dutton & Co., 1901), pp. 70–73.
7. Gordon, *A Book of Saints*, p. 64.
8. Ernest Wood, *Yoga* (Baltimore: MD: Penguin, 1962), p. 30.
9. Mother Tessa Bielecki, from *The Search for Meaning*, in Gordon, *Book of Saints*, p. 65.
10. Author unknown, *The Cloud of Unknowing*.
11. Bertrand Russell, *Mysticism and Logic and Other Essays* (London: Longmans, Green and Co., 1925), p. 9.
12. Evelyn Underhill, *Mysticism* (London: Methuen & Co., 1912), p. 49.
13. William James, in R.M. Bucke, *Cosmic Consciousness* (New York: E.P. Dutton & Co., 1969), Introduction.
14. William James, *Varieties of Religious Experience* (New York: Random House, 1902, 1993).
15. Richard M. Bucke, *Cosmic Consciousness* (New York: E.P. Dutton & Co., 1901, 1969), p. 73.
16. Ibid., p. 70.
17. Melvin Morse with Paul Perry, *Transformed By the Light: The Powerful Effect of Near-Death Experiences on People's Lives* (New York: Villard Books, 1992); and Kenneth Ring, *Heading Toward Omega* (New York: William Morrow, 1984), Foreword.
18. Raymond Moody, *Life After Life* (Atlanta: Mockingbird Books, 1975).
19. Ring, *Heading Toward Omega*.
20. Bruce Greyson, Michael Grosso, Michael Sabom, Cherie Sutherland; see also: IANDS, P.O. Box 502, East Windsor Hill, CT 06028; and Cherie Sutherland, *Reborn in the Light* (New York: Bantam Books, 1992).
21. Raymond Moody, *The Light Beyond* (New York: Bantam Books, 1988), p. 33.
22. Elisabeth Kübler-Ross, in Ring, *Omega*, p. 12.
23. Shafica Karagulla, *Breakthrough to Creativity* (Marina del Rey, CA: DeVorss & Co., 1967).
24. Dora Kunz, *Spiritual Aspects of the Healing Arts* (Wheaton, IL: The Theosophical Publishing House, 1985).
25. Gordon, *Book of Saints*, p. 65.
26. Ibid.
27. Foundation for Inner Peace, *A Course in Miracles, Manual for Teachers* (Glenn Ellyn, CA: Foundation for Inner Peace), p. 3.
28. Ibid., p. 73.
29. Robert Perry, for Miracle Distribution Center, *An Introduction to A Course in Miracles*, (Fullerton, CA, 1987), p. 39.
30. Viktor Frankl, *Man's Search for Meaning* (New York: Simon & Schuster, 1959).
31. Ibid., p. 75.

CHAPTER 8: THE HEALING EXPERIENCE

1. William J. MacMillan, *The Reluctant Healer* (New York: Thomas Crowell Company, 1952).
2. Joel S. Goldsmith, *The Art of Spiritual Healing* (San Francisco: HarperCollins, 1959), p. 83.
3. Dolores Krieger, *Therapeutic Touch* (New York: Prentice-Hall, 1979); and M.D. Borelli and P. Heidt, *Therapeutic Touch* (New York: Springer, 1981).
4. Paramahansa Yogananda, *Autobiography of a Yogi* (Los Angeles: Self-Realization Fellowship, 1946, 1972); and Ambrose Worrall with Olga Worrall, *The Gift of Healing*

(New York: Harper & Row, 1965).

5. O. Carl Simonton, *The Healing Journey* (New York: Bantam, 1992); O.C. Simonton, S. Matthews-Simonton, and J.L. Creighton, *Getting Well Again* (Los Angeles: Tarcher/St. Martins, 1978); and O.C. Simonton and S. Matthews-Simonton, "Cancer and Stress: Counseling the Cancer Patient," *Medical Journal of Australia*, June 1, 1981, pp. 679–683.

6. The Commonweal Cancer Help Program, P.O. Box 316, Bolinas, CA 94924.

7. Jeanne Achterberg, *Imagery in Healing* (Boston: Shambhala, 1985); J. Achterberg, "A Canonical Analysis of Blood Chemistry Variables Related to Psychological Measures of Cancer Patients," *Multivariate Experimental Clinical Research*, vol. 4, 1979, pp. 1–10; J. Achterberg, O.C. Simonton, and S. Simonton, "Psychology of the Exceptional Cancer Patient: A Description of Patients Who Outlive Predicted Life Expectancies," *Psychotherapy: Theory, Research, and Practice*, vol. 14, 1977, pp. 416–422; and Esalen Institute, Highway 1, Big Sur, CA 93920-9616.

8. H.J. Eysenck, "Health's Character," *Psychology Today*, vol. 22, Dec. 1988, pp. 28–32; and H.J. Eysenck, "Personality, Stress, and Cancer: Prediction and Prophylaxis," *British Journal of Medical Psychology*, vol. 61, 1988, pp. 57–75.

9. D. Spiegel, H.C. Kraemer, J.R. Bloom, and E. Gottheil, "The Effect of Psychosocial Treatment on Survival of Patients With Metastatic Breast Cancer," *Lancet*, vol. II (8668), Oct. 14, 1989, pp. 888–891; and David Spiegel, *Living Beyond Limits* (New York: Times Books/Random House, Inc. 1993).

10. Eysenck, "Health's Character."

11. William Nolan, *Healing: Doctor in Search of a Miracle* (New York: Random House, 1974).

12. Brendan O'Regan and Caryle Hirshberg, *Spontaneous Remission: An Annotated Bibliography* (Sausalito, CA: Institute of Noetic Sciences, 1993).

13. Lewis Thomas, *The Youngest Science: Notes of a Medicine Watcher* (New York: Viking Press 1983), p. 205; and O'Regan and Hirshberg, *Spontaneous Remission: An Annotated Bibliography*, Introduction by Hirshberg, p. 1.

CHAPTER 9: MINDING THE BODY

1. Tom Harpur, *The Uncommon Touch: An Investigation of Spiritual Healing* (Toronto: McClelland & Stewart Inc., 1994), pp. 38–73.

2. *Holy Bible.* I Kings 17:20–24; 2 Kings 4:18–37; 2 Kings 5:9–14, 2 Kings 20:1–11; 2 Kings 38:1–6; Numbers 21:4–9.

3. Harpur, *The Uncommon Touch*, pp. 38–73.

4. W. Braud, D. Shafer, K. McNeill, and V. Guerra, "Attention Focusing Facilitated through Remote Mental Interaction," *JASPR*, vol. 89, no. 2, April 1995, p. 113.

5. *Holy Bible.* Numbers 21:4,9; Luke 10:9; Mark 16: 17–18; I Corinthians 12:8–10; and *The Qu'ran*, Sura 44:45.

6. Harpur, *The Uncommon Touch*, p. 38.

7. Ibid., p. 44.

8. Daniel J. Benor, *Healing Research*, vol. I (Munich, Germany: Helix Verlag, 1992).

9. Daniel J. Benor, "Healers and a Changing Medical Paradigm," *Frontier Perspectives*, Center for Frontier Sciences at Temple University, vol. 3, no. 2, Fall 1993, pp. 38–40.

10. The Doctor-Healer Network, May Cottage, 19 Fore Street, Bishopsteignton, South Devon, UK; and Benor, *Healing Research*.

11. Michael Murphy, "Mesmerism and Hypnosis," *The Future of the Body* (Los Angeles: Jeremy P. Tarcher, Inc., 1992), pp. 291–350; and Alan Gauld, *A History of Hypnotism* (Cambridge, England: Cambridge University Press, 1992).

12. Murphy, *The Future of the Body*, pp. 291–350.

13. Ibid.
14. Ibid.
15. *The New Encyclopedia Britannica*, 15th edition, 1995, Volume 6, "Hypnosis," p. 203.
16. Murphy, *The Future of the Body*, pp. 291–350.
17. Ibid.
18. *The New Encyclopedia Britannica*, 15th edition, 1995, Volume 6, "Hypnosis," p. 203.
19. Murphy, *The Future of the Body*, pp. 291–350.
20. L.L. Vasiliev, *Experiments in Mental Suggestion* (Hampshire, Eng.: Gally Hill Press, 1963).
21. Ibid.
22. Ibid.
23. Ibid.
24. Larissa Vilenskaya, in Russell Targ and Keith Harary, *The Mind Race* (New York: Villard Books, 1984), pp. 252–253.
25. Sheila Ostrander and Lynn Schroeder, *Psychic Discoveries Behind the Iron Curtain* (Englewood Cliffs, NJ: Prentice Hall, 1970), p. 13–27.
26. Vilenskaya, in Targ and Harary, *The Mind Race*, pp. 252–253.
27. E.C. May and L. Vilenskaya, "Overview of Current Parapsychology Research in the Former Soviet Union," *Subtle Energies*, vol. 3, no. 3, 1992, pp. 45–67; L. Vilenskaya and E.C. May, "Anomalous Mental Phenomena Research in Russia and the Former Soviet Union: A Follow Up," *Subtle Energies*, vol. 4, no. 3, 1993, pp. 231–250; and E.C. May and L. Vilenskaya, "Some Aspects Of Parapsychological Research in the Former Soviet Union," *Proceedings of the Parapsychological Association*, 1993, Toronto, Canada, 1993, pp. 57–74.
28. E.D. Dean, "Plethysmograph Recordings as ESP Responses," *International Journal of Neuropsychiatry*, vol. 2, 1966, pp. 439–446.
29. E.D. Dean, "Long-Distance Plethysmograph Telepathy with Agent Under Water," *Proceedings of the Parapsychological Association*, 1969, Toronto, Canada, pp. 41–42.
30. Douglas Dean, John Mihalasky, Sheila Ostrander, and Lynn Schroeder, *Executive ESP* (Englewood Cliffs, New Jersey: Prentice-Hall, 1974).
31. W.G. Braud and M.J. Schlitz, "Consciousness Interactions with Remote Biological Systems: Anomalous Intentionality Effects," *Subtle Energies*, vol. 2, no. 1, 1991, pp. 1–6.
32. William Braud, "Mental Techniques for Self-Healing and for Remote Influence," *ASPR Newsletter*, vol. XVIII, no. 1, 1993.
33. W. Braud and M. Schlitz, "Psychokinetic Influence on Electro-Dermal Activity," *Journal of Parapsychology*, vol. 47, 1983, pp. 95–119; and W. Braud, D. Shafer, and S. Andrews, "Reactions to an Unseen Gaze (Remote Attention): A Review, with New Data on Autonomic Staring Detection," *Journal of Parapsychology*, vol. 57, no. 4, 1993, pp. 373–390.
34. Ibid.
35. W. Braud, D. Shafer, and S. Andrews, "Further Studies of Autonomic Detection of Remote Staring: Replication, New Control Procedures, and Personality Correlates," *Journal of Parapsychology*, vol. 57, no. 4, 1993, pp. 391–409.
36. M.J. Schlitz and S. LaBerge, *Autonomic Detection of Remote Observation: Two Conceptual Replications* (Sausalito, CA: Institute of Noetic Sciences, 1994).
37. Marilyn Schlitz and N. Lewis, "Frontiers of Research," *Noetic Sciences Review*, no. 41, Spring 1997, p. 33.
38. W.G. Braud, "Distant Mental Influence of Rate of Hemolysis of Human Red Blood Cells," *JASPR*, vol. 84, no. 1, January 1990, pp. 1–24; and William G. Braud, "Human Interconnectedness: Research indications," *ReVision*, vol. 14, no. 3, Winter 1992, pp. 140–148.

39. Deepak Chopra, *Quantum Healing* (New York: Bantam Books, 1990); and Deepak Chopra, *The Seven Spiritual Laws of Success* (Novato, CA: Amber-Allen Publishing/New World Library, 1994).
40. W. Braud, D. Shafer, K. McNeill, and V. Guerra, "Attention Focusing Facilitated through Remote Mental Interaction," *JASPR*, vol. 89, no. 2, April 1995, pp. 103–115.
41. B. Grad, R.J. Cadoret, and G.I. Paul, "The Influence of an Unorthodox Method of Treatment on Wound Healing in Mice," *International Journal of Parapsychology*, vol. 6, 1961, pp. 472–498; and B. Grad, "Some Biological Effects of the 'Laying On of Hands': A Review of Experiments with Animals and Plants," *JASPR*, vol. 59, 1965, pp. 95–127.
42. Randolph C. Byrd, "Positive Therapeutic Effects of Intercessory Prayer in a Coronary Care Unit Population," *Southern Medical Journal*, vol. 81, no. 7, July 1988, pp. 826–829.
43. Zvi Bentwich and Shulamith Kreitler, "Psychological Determinants of Recovery from Hernia Operations," Unpublished Manuscript, Israel, 1989.
44. Elisabeth Targ, "Healing and the Spirit," *California Pacific Currents*, California Pacific Medical Center, Fall 1997, pp. 8–11.
45. W. Braud, D. Shafer, K. McNeill, and V. Guerra, "Attention Focusing Facilitated through Remote Mental Interaction," *JASPR*, vol. 89, no. 2, April 1995, pp. 113–114.
46. J. Solfvin, "Mental Healing," in S. Krippner, ed., *Advances in Parapsychological Research*, vol. 4 (Jefferson, NC: McFarland & Co., Inc., 1984).
47. William Braud, personal communication, June 24, 1995.
48. Braud, Shafer, and Guerra, "Attention Focusing Facilitated through Remote Mental Interaction."
49. F.W.H. Myers, *Human Personality and Its Survival of Bodily Death* (New Hyde Park, NY: University Books, Inc., 1961), "Hypnotism," pp. 115–161; and Emily W. Cook, "Book Reviews: A History of Hypnotism," *Journal of Scientific Exploration*, vol. 8, no. 4, Winter 1994, pp. 546–553.
50. Brad Lemley, in Larry Dossey, *Meaning & Medicine* (New York: Bantam Books, 1991), p. 178.

CHAPTER 10: WAYS OF HEALING

1. Larry Dossey, *Meaning & Medicine* (New York: Bantam Books, 1991), p. 189.
2. Larry Dossey, *Recovering the Soul* (New York: Bantam Books, 1989); Dossey, *Meaning & Medicine*; Larry Dossey, *Healing Words: The Power of Prayer and the Practice of Medicine* (New York: HarperSanFrancisco, 1993).
3. Dossey, *Meaning & Medicine*.
4. Dossey, *Recovering the Soul*, p. 267.
5. Stanley Krippner and Alberto Villoldo, *The Realms of Healing* (Millbrae, CA: Celestial Arts, 1976), p. 244.
6. Ibid., p. 246.
7. William James, *The Varieties of Religious Experience* (New York: Random House, 1902, 1993); and William James, in Michael Murphy, *The Future of the Body* (Los Angeles: Jeremy P. Tarcher, Inc., 1992), p. 258.
8. Joel S. Goldsmith, *The Art of Spiritual Healing* (San Francisco: HarperCollins, 1959), p. 73.
9. H. Beinfield and E. Korngold, *Between Heaven and Earth: A Guide to Chinese Medicine* (New York: Ballantine, 1991), p. 30.
10. Rosalyn L. Bruyere, *Wheels of Light* (New York: Simon & Schuster, 1994).
11. Ibid., pp. 254–255.

12. Barbara Brennan, in Diane Goldner, "High-Energy Healer," *New Age Journal*, Jan./Feb. 1996, pp. 50–55, pp. 78–81.
13. J.F. Quinn and A.J. Strelkauskas, "Psychoimmunologic Effects of Therapeutic Touch on Practitioners and Recently Bereaved Recipients: A Pilot Study," *AdvNursSci*, vol. 15, no. 4, 1993, pp. 13–26.
14. Dolores Krieger, *Accepting Your Power to Heal* (Santa Fe, NM: Bear & Company, 1993), p. 108.
15. Quinn and Strelkauskas, "Psychoimmunologic Effects of Therapeutic Touch on Practitioners and Recently Bereaved Recipients: A Pilot Study," pp. 13–26.
16. Janet F. Quinn, "Therapeutic Touch as Energy Exchange: Testing the Theory," *AdvNursSci*, Jan. 1984, pp. 42–49.
17. Quinn and Strelkauskas, "Psychoimmunologic Effects of Therapeutic Touch on Practitioners and Recently Bereaved Recipients: A Pilot Study," p. 14.
18. Janet F. Quinn, personal communication, January 31, 1996.
19. Ibid.
20. Quinn and Strelkauskas, "Psychoimmunologic Effects of Therapeutic Touch on Practitioners and Recently Bereaved Recipients: A Pilot Study," p. 14.
21. D.C. McClelland in J. Borysenko, "Healing Motives: An Interview with David C. McClelland," *Advances*, vol. 2, no. 2, 1985, pp. 29–41.
22. Lawrence LeShan, *The Medium, the Mystic, and the Physicist* (New York: Viking, 1974).
23. Ibid., p. 113.
24. Ibid., p. 160.
25. Olga Worrall, in Stanley Krippner and Alberto Villoldo, *The Realms of Healing* (Millbrae, CA: Celestial Arts, 1976), p. 90.
26. Lawrence LeShan, "Larry LeShan: Mobilizing the Life Force, Treating the Individual," *Alternative Therapies*, vol. 1, no. 1, March 1995, p. 67.
27. E. Green and A. Green, *Beyond Biofeedback* (New York: Dell Publishing Co., 1977).
28. Paul Dong and Aristide H. Esser, *Chi Gong* (New York: Marlowe & Co., 1990).
29. Ibid., p. 163.
30. John G. Fuller, *Arigo: Surgeon of the Rusty Knife* (New York: Thomas Crowell Co., 1974); and Rosemary Ellen Guiley, *Harper's Encyclopedia of Mystical & Paranormal Experience* (San Francisco: HarperSanFrancisco, 1991).
31. Dong, *Chi Gong*, pp. 100, 125, 55.
32. Ibid.
33. Tao-Jing, et al., in Dong, p. 163
34. Ernest Wood, *Yoga* (Baltimore, MD: Penguin Books, 1959), p. 177.
35. Diane Goldner, "High-Energy Healer," *New Age Journal*, Jan./Feb. 1996, p. 50.
36. Barbara Brennan, *Hands of Light* (New York: Bantam, 1987); and Barbara Brennan, *Light Emerging* (New York: Bantam, 1993).
37. Myss and Shealy workshop pamphlet. For a presentation entitled "Why People Don't Heal: Understanding the Intimate Language of Wounds," sponsored by The Association for Humanistic Psychology, June 28–29, 1996, Oakland, California.
38. C. Norman Shealy and Caroline M. Myss, *The Creation of Health* (Walpole, NH: Stillpoint Publishing, 1988), p. 159.
39. Ibid., p. 84.
40. Myss and Shealy workshop pamphlet. For a presentation entitled "Why People Don't Heal: Understanding the Intimate Language of Wounds," sponsored by The Association for Humanistic Psychology, June 28–29, 1996, Oakland, California.
41. Shealy and Myss, *The Creation of Health*, p. 159.
42. Jess Stern, *Edgar Cayce — The Sleeping Prophet* (New York: Bantam Books, 1968); Thomas

Sugrue, *There Is a River* (Virginia Beach, VA: ARE Press, 1973); and Guiley, *Harper's Encyclopedia of Mystical & Paranormal Experience.*

43. Candace B. Pert, in S.S. Hall, "A Molecular Code Links Emotions, Mind and Health," *Smithsonian*, June 1989; also Candace B. Pert, "The Wisdom of the Receptors: Neuropeptides, the Emotions, and Bodymind," *Advances*, vol. 3, no. 3, 1986, pp. 8–16.
44. Candace B. Pert, *Molecules of Emotion* (New York: Scribner, 1997).
45. S.M. Levy, R.B. Herberman, M. Lippman, and T. D'Angelo, "Correlation of Stress Factors with Sustained Depression of Natural Killer Cell Activity with Predicted Prognosis in Patients with Breast Cancer," *Journal of Clinical Oncology*, vol. 5, no. 3, 1987, pp. 348–353; and S.M. Levy, "Host Differences in Neoplastic Risk: Behavioral and Social Contributors to Disease," *Health Psychology*, vol. 2, 1983, pp. 21–44.
46. Candace B. Pert, in a promotional letter for a presentation entitled "The Matter of Mind: Emotions, Immunity & the Psychosomatic Network" given at the 12th annual Gardner Murphy Memorial Lecture sponsored by The American Society for Psychical Research, June 7, 1996, Hotel St. Moritz, New York City.
47. Candace B. Pert, in Hall, "A Molecular Code Links Emotions, Mind and Health."
48. Francis O. Schmidt, as quoted in Hall, "A Molecular Code Links Emotions, Mind and Health."
49. Lydia Temoshok and Henry Dreher, *The Type C Connection: The Mind-Body Link to Cancer and Your Health* (New York: Penguin Group/Plume, 1992), p. 193.

CHAPTER 11: PRAYER AND THE HEALING CONNECTION

1. Olga Worrall, in Edwina Cerutti, *Olga Worrall: Mystic With the Healing Hands* (New York: Harper & Row, 1975), p. 40.
2. Ibid, p. 43.
3. Olga Worrall, in Caryl Hirshberg and Marc Ian Barasch, *Remarkable Recovery* (New York: Riverhead Books, 1995), p. 129.
4. Joyce Goodrich, Project Director, Consciousness Research and Training Project, Inc., 315 East 68th Street, Box 9G, New York, NY 10021.
5. Joel Goldsmith, *Spiritual Interpretation of Scripture* (Marina del Rey, CA: DeVorss & Co., 1947, 1994), p. 179.
6. Lawrence LeShan, *The Medium, the Mystic, and the Physicist* (New York: Viking, 1974), p. 161.
7. Gerald Jampolsky, *Love Is Letting Go of Fear* (Berkeley, CA: Celestial Arts, 1979); also Gerald G. Jampolsky and Diane V. Cirincione, *Change Your Mind, Change Your Life* (New York: Bantam, 1993).
8. The Center for Attitudinal Healing, 33 Buchanan Drive, Sausalito, CA 94965, 1996 promotional brochure.
9. The Network for Attitudinal Healing International, Inc., 1301 Capital of Texas Highway, South; Suite B-122, Austin, TX 78746.
10. Jampolsky, *Love Is Letting Go of Fear.*
11. Susan S. Trout, *To See Differently.* (Washington, DC: Three Roses Press, 1990).
12. M. Scott Peck, *The Road Less Traveled* (New York: Simon & Schuster, Inc., 1978), p. 81.
13. The Center for Attitudinal Healing, Sausalito, CA.
14. Alan Young, *Spiritual Healing: Miracle or Mirage?* (Marina del Rey, CA: DeVorss & Co., 1981), p. 49.
15. Alan Young, *Cosmic Healing: A Comparative Study of Channeled Teachings on Healing* (Marina del Rey, CA: DeVorss & Co., 1988).
16. Ambrose Worrall, in Harold Sherman, *Your Power to Heal* (New York: Harper & Row,

1972), p. 120.
17. Ibid., p. 117.
18. Lawrence LeShan, "Larry LeShan: Mobilizing the Life Force, Treating the Individual," *Alternative Therapies*, vol. 1, no. 1, March 1995, pp. 62–69.
19. Ibid.
20. Joel S. Goldsmith, *The Art of Spiritual Healing* (San Francisco: HarperCollins, 1959), p. 119.
21. Ibid., p. 186.

CHAPTER 12: THE PHYSICS OF MIRACLES AND THE MAGIC OF MIND

1. Patanjali, *Sutras*, in Swami Prabhavananda, *How to Know God*, translated by Christopher Isherwood, (Hollywood, CA: Vedanta Press, 1983).
2. John Palmer, "Extrasensory Perception: Research Findings," in Stanley Krippner, ed., *Advances in Parapsychological Research* (New York: Plenum Press, 1978), pp. 59–243.
3. C.W. Misner and J. Wheeler, "Gravitation, Electromagnetism, Unquantized Charge, and Mass as Properties of Curved Empty Space," *Annals of Physics*, vol. 2, Dec. 1957, pp. 525–603.
4. A. Einstein, B. Podolsky, and N. Rosen, "Can a Quantum Mechanical Description of Physical Reality Be Considered Complete?" *Physical Review*, vol. 47, May 15, 1935, pp. 777–780.
5. Brian Josephson, "Biological Utilization of Quantum Nonlocality," *Foundations of Physics*, vol. 21, 1991, pp. 197–207.
6. S. Freedman and J. Clauser, "Experimental Test of Local Hidden Variable Theories," *Physical Review Letters*, vol. 28, 1972, pp. 934–941; and A. Aspect, et al., "Experimental Tests of Bell's Inequalities Using Time-Varying Analyzers," *Physical Review Letters*, vol. 49, December 20, 1982, pp. 1804–1907; and Malcolm Browne, "Signal Travels Farther and Faster than Light," *New York Times*, July 22, 1997.
7. Brian Josephson, "Biological Utilization of Quantum Nonlocality."
8. Ken Wilber, *No Boundary* (Boston: Shambhala, 1979).
9. Aldous Huxley, *The Perennial Philosophy* (New York: Harper and Row, 1945).
10. Prabhavananda and Isherwood, *How to Know God*.
11. Plato, *The Republic-Book VII. The Allegory of the Cave*, translated by B. Jowett (New York: Vintage, 1994).
12. George Leonard and Michael Murphy, *The Life We Are Given* (New York: Jeremy Tarcher/Putnam, 1995), p. 176.
13. Lawrence Kushner, *The River of Light* (Woodstock, VT: Jewish Lights Publishing, 1981, 1990), pp. 82–83.
14. D. Bohm and B.J. Hiley, *The Undivided Universe* (New York: Routledge, 1993), p. 382.
15. Rupert Sheldrake, *A New Science of Life* (London: Blond & Briggs, 1981).
16. Peter Russell, *The Global Brain* (Los Angeles: Jeremy Tarcher, 1983), p. 129.
17. Bohm and Hiley, *The Undivided Universe*, p. 382.
18. Ibid., p. 386.
19. Ibid.
20. Michael Talbot, *The Holographic Universe* (New York: HarperPerennial, 1991), p. 81.
21. Kenneth Ring, in R. Walsh and F. Vaughan, *Beyond Ego: Transpersonal Dimensions in Psychology* (Los Angeles: Jeremy Tarcher, 1980), p. 198.
22. Kenneth Ring, "Near-Death Experiences: Implications for Human Evolution and Planetary Transformation," *Revision*, vol. 8, no. 2, 1986, pp. 75–85; Bruce Greyson, "Near-Death Studies, 1981-82: A Review," *Anabiosis*, vol. 2, 1982, pp. 150–158;

Bruce Greyson, "Increase in Psychic Phenomena Following Near-Death Experiences," *Theta*, 2, 1983, p. 1016; R.L. Kohr, "Near-Death Experience and Its Relationship to Psi and Various Altered States," *Theta*, vol. 10, no. 3, 1982, pp. 50–53; R.L. Kohr, "Near-Death Experiences, Altered States and Psi Sensitivity," *Anabiosis*, vol. 3, 1983, pp. 157–174; and Melvin Morse with Paul Perry, *Transformed by the Light: The Powerful Effect of Near-Death Experiences on People's Lives* (New York: Villard Books, 1992).

23. George Gallup, Jr., *Adventures in Immortality* (New York: McGraw-Hill, 1982), pp. 198–200.
24. Kenneth Ring, *Heading Toward Omega* (New York: William Morrow, 1984), p. 35.
25. Ibid.
26. An NDEr, in Kenneth Ring, *Heading Toward Omega* (New York: William Morrow, 1984), p. 109.
27. Michael Sabom, *Recollections of Death* (New York: Harper & Row, 1982), Chapter 7.
28. Ring, in Walsh and Vaughan, *Beyond Ego: Transpersonal Dimensions in Psychology*, p. 198.
29. George Leonard and Michael Murphy, *The Life We Are Given* (New York: Jeremy Tarcher/Putnam, 1995).
30. Ibid., p. 170.
31. Ernest Wood, *Yoga* (Baltimore, MD: Penguin Books, 1959), p. 78.
32. The Dalai Lama, in Jean-Claude Carriere, "Facing the future," *New Age Journal*, Nov./Dec. 1995, p. 146.
33. Ibid., p. 147.
34. Foundation for Inner Peace, *A Course in Miracles*. Glen Ellen, CA, 1975.
35. Foundation for Inner Peace, *A Course in Miracles: Manual for Teachers*, p. 73.
36. Ibid., p. 5.
37. Foundation for Inner Peace, *A Course in Miracles*, p. 315.

Bibliography

Achterberg, Jeanne. "A Canonical Analysis of Blood Chemistry Variables Related to Psychological Measures of Cancer Patients." *Multivariate Experimental Clinical Research* 4 (1979): 1–10.

Achterberg, Jeanne. *Imagery in Healing*. Boston: Shambhala, 1985.

Achterberg, J., O.C. Simonton, and S. Simonton. "Psychology of the Exceptional Cancer Patient: A Description of Patients Who Outlive Predicted Life Expectancies." *Psychotherapy: Theory, Research, and Practice* 14 (1977): 416–422,.

Aspect, A., et al. "Experimental Tests of Bell's Inequalities Using Time-Varying Analyzers." *Physical Review Letters* 49 (December 20, 1982): 1804–1907.

Ayer, Alfred J. *Language, Truth and Logic*. New York: Dover Publications, Inc., 1952.

Bach, Richard. *Psychic*. October 1974.

Batten, Alan H. "A Most Rare Vision: Eddington's Thinking on the Relation Between Science and Religion." *Journal of Scientific Exploration* 9, no. 2 (Summer 1995): 231–234.

Beinfield, H. and E. Korngold. *Between Heaven and Earth: A Guide to Chinese Medicine*. New York: Ballantine, 1991.

Bem, D., and C. Honorton. "Does Psi Exist? Replicable Evidence for an Anomalous Process of Information Transfer." *Psychological Bulletin*, January 1994.

Benor, Daniel J. *Healing Research*. Volume I. Munich, Germany: Helix Verlag, 1992.

Benor, Daniel J. "Healers and a Changing Medical Paradigm." *Frontier Perspectives* 3, no. 2 (Fall 1993): 38–40,

Benson, Herbert. *The Relaxation Response*. New York: William Morrow, 1975.

Benson, Herbert. *Beyond the Relaxation Response*. New York: Times Books, 1984.

Bentwich, Zvi and Shulamith Kreitler. "Psychological Determinants of Recovery from Hernia Operations." Israel, Unpublished Manuscript, 1989.

Bielecki, Mother Tessa, *The Search for Meaning*. In Gordon, Anne. *A Book of Saints*. New York: Bantam, 1994.

Blom, J.G. and J.G. Pratt. "A Second Confirmatory Experiment with Pavel Stepanek as a 'Borrowed Subject,'" *Journal of the ASPR* 62 (1969): 28–45.

Bohm, D. and B.J. Hiley. *The Undivided Universe*. New York: Routledge, 1993.

Borelli, M.D. and P. Heidt. *Therapeutic Touch*. New York: Springer, 1981.

Borysenko, J. "Healing Motives: An Interview with David C. McClelland." *Advances* 2, no. 2 (1985): 29–41.

Braud, W. "On the Use of Living Target Systems in Distant Mental Influence Research." In Coly, L., ed. *Psi Research Methodology:A Re-examination.* New York: Parapsychology Foundation, 1993.

Braud, W. "A Role of Mind in the Physical World." *European Journal of Parapsychology* 10 (1994): 66–77.

Braud, W. "Direct Mental Influence on the Rate of Hemolysis of Human Red Blood Cells." *The Journal of the ASPR* (January 1990): 1–24.

Braud, W., D. Shafer, K. McNeill, and V. Guerra. "Attention Focusing Facilitated Through Remote Mental Interaction." *JASPR* 89, no. 2 (April 1995): 113.

Braud, W.G. and M.J. Schlitz. "Consciousness Interactions with Remote Biological Systems: Anomalous Intentionality Effects." *Subtle Energies* 2, no. 1 (1991): 1–46.

Braud, William. "Mental Techniques for Self-Healing and for Remote Influence." *ASPR Newsletter* 18, no. 1 (1993).

Braud, W. and M. Schlitz. "Psychokinetic Influence on Electro-Dermal Activity." *Journal of Parapsychology* 47 (1983): 95–119.

Braud, W., D. Shafer, and S. Andrews. "Reactions to an Unseen Gaze (Remote Attention): A Review, with New Data on Autonomic Staring Detection." *Journal of Parapsychology* 57, no. 4 (1993): 373–390.

Braud, W., D. Shafer, and S. Andrews. "Further Studies of Autonomic Detection of Remote Staring: Replication, New Control Procedures, and Personality Correlates." *Journal of Parapsychology* 57, no. 4 (1993): 391–409.

Braud, W.G. "Distant Mental Influence of Rate of Hemolysis of Human Red Blood Cells." *JASPR* 84, no. 1 (January 1990): 1–24.

Braud, William G. "Human Interconnectedness: Research Indications." *ReVision* 14, no. 3 (Winter 1992): 140–148.

Braud, William G. "Empirical Explorations of Prayer, Distant Healing, and Remote Mental Influence." *The Journal of Religion and Psychical Research* 17, no. 2 (April 1994): 62–73.

Braud, W., D. Shafer, K. McNeill, and V. Guerra. "Attention Focusing Facilitated Through Remote Mental Interaction." *JASPR* 89, no. 2 (April 1995): 103–115.

Braud, William. Personal communication with Russell Targ, June 24, 1995.

Braude, S.E. *ESP and Psychokenisis: A Philosophical Examination.* Philadelphia, PA, Temple University Press, 1979.

Brennan, Barbara, in Diane Goldner. "High-Energy Healer." *New Age Journal.*, Jan./Feb. 1996, 50–55, 78–81.

Brennan, Barbara. *Hands of Light.* New York: Bantam, 1987.

Brennan, Barbara. *Light Emerging.* New York: Bantam, 1993.

Brown, Dean. *Direct from Sanskrit: New Translations of Seven Upanishads, the Aphorisms of Patanjali, and Other Microcosmic Texts of Ancient India.* Los Angeles: Philosophical Research Society, 1996.

Browne, Malcolm. "Signal Travels Farther and Faster than Light," *New York Times*, July 22, 1997.

Bruyere, Rosalyn L. *Wheels of Light.* New York: Simon & Schuster, 1994.

Bucke, Richard M. *Cosmic Consciousness.* New York: E.P. Dutton & Co, 1969.

Byrd, Randolph C. "Positive Therapeutic Effects of Intercessory Prayer in a Coronary Care Unit Population." *Southern Medical Journal* 81, no. 7 (July 1988): 826–829

Carpenter, James. 1975. "Toward the Effective Utilization of Enhanced Weak-Signal Esp Effects," Paper delivered at AAAS meeting in New York, and ("Prediction of

Forced-Choice ESP Performance, Part-3," *Journal of Parapsychology* 55 (Sept. 1991): 227–280.

Carriere, Jean-Claude. "Facing the Future." *New Age Journal*, Nov./Dec. 1995, 146.

Cayce, Edgar, in Thomas Sugrue. *There Is a River.* Virginia Beach, VA: ARE Press; and Stern, Jess. 1968. *Edgar Cayce — The Sleeping Prophet.* New York: Bantam Books, 1973.

Chopra, Deepak. *Quantum Healing.* New York: Bantam Books, 1990.

Chopra, Deepak. *The Seven Spiritual Laws of Success.* San Rafael, CA: Amber-Allen Publishing/ New World Library, 1994.

Clark, Arthur C. *Childhood's End.* New York: Ballantine Books/Random House, 1953.

Cook, Emily W. "Book reviews: A History of Hypnotism." *Journal of Scientific Exploration* 8, no. 4 (Winter 1994): 546–553.

Cooper, Rabbi David A., in Eliezer Sobel. "Contemplative Judaism." *the Quest*, Winter 1995, 68.

Dalai Lama, in Jean-Claude Carriere. "Facing the future." *New Age Journal*, Nov./Dec. 1995, 146.

Dean, Douglas. "Infrared and Ultraviolet Techniques to Test for Changes in Water Following the Laying on of Hands." Doctoral dissertation, Saybrook University, San Francisco, CA, 1983. International microfilm number 8408650.

Dean, E.D. "Plethysmograph Recordings as ESP Responses." *International Journal of Europsychiatry* 2 (1966): 439–446.

Dean, E.D. "Long-Distance Plethysmograph Telepathy with Agent Under Water." *Proceedings of the Parapsychological Association* 6 (1969): 41–42.

Dean, Douglas, John Mihalasky, Sheila Ostrander, and Lynn Schroeder. *Executive ESP.* Englewood Cliffs, New Jersey: Prentice-Hall, 1974.

Dixon, N.F. *Subliminal Perception,* London: McGraw-Hill, 1971.

Dong, Paul, and Aristide H. Esser. *Chi Gong.* New York: Marlowe & Co., 1990.

Dossey, Larry. "Healing Happens." *Utne Reader*, Sept./Oct. 1995, 52–59.

Dossey, Larry. *Recovering the Soul.* New York: Bantam Books, 1989.

Dossey, Larry. *Healing Words: The Power of Prayer and the Practice of Medicine.* San Francisco: HarperCollins, 1993.

Dossey, Larry. *Meaning & Medicine.* New York: Bantam Books, 1991.

Duncan, Lois and William Roll. *Psychic Connections.* New York: Delacourt Press, 1995.

Dunne, B.J., R.G. Jahn, and R.D. Nelson. "Precognitive Remote Perception." Princeton Engineering Anomalies Research Laboratory (Report), August 1983.

Dunne, J.W. *An Experiment with Time.* London: Faber & Faber, 1969.

Dyson, Freeman. "The Scientist as Rebel." *The New York Review of Books*, May 25, 1995, 31–33.

Eccles, John C. *Facing Reality.* New York: Springer-Verlag, 1970.

Eddy, M.B. *Science and Health.* Also *Science and Health with Key to the Scriptures.* First Church of Christ Scientist, 1875, 1971.

Einstein, A., B. Podolsky, and N. Rosen. "Can Quantum Mechanical Description of Physical Reality Be Considered Complete?" *Physical Review* 47 (May 15, 1935): 777–780.

Einstein, Albert. *Living Philosophies.* New York: Simon & Schuster, 1931.

Einstein, Albert. *The World as I See It.* New York: Citadel Press, 1979.

Einstein, Albert. *Ideas and Opinions.* New York: Bonanza Books/Crown Publishing, 1954.

Einstein, Albert. *Out of My Later Years.* Secaucus, NJ: Citadel Press, 1950.

Eisenbud, J. *Psi and Psychoanalysis.* New York: Grune and Stratton, 1970.

Eisenbud, J. *Paranormal Foreknowledge.* New York, Human Science Press, 1982.

Eysenck, H.J. "Health's Character." *Psychology Today*, December 1988, 28–32.

Eysenck, H.J. "Personality, Stress, and Cancer: Prediction and Prophylaxis." *British Journal of Medical Psychology* 61 (1988): 57–75.

Feinberg, Gerald. "Precognition — Memory of Things Future," in proceedings of conference on quantum physics and parapsychology (Geneva). New York: Parapsychology Foundation, 1975, 4–75.

Ferrini, Paul. "The Door to the House of Love." *Miracles Magazine* I (Autumn 1991): 53.

Foundation for Inner Peace. *A Course in Miracles.* Glen Ellen, CA: Foundation for Inner Peace, 1975.

Frankl, Viktor. *Man's Search for Meaning.* New York: Simon & Schuster, 1959.

Freedman, S. and J. Clauser. "Experimental test of local hidden variable theories." *Physical Review Letters* 28 (1972): 934–941.

Freud, S. "Dreaming and Telepathy" in G. Devereux, ed. *Psychoanalysis and the Occult.* New York: International Universities Press, 1953, 69–86.

Friedman, Norman. *Bridging Science and Spirit: Common Elements of David Bohm's Physics, the Perennial Philosophy, and Seth.* St. Louis, MO: Living Lake Books, 1994.

Fuller, John G. *Arigo: Surgeon of the Rusty Knife.* New York: Thomas Crowell Co., 1974.

Gallup, George, Jr. *Adventures in Immortality.* New York: McGraw-Hill, 1982.

Gauld, Alan. *A History of Hypnotism.* Cambridge, England: Cambridge University Press, 1992.

Goldner, Diane. "High-Energy Healer." *New Age Journal,* Jan./Feb 1996, 50.

Goldsmith, Joel S. *The Art of Spiritual Healing.* San Francisco: HarperCollins, 1959.

Goldsmith, Joel S. *Consciousness Unfolding.* New York: Citadel Press/Carol Publishing Group, 1994.

Goodrich, Joyce. Project Director, Consciousness Research and Training Project, Inc., 315 East 68th Street, Box 9G, New York, NY 10021.

Gordon, Anne. *A Book of Saints.* New York: Bantam, 1994.

Grad, B. "A Telekinetic Effect On Plant Growth." *International Journal of Parapsychology* 6 (1964): 472–498.

Grad, B. "Some Biological Effects of the 'Laying-On of Hands:' A Review of Experiments with Animals and Plants." *JASPR* 59 (1965): 95–127

Grad, B., R.J. Cadoret, and G.I. Paul. "The Influence of Unorthodox Methods of Treatment On Wound Healing in Mice." *International Journal of Parapsychology* 3 (1961): 5–24.

Green, E. and A. Green. *Beyond Biofeedback.* New York: Dell Publishing Company, 1977.

Greyson, Bruce. "Increase in Psychic Phenomena Following Near-Death Experiences." *Theta* 2 (1983): 1016.

Greyson, Bruce. "Near-Death Studies, 1981–82: A review." *Anabiosis* 2 (1982): 150–58.

Grof, Stanislav and Christina Grof, eds. *Spiritual Emergency: When Personal Transformation Becomes a Crisis.* Los Angeles: J.P. Tarcher, 1989.

Guiley, Rosemary Ellen. *Harper's Encyclopedia of Mystical & Paranormal Experience.* New York: HarperSanFrancisco, 1991.

Hall, S.S. "A Molecular Code Links Emotions, Mind and Health." *Smithsonian,* June 1989.

Hansen, G., M. Schlitz, and C. Tart. "Remote Viewing Research 1973–1982." In Targ, R. and Harary, K., *The Mind Race.* New York: Villard, 1984.

Harpur, Tom. *The Uncommon Touch: An Investigation of Spiritual Healing.* Toronto: McClelland & Stewart Inc., 1994.

Holy Bible. King James Version. New York: The World Publishing Company.

Honorton, C. "Meta-Analysis of Psi Ganzfeld Research: A Response to Hyman." *Journal of Parapsychology* 49 (1985): 51–91.

Honorton, Charles and Diane C. Ferari. "Future-Telling: A Meta-Analysis of Forced-Choice Precognition Experiments." *Journal of Parapsychology* 53 (1989): 281–309.

Huxley, Aldous. *The Perennial Philosophy*. New York: Harper and Row, 1945.

Hyman, R. and C. Honorton. "A Joint Communiqué: The Psi Ganzfeld Controversy," *Journal of Parapsychology* 50 (1986): 251–264.

Inglis, Brian. *Natural and Supernatural*. London: Hodder and Stoughton, 1977.

James, William, from the foreward to R.M. Bucke. *Cosmic Consciousness*. New York: E.P. Dutton & Co., 1969.

James, William. *Varieties of Religious Experience*. New York: Random House, 1993. Originally published in 1902.

James, William, in Michael Murphy. *The Future of the Body*. Los Angeles: Jeremy P. Tarcher, Inc., 1992.

Jampolsky, Gerald. *Love Is Letting Go of Fear*. Berkeley, CA: Celestial Arts, 1979.

Jampolsky, Gerald G. and Diane V. Cirincione. *Change Your Mind, Change Your Life*. New York: Bantam, 1993.

Josephson, Brian. "Biological Utilization of Quantum Nonlocality." *Foundations of Physics* 21 (1991): 197–207.

Karagulla, Shafica. *Breakthrough to Creativity*. Marina del Rey, CA: DeVorss & Co., 1967.

Kason, Yvonne. *A Farther Shore*. Toronto: HarperCollins, 1994.

Koestler, Arthur. *The Roots of Coincidence*. New York: Random House, 1972.

Kohr, R.L. "Near-Death Experience and Its Relationship to Psi and Various Altered States." *Theta* 10, no. 3 (1982): 50–53.

Kohr, R.L. "Near-Death Experiences, Altered States and Psi Sensitivity." *Anabiosis* 3 (1983): 157–174.

Krieger, Dolores. *Therapeutic Touch*. New York: Prentice-Hall, 1979.

Krieger, Dolores. *Accepting Your Power to Heal*. Santa Fe, NM: Bear & Company, 1993.

Krippner, S., C. Honorton, M. Ullman, and M. Masters. "A Long-Distance 'Sensory Bombardment' Study of ESP in Dreams." *Journal of the ASPR* 65 (1971): 468–475.

Krippner, S., M. Ullman, and C. Honorton. "A Precognitive Dream Study with a Single Subject." *Journal of the ASPR* 65 (1971): 192–203; and "A Second Precognitive Dream Study With Malcolm Besant." *Journal of the ASPR* 66 (1972): 269–279.

Krippner, Stanley and Alberto Villoldo. *The Realms of Healing*. Millbrae, CA: Celestial Arts, 1976.

Kunz, Dora. *Spiritual Aspects of the Healing Arts*. Wheaton, IL: The Theosophical Publishing House, 1985.

Kushner, Lawrence. *The River of Light*. Woodstock, VT: Jewish Lights Publishing, 1981, 1990.

Leadbeater, C.W. *Occult Chemistry*. London: Theosophical Society, 1898.

Lemley, Brad, in Larry Dossey. *Meaning & Medicine*. New York: Bantam Books, 1991.

Leonard, George and Michael Murphy. *The Life We Are Given*. New York: Jeremy Tarcher/Putnam, 1995.

LeShan, Lawrence. *The Medium, the Mystic, and the Physicist*. New York: Viking, 1974.

LeShan, Lawrence. "Larry LeShan: Mobilizing the Life Force, Treating the Individual." *Alternative Therapies* 1, no. 1 (March 1995): 62–69.

Levy, S.M. "Host Differences in Neoplastic Risk: Behavioral and Social Contributors to Disease." *Health Psychology* 2 (1983): 21–44.

Levy, S.M., R.B. Herberman, M. Lippman, and T. D'Angelo. "Correlation of Stress Factors with Sustained Depression of Natural Killer Cell Activity with Predicted Prognosis in Patients with Breast Cancer." *Journal of Clinical Oncology* 5, no. 3 (1987): 348–353

MacMillan, William J. *The Reluctant Healer*. New York: Thomas Crowell Company, 1952.

May, E.C. "AC Technical Trials: Inspiration for the Target Entropy Concept." Proceedings

1995 Parapsychology Association Conference, Durham, NC, 1995.

May, Edwin C. "The American Institutes of Research Review of the Department of Defense's STAR GATE Program: A Commentary." *Journal of Scientific Exploration* 10 (1996): 89–107.

May, Edwin C., James Spottiswoode, and Jessica Utts. "Decision Augmentation Theory: Toward a Model of Anomalous Mental Phenomena." *Journal of Parapsychology* 59 (September 1995): 195–221.

May, E.C. and J. Spottiswoode. "Managing the Target Pool Bandwidth: Possible Noise Reduction for Anomalous Cognition Experiments." *Journal of Parapsychology* 58 (1994): 305–315.

May, E.C. and L. Vilenskaya. "Some Aspects of Parapsychological Research in the Former Soviet Union." Toronto: Canada, *Proceedings of the Parapsychological Association*, 1993, 57–74.

McClelland, D.C., in Joan Borysenko. "Healing Motives: An Interview with David C. McClelland." *Advances* 2, no. 2 (1985): 29–41.

McKim, Robert. *Experiences in Visual Thinking*. Monterey, CA: Brooks/Cole, 1972.

McMoneagle, Joseph. *Mind Trek*. Norfolk, VA: Hampton Roads Publishing Co., 1993.

Mishlove, Jeffrey. *The Roots of Consciousness*. Tulsa, OK: Council Oak Books, 1993.

Misner, C.W. and J. Wheeler. "Gravitation, Electromagnetism, Unquantized Charge, and Mass, as Properties of Curved Empty Space." *Annals of Physics* 2 (December 1957): 525–603.

Mitchell, Edgar D. "An ESP Test from Apollo 14." *Journal of Parapsychology* 35, no. 2 (1971).

Moody, Raymond. *Life After Life*. Atlanta: Mockingbird Books, 1975.

Moody, Raymond. *The Light Beyond*. New York: Bantam, 1988.

Morse, Melvin, with Paul Perry. *Transformed by the Light: The Powerful Effect of Near-Death Experiences on People's Lives*. New York: Villard Books, 1992.

Murphy, Michael. "Mesmerism and Hypnosis." *The Future of the Body*. Los Angeles: Jeremy P. Tarcher, Inc., 1992.

Myers, F.W.H. "Hypnotism." *Human Personality and Its Survival of Bodily Death*. New Hyde Park, New York: University Books, Inc., 1961, 115–161.

Myss, Caroline, in Larry Dossey. *Meaning & Medicine*. New York: Bantam, 1991.

Myss, C. and C.N. Shealy. Workshop pamphlets. 1995, 1996.

Nagarjuna, philosophy of, in Richard P. Hayes. "Nagajuna's Appeal." *Journal of Indian Philosophy* (1994): 299–378.

New Encyclopedia Britannica. 15th edition, Volume 6, "Hypnosis," 1995, p. 203.

New Jerusalem Bible. New York: Doubleday, 1985.

Nolan, William. Healing: *Doctor in Search of a Miracle*. New York: Random House, 1974.

O'Regan, Brendan, and Caryle Hirshberg. *Spontaneous Remission: An Annotated Bibliography*. Sausalito, CA: Institute of Noetic Sciences, 1993.

Ornish, Dean. *Dr. Dean Ornish's Program for Reversing Heart Disease*. New York: Random House, Inc., 1990.

Ostrander, Sheila and Lynn Schroeder. *Psychic Discoveries Behind the Iron Curtain*. Englewood Cliffs, NJ: Prentice Hall, 1970.

Palmer, John. "Extrasensory Perception: Research Findings," in Krippner, Stanley, ed. *Advances in Parapsychological Research*. New York: Plenum Press, 1978, 59–243.

Patanjali, *Sutras*, in Prabhavananda, Swami *How to Know God*. Translated by Christopher Isherwood. Hollywood, CA: Vedanta Press, 1983.

Patanjali, *Yoga Sutras* iii: 16–48, iii: 36, iv: I, in Wood, *Yoga*. Baltimore, Maryland: Penguin, 78–79.

Penrose, Roger. *Shadows of the Mind: A Search for the Missing Science of Consciousness*. New York:

Oxford University Press, 1994.

Perry, Robert. *An Introduction to A Course in Miracles.* Fullerton, CA: Miracle Distribution Center, 1987.

Pert, Candace B. "The Wisdom of The Receptors: Neuropeptides, the Emotions, and Bodymind." *Advances* 3, no. 3 (1986): 8–16.

Pert, Candace B., in S.S. Hall. "A Molecular Code Links Emotions, Mind and Health." *Smithsonian*, June 1989.

Pert, Candace B. In a promotional letter for a presentation entitled "The Matter of Mind: Emotions, Immunity & the Psychosomatic Network" given at the 12th annual Gardner Murphy Memorial Lecture sponsored by The American Society for Psychical Research, Friday, June 7th, 1996, Hotel St. Moritz, New York City.

Pert, Candace B. *Molecules of Emotion.* New York: Scribner, 1997.

Plato, *The Republic—Book VII.* Translated by B. Jowett. New York: Vintage, 1994.

Prabhavananda, Swami. *How to Know God.* Translated Christopher Isherwood. Hollywood, CA: Vedanta Press, 1983.

Price, G.R. "Science and the Supernatural," *Science* 122 (1955): 359–367.

Puthoff, Harold and Russell Targ. "Perceptual Augmentation Techniques." *SRI Final Report,* Covering the period January, 1974 through February, 1995. December 1, 1975.

Puthoff, H.E. and R. Targ. "A Perceptual Channel for Information Transfer Over Kilometer Distances: Historical Perspective and Recent Research." *Proceedings of IEEE* 64, no. 3 (March 1976): 229–254.

Puthoff, H.E., R. Targ, and C.T. Tart. "Resolution in Remote Viewing Studies." *Research in Parapsychology 1979.* Metuchen, NJ: Scarecrow Press, 1980.

Puthoff, H.E. "ARV Associational Remote Viewing Applications." *Research in Parapsychology 1984.* Metuchen, NJ: Scarecrow Press, 1985, 121–122.

Quinn, Janet F. "Therapeutic Touch as Energy Exchange: Testing the Theory." *AdvNursSci* (January 1984): 42–49.

Quinn, J. and Strelkauskas. "Psychoimmunologic Effects of Therapeutic Touch on Practitioners and Recently Bereaved Recipients: A Pilot Study." *AdvNursSci* 15, no. 4 (1993): 13–26.

Radin, Dean. *The Conscious Universe.* New York: HarperEdge, 1997.

Radin, Dean. "Unconscious Perceptions of Future Emotions: An Experiment in Presentiment." *Proceedings of Parapsychological Association*, 39th Annual Convention, San Diego, CA, 1996.

Rao, R.K. *The Basic Experiments in Parapsychology.* Jefferson, NC: McFarland & Co., 1984.

Remen, Rachel Naomi. "Is Psi Sacred?" *Noetic Sciences Review* 35 (Autumn 1995): 34.

Rhine, J. B., and J.G. Pratt. "A Review of the Pearce-Pratt Distance Series of ESP Tests." *Journal of Parapsychology* 18 (1954): 165–177.

Rhine, Louisa. "Frequency and Types of Experience in Spontaneous Precognition." *Journal of Parapsychology* 16 (1954): 93–123.

Ring, Kenneth, in R. Walsh and F. Vaughan. *Beyond Ego: Transpersonal Dimensions in Psychology.* Los Angeles: J.P. Tarcher, 1980, 198.

Ring, Kenneth. "Near-Death Experiences: Implications for Human Evolution and Planetary Transformation." *Revision* 8, no. 2 (1986): 75–85.

Ring, Kenneth. *Heading Toward Omega.* New York: William Morrow, 1984.

Robinson, C.A., Jr. "Soviets Push for Beam Weapon." *Aviation Week*, May 2, 1977.

Roll, William, in Lois Duncan and William Roll. *Psychic Connections.* New York: Delacourt Press, 1995.

Rose, Charles. Chairman of the House Sub-Committee on Intelligence Evaluation and Oversight, interviewed on the subject of the SRI long-distance remote viewing experiments. *Omni,* July 1979.

Rubik, B. and E. Rauscher. "Effects on Motility Behavior and Growth Rate of Salmonella Typhimurium in the Presence of a Psychic Subject." In Roll, W.G., ed. *Research in Parapsychology 1979.* Metuchen, NJ: Scarecrow, 1980, 140–142.

Rumi, Jelaluddin Balkhi. *The Essential Rumi.* Translated by Coleman Barks with J. Moyne. San Francisco: HarperSanFrancisco, 1995.

Russell, Bertrand. *Mysticism and Logic and Other Essays.* London: Longmans, Green and Co., 1925.

Russell, Peter. *The Global Brain.* Los Angeles: Jeremy Tarcher, 1983.

Ryzl, Milan. "A Model of Parapsychological Communication," *Journal of Parapsychology* (1966): 18–30.

Sabom, Michael. *Recollections of Death.* New York: Harper & Row, 1982.

Saint John of the Cross. trans. *Dark Night of the Soul.* New York: Doubleday, 1959.

Schlitz, M., and C. Honorton. "Ganzfeld Psi Performance Within an Artistically Gifted Population." *Journal ASPR* 86 (1992): 83–98.

Schlitz, M. and E. Grouber. "Transcontinental Remote Viewing." *Journal of Parapsychology* 44 (1980): 305–317.

Schlitz, M.J. and S. LaBerge. "Autonomic Detection of Remote Observation: Two Conceptual Replications." Sausalito, CA: Institute of Noetic Sciences (preprint), 1994.

Schlitz, M. and N. Lewis, "Frontiers of Research." *Noetic Sciences Review* 41 (Spring 1997): 33.

Schmeidler, G.R. "An Experiment in Precognitive Clairvoyance: Part-1, The Main Results" and "Part-2. The Reliability of the Scores." *Journal of Parapsychology* 28 (1964): 1–27.

Schmidt, Francis O. in S.S. Hall. "A Molecular Code Links Emotions, Mind and Health." *Smithsonian,* June 1989.

Schmidt, Helmut. "Random Generators and Living Systems as Targets in Retro-PK Experiments," *Journal of ASPR* 91 (1997): 1–14.

Schnabel, Jim. *Remote Viewers: The Secret History of Americas Psychic Spies.* New York: Dell Books, 1997, 244–247.

Schwartz, Stephan, Rand DeMattei, James Spottiswoode, and Edward Brain, Jr. "Infrared Spectra Alteration in Water, Proximate to the Palms of Therapeutic Practitioners." *Subtle Energies* 1 (1990): 43–72.

Schwartz, Stephan. *The Secret Vaults of Time.* New York: Grosset & Dunlap, 1978.

Schwartz, Stephan. *The Alexandria Project.* New York: Delacorte/Friede, 1983.

Shankara, in Prabhavananda, Swami. *Crest-Jewel of Discrimination.* Translated by Christopher Isherwood. Hollywood, CA: Vedanta Press, 1975.

Shankara, *Ode to the South-Facing Form,* in Wood, *The Glorious Presence.* Wheaton, IL: The Theosophical Publishing House, 1974.

Shealy, C. Norman and Caroline M. Myss. *The Creation of Health.* Walpole, NH: Stillpoint Publishing, 1988.

Sheldrake, Rupert. *A New Science of Life.* London: Blond & Briggs, 1981.

Sherman, Harold. *Your Power to Heal.* New York: Harper & Row, 1972.

Simonton, O. Carl. *The Healing Journey.* New York: Bantam, 1992.

Simonton, O.C., S. Matthews-Simonton, and J.L. Creighton. *Getting Well Again.* Los Angeles: Tarcher/St. Martin's, 1978.

Simonton, O.C. and S. Matthews-Simonton. "Cancer and Stress: Counseling the Cancer Patient." *Medical Journal of Australia* 1 (June 1981): 679–683.

Sinclair, Upton. *Mental Radio.* New York: Collier, 1971.

Solfvin, J. "Mental Healing." In S. Krippner, ed., *Advances in Parapsychological Research*. Vol. 4. Jefferson, NC: McFarland & Co., Inc., 1984.

Spiegel, David. *Living Beyond Limits*. New York: Times Books/Random House, Inc., 1993.

Spiegel, D., H.C. Kraemer, J.R. Bloom, and E. Gottheil. "The Effect of Psychosocial Treatment on Survival of Patients with Metastatic Breast Cancer." *Lancet*, October 14, 1989, 888–891.

Spottiswoode, James. "Geomagnetic Fluctuations and Free-Response Anomalous Cognition: A New Understanding." *Journal of Parapsychology* 61 (March 1997).

Stern, Jess. *Edgar Cayce — The Sleeping Prophet*. New York: Bantam Books, 1968.

Sugrue, Thomas. *There Is a River*. Virginia Beach, VA: ARE Press, 1973.

Sutherland, Cherie. *Reborn in the Light*. New York: Bantam Books, 1992.

Taimni, I.K. *The Science of Yoga*. Wheaton, IL: Quest/Theosophical Publishing House, 1961.

Talbot, Michael. *The Holographic Universe*. New York: HarperPerennial, 1991.

Targ, Elisabeth and Russell Targ. "Accuracy of Paranormal Perception as a Function of Varying Target Probabilities," *Journal of Parapsychology* 50 (March 1986): 17–27.

Targ, Elisabeth, Russell Targ, and Oliver Lichtarg. "Realtime Clairvoyance: A Study of Remote Viewing Without Feedback." *Journal of ASPR* 79 (October 1985): 494–500.

Targ, Elisabeth. "Healing and the Spirit," *California Pacific Currents*, Fall 1997, pp. 8–11.

Targ, Russell. "Remote Viewing Replication Evaluated by Concept Analysis." *Journal of Parapsychology* 58 (September 1994).

Targ, Russell, Elisabeth Targ, and Keith Harary. "Moscow - San Francisco Remote Viewing Experiment." *Psi Research* 3, no. 3–4 (September/December 1984).

Targ, Russell and David Hurt. "Learning Clairvoyance and Precognition with an ESP Teaching Machine." *Parapsychology Review*, July–August 1972.

Targ, Russell and Harold E. Puthoff. "Information Transmission Under Conditions of Sensory Shielding." *Nature* 252 (Oct. 1974): 602–607.

Targ, Russell, Phyllis Cole, and Harold Puthoff. "Development of Techniques to Enhance Man/Machine Interactions." *SRI Final Report for NASA*, 1976.

Targ, Russell, William Broad, Marilyn Schlitz, Rex Stanford, and Charles Honorton. "Increasing Psychic Reliability," a panel discussion presented at the 33rd annual conference of the Parapsychological Association, Chevy Chase, MD, Aug. 16–20, 1990," *Journal of Parapsychology* 55 (1991): 59.

Targ, Russell, E.C. May, and H.E. Puthoff. "Direct Perception of Remote Geographic Locations." *Mind At Large: Proceedings of IEEE Symposia on Extrasensory Perception*. New York: Praeger, 1979.

Targ, Russell and Keith Harary. *The Mind Race*. New York: Villard, 1994.

Targ, Russell and Harold Puthoff. *Mind-Reach: Scientists Look at Psychic Abilities*. New York: Delacorte, 1977.

Targ, Russell, Jane Katra, Dean Brown, and Wenden Wiegand. "Viewing the Future: A Pilot Study with an Error-Detecting Protocol." *Journal of Scientific Exploration* 9, no. 3 (1995): 367–380.

Temoshok, Lydia, and Henry Dreher. *The Type C Connection: The Mind-Body Link to Cancer and Your Health*. New York: Penguin Group/Plume, 1992, 193.

Terry, James C. and Charles Honorton. "Psi Information Retrieval in the Ganzfeld: Two Confirmatory Studies," *Journal ASPR* 70 (1976): 207–219.

Thomas, Lewis. *The Youngest Science: Notes of a Medicine Watcher*. New York: Viking Press, 1983.

Ullman, M., S. Krippner, and A. Vaughan. *Dream Telepathy*. New York: Macmillan.

Underhill, Evelyn. *Mysticism*. London: Methuen & Co., 1912 & 1973.

Utts, Jessica. "An Assessment of the Evidence for Psychic Functioning." Prepared for the U.S. Central Intelligence Agency through the American Institute of Research.

Division of Statistics, University of California, Davis, 1995.

Vasiliev, L.L. *Experiments in Mental Suggestion.* Hampshire, England: Gally Hill Press, 1963.

Vilenskaya, Larissa, in Russell Targ and Keith Harary. *The Mind Race.* New York: Villard Books, 1984.

Vilenskaya, L., and E.C. May. "Anomalous Mental Phenomena Research in Russia and the Former Soviet Union: A Follow Up." *Subtle Energies* 4, no. 3 (1993): 231–250.

Walsh, R. and F. Vaughan. *Beyond Ego: Transpersonal Dimensions in Psychology.* Los Angeles: J.P. Tarcher, 1980.

Wapnick, Kenneth. *Forgiveness and Jesus.* Farmingdale, NY: Coleman Publishing, 1983.

Warcollier, René. *Mind to Mind.* New York: Collier, 1963.

Weber, Renèe. "Meaning as Being in the Implicate Order Philosophy of David Bohm: A Conversation." In B.J. Hiley and F. David Peat, eds. *Quantum Implications: Essays in Honor of David Bohm.* New York: Routledge, 1987, 436.

Whitehead, Alfred North, and Bertrand Russell. *Principia Mathematica.* Cambridge, England: Cambridge University Press, 1910.

Wilber, Ken. *The Spectrum of Consciousness.* Wheaton, IL: Quest Books, 1993.

Wilber, Ken. *No Boundary.* Boston, Shambhala, 1979.

Wolman, Benjamin B., ed. *Handbook of Parapsychology.* New York: Van Nostrand Reinhold Company, 1977.

Wood, Ernest. *The Glorious Presence.* Wheaton, IL: The Theosophical Publishing House, 1974.

Wood, Ernest. *Yoga.* Baltimore, MD: Penguin, 1962.

Worrall, Ambrose, in Harold Sherman. *Your Power to Heal.* New York: Harper & Row, 1972.

Worrall, Ambrose, with Olga Worrall. *The Gift of Healing.* New York: Harper & Row, 1965.

Worrall, Olga, in Stanley Krippner and Alberto Villoldo. *The Realms of Healing.* Millbrae, CA: Celestial Arts, 1976.

Worrall, Olga, in Edwina Cerutti. *Olga Worrall: Mystic With the Healing Hands.* New York: Harper & Row, 1975.

Worrall, Olga, in Caryl Hirshberg and Marc Ian Barasch. *Remarkable Recovery.* New York: Riverhead Books, 1995, 129.

Yogananda, Paramahansa. *Autobiography of a Yogi.* Los Angeles: Self Realization Fellowship, 1946 & 1972.

Young, Alan. *Spiritual Healing: Miracle or Mirage?* Marina del Rey, CA: DeVorss & Co., 1981.

Young, Alan. *Cosmic Healing: A Comparative Study of Channeled Teachings on Healing.* Marina del Rey, CA: DeVorss & Co., 1988.

Index

About the Authors

RUSSELL TARG is a physicist and author who was a pioneer in the development of the laser and co-founder of the Stanford Research Institute's investigation into psychic ability in the 1970s and 1980s. He is co-author of *Mind-Reach: Scientists Look at Psychic Abilities* and *The Mind Race: Understanding and Using Psychic Abilities*. Targ recently retired as a senior staff scientist for Lockheed Martin, where he developed laser technology for peaceful applications. Targ lives in Palo Alto, CA.

JANE KATRA holds a doctorate in public health education and has been a spiritual healer for more than twenty years. She has taught nutrition and health classes at the University of Oregon, and Therapeutic Touch at Lane Community College in Eugene. Dr. Katra presently works part-time as an "immune-system coach," while writing and participating in consciousness research. She lives in the Pacific Northwest.

New World Library is dedicated to
publishing books and cassettes that inspire
and challenge us to improve the quality
of our lives and our world.

Our books and tapes are available
in bookstores everywhere.
For a catalog of our complete library
of fine books and cassettes, contact:

New World Library
14 Pamaron Way
Novato, CA 94949

Phone: (415) 884-2100
Fax: (415) 884-2199
Or call toll-free (800) 972-6657
Catalog requests: Ext. 900
Ordering: Ext. 902

E-mail: escort@nwlib.com
http://www.nwlib.com